Marriage, Sex, and the Family in England 1660-1800

A Forty-four Volume Facsimile Series

edited by
Randolph Trumbach
Baruch College

A Garland Series

An Essay on the Government of Children

James Nelson

Garland Publishing, Inc.
New York & London
1985

For a complete list of the titles in this series see the final pages of this volume.

This facsimile was made from a copy in the Seeley G. Mudd Library of Yale University.

Library of Congress Cataloging in Publication Data

Nelson, James, 1710-1794.
An essay on the government of children.

(Marriage, sex, and the family in England, 1660-1800)
Reprint. Originally published : London : Printed for R. and J. Dodsley, 1756.
1. Child rearing—England—History—18th century.
I. Title. II. Series.
HQ792.G7N35 1985 649'.1'0942 83-48604
ISBN 0-8240-5929-8 (alk. paper)

The volumes in this series are printed on acid-free, 250-year-life paper.

Printed in the United States of America

A N

E S S A Y

O N T H E

Government of Children,

Under Three General Heads:

V I Z.

Health, Manners and Education.

By J A M E S N E L S O N, Apothecary.

THE SECOND EDITION.

Juſt as the Twig is bent, the Tree's inclin'd. POPE.

L O N D O N:
Printed for R. and J. DODSLEY in Pall-mall;
And Sold by M. COOPER in Pater-noſter-row. 1756.

TO THE

RIGHT HONOURABLE

THE

Counteſs of - - - - -.

MADAM,

HAPPINESS being the grand Object of human Purſuit, it may, I imagine, be modeſtly preſumed, that every Attempt, however ineffectual, to render That univerſal, muſt be univerſally well received. And yet, conſcious as I am that the following Eſſay aims ſolely at this Point, the Fear of it's being too feeble to ſtand alone, makes me deſirous of procuring it the additional Strength of your Ladyſhip's Countenance and Protection.

The Subject is undoubtedly of great Moment, namely, the proper Government of Children; which being ranged under the Heads of HEALTH, MANNERS, and EDUCATION, affords not only the Opportunity of expoſing many Errors, too generally adopted, but alſo of pointing out a more natural and rational Method of attaining the End propoſed, than is uſually purſued. And I cannot but think, that, if this Method were ſeriouſly attended

attended to, the Happineſs of all Mankind would be built on a more ſolid Baſis, than it has in common hitherto been.

Works of this Kind naturally calling on the Great and Good for Patronage; it cannot be thought ſtrange that I aſpire to the Honour of your Ladyſhip's. Protection is the Privilege of the Powerful: And therefore, where Power is happily joined with Goodneſs, the Recourſe of the Weak to it's beneficent Influence, is but a juſt Tribute of that Homage which is due to ſuperior Merit: And ſuch is the unfeigned Reſpect I mean to pay your Ladyſhip by this Addreſs.

I have

I have yet another Motive for presuming to offer this Performance to your Ladyship; namely, the Hopes that it's Use may, by this Means, be farther extended. The World, Madam, has it's Eyes upon You: The many Excellencies of Mind and Heart so conspicuous in Yourself; and the uncommon Lustre of every eminent Virtue in the noble Lord, with whom you have wisely chosen to share the Dignity and Duties of the Matrimonial and Parental State, have justly gained you, not only general Admiration, but general Esteem.

When the World shall behold you declining many of it's Allurements, to yield to the stronger

ger Attraction of Parental Affection; when it shall see you often decline the Assemblies of the Great, and retreat from the Splendor of a Court, to take upon you the Office of a tender Mother, by cherishing, watching over, and instructing your Offspring; when the World, I say, shall behold you employed in Actions like these, it will not only be charmed with the pleasing Task you have undertaken, but be powerfully animated to pursue the same Measures; which alone can procure that solid Happiness all seek, or seem to seek, yet so few find.

That nothing may ever interrupt your present Felicity; but

but that it may be augmented to the moſt exalted Degree, by the additional Bleſſing of wiſe and virtuous Children, is the ſincere and fervent Wiſh of,

Madam,

Your Ladyſhip's

moſt obliged, and

moſt obedient

humble Servant,

Red-lion-ſtreet,
HOLBORN,
Dec. 1, 1755.

James Nelſon.

ADVERTISEMENT.

THE important Business of the Management of Children, thro' every Stage of our Dominion over them, has led many Writers to handle the Subject: but on this, as on other Occasions, each has had some particular Point in View; and each has directed his Steps to that End. One has considered only the State of Infancy, and, with an Eye to their Health chiefly, laboured to point out the Means of preserving it: another has passed over that State, as if of no Consequence; and, while nobly aiming at regulating the Passions, has inadvertently suffered them to be too deeply rooted from an Inattention to their first Appearance: a third has made it his principal Business to conduct their Education; and has either omitted altogether the forming their

Manners, or has ſuppoſed, what is very far from being generally true, that the one is a neceſſary Conſequence of the other; or in other Words, that good Education will always produce good Manners. Others have confined themſelves to one Species of Education; or, if they aimed at a perfect Piece, it was for an Individual only, or at moſt, for one Claſs of a whole Kingdom.

Yet, of the many excellent Performances on theſe Heads, no one, that can here be recollected, has either been extended to general Life, or has comprehended the Whole of a Parent's Care for their Offſpring. In one we ſee delineated the Education of a Prince; in another, of an able Stateſman; in a third, of a great Commander; and ſo on: but theſe are too narrow to inſtruct the Whole, and too confined to become general Rules. They reſemble, if the Compariſon may be allowed, ſome great Maſters in Painting; one is happy in hitting the Likeneſs; another gives an exquiſite Softneſs and Eaſe to the Fall of the Arms; a third has a

peculiar

peculiar Grace in his Attitudes; yet all, perhaps, are obliged to a fourth for the Delicacy of the Drapery: while he too, who excels in this, is unable to reach any Degree of Perfection in the rest.

But here the Reader is presented with a more extensive Plan on the Government of Children; a Plan adapted to general Use; calculated for familiar Life: and which, without a Thought of Arrogance, or once supposing it perfect, aims at the Good of all. The first *Part treats of the general Means of preserving Health; in which every one is equally concerned. The* next *relates to forming the Mind; that is, shews the Use of Manners, and points out the most rational Method of acquiring them: to the End, not only that good Habits may be obtained, but that Reason may always have the Ascendant of the Passions. The* last *Part treats of Education; which, tho' here it makes a distinct Head from Manners, yet are they to be considered as very strictly connected; because the more exalted the one is, the more conspicuous should the other be. As in every State or Kingdom there are many Degrees of Rank and Fortune; ſo great Pains have been taken to conſider the Propriety of Education; and to point out a judicious Degree of it for each Individual.*

Thus it is to be obſerved, that the Piece here preſented is not deſigned to direct the Fathers, and exclude the Mothers; to govern the Boys, and neglect the Girls; nor to addreſs the Great, and diſregarded the Little; by no Means: it aſpires at offering Advice to all; and, with equal Zeal, aims at giving Aid to Parents of every Rank, Sex and Degree. It regards the Care of Children as long as the Dominion of Parents may be ſaid to laſt; and neither neglects the Infant of a Day, nor gives up unconcernedly, a Youth of either Sex, at twenty Years old.

The Point moſt laboured at is indeed that of Manners; not only becauſe they are of the utmoſt Conſequence in themſelves, and furniſh the ſureſt Means of being happy, and excelling in Life, but becauſe

becauſe the preſent too general Depravity of them ſtands publicly confeſſed.

Should it be urged, that as a great deal has already been wrote on the ſame Topics, and in a maſterly Manner too, all farther Attempts of the like Nature ſeem needleſs; it may be anſwered, (beſides what has already been obſerved) that ſo fertile a Subject cannot eaſily be exhauſted; and being Points of the moſt weighty Concern, they will undoubtedly always furniſh thinking Men with Matter to expatiate on.

The Thoughts here given are the Reſult of Reaſon, Obſervation and Experience; and ſhould it be ſaid that they are not new, ſtill it is hoped they have a Claim to ſome Degree of Regard, as there is always both Uſe and Entertainment in diſplaying even the ſame Sentiments in a different Manner.

INTRODUCTION.

NOTHING is more evident, than that a Love of our Children is a great ruling Principle in human Nature; and that it makes a large Part of that Self-love which ſticks ſo cloſely to us. For them we aim at Wealth, Power, and Dignity; for them our Views are endleſs, our Deſires boundleſs. Nor do we ſtop here; for, eager as we are in purſuing the real or ſeeming Good of our Children, we extend our Views ſtill farther, even to their Children. And it is certain, that Mankind in general do not think the great Buſineſs of Life compleat, unleſs they live (as it is uſually termed) to ſee their Children ſettled, and in a Way of contributing to the great Family of the World. But were none to engage in a State of Wedlock in order to become Parents, till their Abilities to train up their little Off-ſpring were try'd and approv'd, I am of Opinion the Number of Marriage Licences would be greatly abridg'd.

Many run precipitately into this important State, without any Fore-thought at all; but even among the wary, the discreet, and the wise, how very few are there who reflect on the Duty of first acquiring such a Degree of Knowledge as may serve to make their Children happy in them, and themselves happy in their Children? It is this general Defect in human Life, which has induced me to offer my own Thoughts on the Government of Children; and my Aim herein is, to point out the Errors committed in this important Work, and propose some Means of preventing them for the future. A learned Writer on the Art of Medicine * says, that he who advances the Knowledge of it, tho' but a Step, deserves the Thanks of the whole Species; if then I am but happy enough to give one useful Hint, one helping Hand for the Public Good, I shall esteem my Labours abundantly rewarded. But before I go any farther, let me be understood: I am not giving Laws, but Counsel. The Experience I have gained in the tutoring seven Children of my own, joined to the Observations I have made on the Management of others of every Age and Degree, seem to give me

* Dr. *Shaw*. See *Quincy*'s Prælectiones Pharmaceuticæ.

some

ſome Title to hope my Thoughts may prove uſeful; if ſo, my End is anſwered.

Mr. *Pope*, in his moral Eſſays, tells us, that all Happineſs lies in three Words; Health, Peace, and Competence. May we not then hope, that an Endeavour to point out the Way to Health, Manners, and Education, will help us in the Purſuit of this great Object? For theſe rightly underſtood and well conducted, Peace and Competence will ſeldom fail to follow.

Manners however is the grand Point I aim at; every thing elſe is ſecondary to that. Health, it may not be in our Power to ſecure; and School Education, all cannot reach to in any conſiderable Degree. The Government of our Children is indeed an univerſal Obligation; but all Men are not therefore obliged to be Phyſicians or Pedagogues. Still, as neither Health nor liberal Inſtruction, where proper, are to be neglected, I ſhall in their due Place ſpeak of both, ſo far as ſeems neceſſary for every Parent to know.

By Manners I do not mean that external Shew of good Breeding, which conſiſts only in a Bow, or Curtſy, or other perſonal Carriage,

Carriage, tho' this too is of Importance; but I mean, ſuch a uniform Deportment, ſuch a ready engaging Behaviour, and ſuch a Propenſity to do what is right, as teſtify a happy Diſpoſition of the Mind and Heart; and appear, what they really are, the Fruits of good Habits, either natural, or acquired, or both.

The grand Source of the too general Defect, we cannot but obſerve and lament in the Manners of Children, is partly in themſelves, but chiefly in their Parents. In themſelves it ariſes from a natural Love of Eaſe and Liberty; in Parents, from a ſupine Neglect of that neceſſary Knowledge already hinted at: in ſhort, from want of reflecting why they are Parents, and what is incumbent on them to do, in order to make their Children happy in themſelves, and uſeful to Society. But how ſhall I be ſheltered from the Imputation of Vanity? I am well aware how liable a Man is to be cenſured, for attempting to point out to others, what every one ſuppoſes himſelf to be already acquainted with: and where are the Parents who once ſuſpect, that they are ſo little acquainted with the Duties of their State, as to be themſelves the Cauſes of their Children's Miſconduct?

That

That there are many whofe Ability in this important Work is far fuperior to any thing I can pretend to, I am convinc'd; many who are happily endowed with a competent Penetration and Skill to manage the Tempér, Genius, and Paffions of Children, and who are equally affiduous in the Exercife of thofe Gifts for the Benefit of the rifing Generation: neither is it for thefe I write; rather do I wifh to receive their Inftructions myfelf. But, that the Bulk of Mankind are wholly thoughtlefs of, or unacquainted with, the proper Methods of managing Children, is, I think, very evident. In proof of which I appeal to every one's own Obfervation. Let the Generality of People look round them, and reflect how they find the Majority of Children of every Rank among their Acquaintance. Are they innocent, tractable, orderly, and courteous? Are they tolerably inftructed in the Knowledge neceffary for their Age and Station? Or are they not rather corrupt and untoward? Are they not rather unruly to a Degree of Pity? Incorrigibly rude, or tolerably civil only by Starts; grofsly ignorant in many Things they ought to have been taught, and but too knowing in others it were perhaps better they never knew at all? If they really find this to be

true

true in the Children of others, let them turn their Eyes homewards, and impartially canvas their own Children's Deportment; and if upon discovering any of the like Deformities, they can resolve to be just to themselves, I am confident they will to their great Surprize awaken to the Consciousness of one Truth, which perhaps they hitherto never so much as suspected; namely, that what they have the most Reason to be displeased with in the Conduct of their Offspring, is chiefly owing to their own want of Skill, or want of Thought, in the Management of those tender Plants.

As Men are sometimes seen to forget the Husband and act the Sovereign only, so are they apt to think themselves supreme and independent in the Power they have over their Children. But can we, upon Reflection, take it to be the Intention of Nature, that Children be govern'd by Fathers alone, while they are in Possession of the Blessing of having Mothers to share a Part in that Government? Or can we consider paternal Sway as an arbitrary Power, absolutely presiding over, and giving Laws to Children without any Controul? No. Lest Fathers thus impower'd should invert the Intention of the Creation by becoming Tyrants, the providential

providential Laws of Nature have wifely affigned a joint Portion of Power to the Mothers; that the Father's Authority and the Mother's Sweetnefs being feafonably and difcreetly blended, both might equally contribute to one and the fame great End, the future Welfare of their Offspring: where the Roughnefs of the one ferving as a Spur to egg them on to the Purfuit of Happinefs from a Principle of Awe, the Smoothnefs of the other may footh them forward, from Motives of Affection; or, in a Word, that the Sternnefs of the Father may ferve as a Quickener to maternal Endearments, and the Mildnefs of the Mother fweeten and render palatable the more bitter Draughts of paternal Harfhnefs.

It is no fmall Difficulty to fix the Time in which Parents fhould take the Reins of Government into their Hands; but if it be confidered that we are by the Perverfenefs of our Nature prone to err, I think they cannot begin too foon; in fhort, they fhould begin as foon as they become Parents, that is, as foon as their Childen have a Being. This will appear to be ftrange Doctrine to thofe who have not reflected how very early Children fhew themfelves. The Source of many of our Errors with Regard to the Govern-

Government of Children, ſeems owing to a miſtaken Notion of their Incapacity; whereas in Reality they have ſome Reaſon much earlier than is commonly imagined; but till that dawns out, the Paſſions alone are their Guides. Now if the Paſſions are ſuffered to gather Strength, by cheriſhing and indulging them, (which is too commonly the Caſe) and Reaſon remains feeble for want of being exercis'd, the natural Conſequence muſt be, that Children will grow obſtinate, perverſe, and ungovernable in their Paſſions, before Reaſon is called forth to their Aſſiſtance; and it will often prove a very unſucceſsful Taſk to hinder them when grown up, from being Slaves to themſelves, and Plagues to all about them.

Parents then, to obviate theſe Evils, have two principal Points to aim at, for their own and Children's Happineſs; and indeed for the Happineſs of all Poſterity; *viz.* weakening their Paſſions, and ſtrengthening their Reaſon. And that this is greatly in their Power to effect, is an undoubted Truth, tho' it may often prove an arduous Taſk to reduce to practice. Still it may, and ought to be aim'd at; and, if I may be allowed to ſpeak my Sentiments, I think I may confidently aſſert, that all ſocial Virtues, and the genuine

genuine Happineſs which they are productive of, will inſenſibly flow from a conſtant due Exerciſe of that Dominion over our Children, which all Laws divine and human have entruſted to us.

'Tis wonderful to obſerve how very early a Wilfulneſs is diſcernable in Children; and with what ſwift Progreſs it gathers Strength, if not immediately and carefully check'd. I have ſeen a Child not above ſix Months old, obſtinately contending for a certain Poſition to be ſuckled in, and the tender (ſimply tender) Mother painfully diſtorting her Limbs, and ſtraining her whole Frame, in Compliance to it, or it would not ſuck at all: and I have ſeen too a Child, before one Year of Life was compleated, ſo fantaſtically, and yet ſo obſtinately humourſome, that all that could be deviſ'd to give it, was not ſufficient to gratify it: it would roar for the firſt Thing it ſaw, then throw it away and fight for another, and ſo on without Meaſure; and this at the Expence not merely of Baubles, but of Glaſſes, China, and other valuable Things; and often at the ſtill greater Expence of the Mother's Peace and Reſt.

The next Advance is to the Uſe of Speech; and this Faculty is no ſooner acquired,

quired, but immediately follows the Abuſe of it. Many Children, indeed, are ſlow and backward in the Acquiſition of it, but few are thoſe who are not too forward in miſapplying this noble Gift. Let a Child of three Years old, who has been much indulged, be bid to do any thing, and how ready is it to anſwer, *I won't!* And if forbid a thing, how pert to ſay, *I will!* Yet let the fondling Parent aſk it ever ſo plain and eaſy a Queſtion, it is a thouſand to one, if a Word of Anſwer be obtained: the cunning, obſtinate Urchin is inſtantly dumb, and nothing ſhall reſtore it to the Uſe of its Tongue, but the Gratification of its Humour with a Cake or a Play-thing.

Thus are they generally ſuffered to run on to near the Age of Seven, with little or no Variation, except that of their Appetites gaining head of their Reaſon, and multiplying in proportion to the Objects which excite them. And as during that Term of Life which we diſtinguiſh by the Name of Childhood, Parents look upon the infant Reaſon of their Children, as incapable of producing Fruits, they are but too apt to leave that uncultivated, and to overlook, with an injudicious Contempt, their early Deviations from it. But ſurely it were in-

juring

juring human Underſtanding, to agree with ſuch Parents, in an Opinion which condemns itſelf; and which they themſelves are univerſally the firſt to contradict. For let the Topic of Children be but broach'd to any of them, and what Encomiums are we not ſure to be tir'd with upon their own! What Enlargements on their Comprehenſion, their Judgment, their Wit, and the ſurprizing Products of all theſe, in the many excellent things they ſay and do! In the mean time not a ſingle Step is taken to improve all theſe boaſted Talents, nor to check the growing Humours which threaten them with Deſtruction; and may, if neglected, grow into Habits more difficult to eradicate than an hereditary Diſeaſe.

Leſt this ſhould affect but little thoſe Parents, who are more ſolicitous that their Children ſhould be fair in Face, and ſtrong in Body, than beauteous in Mind, and pure of Heart, let me convince even theſe, that it is dangerous too to the bodily Welfare of Children, to neglect cultivating their Reaſon from their earlieſt Infancy; or to be careleſs of eradicating their little Humours, as ſoon as diſcover'd. And to this end they need only view the Majority of them on a ſick Bed; where they will ſee this melan-

choly

choly Truth (for ſuch indeed we may call it) in its full Light.

Diſeaſes are one Part of the Portion of human Nature, in a State of Mortality: no Stage of our Exiſtence is exempt from them, and Childhood as little as any. Let then an unmanag'd, humour'd, pamper'd Child be ſick; and beſides the Abundance of otherwiſe unneceſſary Trouble and Affliction it brings on the Parents and the whole Family, what Danger is not the Child itſelf expoſed to, beyond what the Diſeaſe brings with it!

All wiſe Men agree, that Providence has furniſhed the World with Remedies for moſt human Diſeaſes, at leaſt in their firſt Stages, and Men with Knowledge to apply them. When ſkilful People are conſulted in Time, the Medicines good, duly prepared and given, the Nurſe attentive, and the Patient tractable, there is but little to be apprehended from the firſt Stage of any Diſeaſe which is not mortal of itſelf, where the Habit of Body is otherwiſe ſound; barring ſuch Accidents as cannot be foreſeen, nor conſequently obviated. But what can Phyſicians, Medicines, Nurſes, all avail, in the Diſeaſe (otherwiſe ever ſo curable) of an untoward

toward Creature, againſt whom perhaps there are great Odds that it ſhall not be conquered to ſwallow the leaſt Portion of the moſt abſolutely neceſſary Remedy; nor to ſubmit in Sickneſs to the leaſt Controul; indulged, perhaps, as it has been, in a Habit of ſlighting and baffling all Authority while in Health? Juſt nothing. No; the Trouble indeed of attending it, is doubled and trebled to thoſe who are conſtantly about it; the Expence is at leaſt the ſame, if not conſiderably augmented; and the Confuſion, Affliction, and Alarms of the Parents, at the growing Danger of their ſpoil'd Darling, immoderately encreas'd, on finding all Remedies rendered ineffectual to it, by an Obſtinacy which they (whether conſcious of it or not) have heretofore been the fooliſh Encouragers of. In the mean time, the Diſeaſe gathers Strength, and the Child's Wilfulneſs with it; and the little ungovernable Patient falls an untimely Victim to the former Miſmanagement of the miſtakenly fond Parents, and its own preſent Unrulineſs. To ſee a fond Father, in Spite of the Impotence of Tears, ſo general to his Sex, weeping over his Child, his Heir, his only Hope of Joy, and vainly entreating him, whom he might command, to take an eaſy Remedy! To behold a tender Mother,

herſelf

herſelf half ſpent with Grief and Fears, proſtrate at her ſick Favourite's Pillow, expoſtulating with all the Eloquence of maternal Anxiety, and entreating, praying, coaxing it to ſwallow a neceſſary Medicine, but ſtill in vain! To view the Parents at ſuch a Juncture, inwardly divided, torn, and almoſt conſumed, between the alternate Motions of Tenderneſs, Impatience, Love, and Anger, fruitleſsly inſiſt, where a Habit of Subjection ſhould have already made a Word or a Look ſufficient; and yet to find the humour'd Thing as reſolutely bent on refuſing, merely, perhaps, becauſe ſo much entreated! To eye all this, I ſay, were ſurely ſufficient to convince us, that it is a ſtrange Inverſion of the natural Order of Things; and has a ſomething in it extremely abſurd: and the more ſo, when we reflect, that the whole is an Effect of Folly in the Parents, and chiefly owing to their former Neglect of exerting a little prudential Authority.

If this be too frequent a Caſe, as the Experience of many People muſt convince them it is, let Parents in general remember, that their watchful Induſtry to conquer and regulate the little growing Paſſions and Humours of their tender Offspring, is as neceſſary towards the Preſervation of their Bodies, as for the Culture of their Minds.

That this Difficulty of conquering Children, and rendering them tractable while ſick, is no Exaggeration, I might appeal to the Conſciouſneſs of moſt Parents throughout the Kingdom; nay, I could ſupport the Charge by many Inſtances within my own Knowledge; but ſhall content myſelf with producing a very few from the Relation of others. A Friend of mine, who had the Care of a young Gentleman, lately received a Letter from his Boarding School, with this Information; "Maſter has been much "out of order, and what is worſe, was out "of the Reach of the Means of being eaſily "made better. He had indeed three Doſes "of Phyſic preſcrib'd him, but could not "be prevailed on to ſwallow one; in ſhort, "they were all ſpilt on the Sheets, for not "a Drop went down his Throat." A little Miſs not yet able to ſpeak plain (as I was informed by a Perſon preſent) had a Medicine to take which ſhe obſtinately refus'd; Mamma interferes, and after many fruitleſs Entreaties gently corrects her; Miſs ſtill perſiſts in the Refuſal, and is chaſtiſed with additional Severity, even to the ſixth time; at length, half breathleſs with crying, and ready

ready in appearance to burſt with Paſſion, ſhe has ſtill her Spirit ſo little conquered as to ſay in her imperfect Gibberiſh, "Well, "if you *till* me, I won't take it." So Mamma overcome, lays down the Rod; and obſtinate Miſs coming off with the Victory, ſhewed ſhe had more Courage to receive Correction, than the Mother Reſolution to beſtow it. The Truth was, that Mamma had never had a Diſpute with the Child, in which ſhe had not the Weakneſs to ſuffer it to get the better of her. A Lady of Rank I have the Honour to be acquainted with, and who I'm ſure in other Reſpects has good Underſtanding, forfeited it greatly on a like Occaſion. She told me her Daughter, when in the Country, having a Fever, all uſual Means were try'd to prevail on her to take the neceſſary Remedies, but in vain! So far from being mov'd to Compliance, ſhe was thrown into ſuch vehement Fits of crying, whenever they were offered to her, that it was apprehended her Fever would encreaſe, and endanger her Life: 'till at length by good Fortune the Lady reflecting ſhe had a Kitten which Miſs was extravagantly fond of, ſhe reſolved to try an Experiment. Accordingly, as often as any thing was to be taken by Miſs, Mamma holding Puſs in her Hands, proteſted it

ſhould

ſhould be thrown out of the Window and killed, if ſhe did not take what was given her; and by this Stratagem brought the Child to a Compliance, which nothing elſe could effect. I own the Expedient was ingenious, and the Lady gave a Proof of her great Preſence of Mind in turning to the Child's Advantage an innocent Foible ſhe had been indulg'd in. But ſurely at the ſame time ſhe betrayed how much ſhe had before forfeited her Underſtanding as well as the true Tenderneſs of the Parent, by the little Care ſhe had taken to inculcate and enforce ſuch Principles of Obedience and Gratitude, as ſhould have taught her on the like Occaſions to do at leaſt as much out of Love and Duty to a fond Parent, as ſhe did out of childiſh Attachment to a Kitten. Now however lightly People may think of theſe Things, who are not immediately concerned, they muſt and will be acknowledged great Afflictions to all Parents who love their Children, and ſee them in ſuch Circumſtances.

'Tis certain that Children may have Diſorders which are not of a dangerous Nature, and may therefore be got through without a nice Obſervance of Rule; but then it is equally certain, that they have oftentimes very dangerous ones, which neceſſarily require both Medicines and Rule. And very eminent Phyſicians have declared it as their Opinion, that many of theſe tender Lives have been loſt, purely for want of Submiſſion to the Medicines and Rules preſcribed them. Who then can look back on the Cauſes of a Loſs ſo detrimental to Society, and not be offended at the general Neglect of Parents to remove them?

Nor can one, reaſonably ſpeaking, be leſs offended and concerned at the univerſal Cuſtom among Parents of remedying on ſuch Occaſions their former Neglects, by preſent Falſehoods: that is, I mean, by attempting to impoſe on their Children's Senſes and Underſtandings by manifeſt Untruths. When a Child is to take a Medicine, is it not ridiculous to call a bitter Draught ſour, or a ſour one ſweet? Is it leſs abſurd to inſiſt on a nauſeous thing's being pleaſant, than it is to ſhew them what is black, and endeavour to perſuade them it is white? And yet this is the Method commonly made uſe of with Children, to beguile down their Medicines. It is true it may furniſh People with an eaſy Pretext to expatiate on their Children's Capacity; but I am ſure it adds no Honour to their own. They may tell their Apothecary how much Pains they took to cheat the Child, but the little Rogue was ſo cunning it would not be cheated! They may diſplay his Genius by telling how they called it Wine, and gave it in the dark; or ſaid it was Tea, and put it into his own Cup; ſtill nothing could deceive him: Oh! it is a ſenſible little Creature! But what all this while is become of the Senſe of the Parents? For after all this Addreſs, this mighty Juggle, it muſt ſtill perhaps be owned, that the Child does not take the Doſe: or if it ſhould, with a Superiority of Senſe, it juſtly reproaches the Parents with having told it a Falſehood. "You ſaid it "was good, but I find it is naſty Stuff, "and I'll take no more of it." And too generally do they keep their Word. Can Parents ſo palpably miſlead their Children, and not be ſenſible of their Miſtake? Or can they be ſenſible of it, and not bluſh at their own Folly?

Thus far we have conſidered the Untowardneſs of Children, with ſome of its Conſequences, in that Stage of Life we uſually call their Childhood; that is, to ſeven Years old; for according to the Cuſtom of familiar Life, every Septenary is reckoned a Stage; tho' Phyſical Writers divide Life otherwiſe. With them there are eight

Stages. From the Birth to three Years old, is one; viz. the Infancy; from three to ten another; and ſo on to Decrepidity. But as this Treatiſe attempts to reach no farther than the Dominion of Parents generally extends, that is, till they become Men and Women; it will not be conſiſtent with my Deſign, to carry on either Obſervation or Precept beyond the third Stage of Life.

Let us therefore proceed to take ſome Obſervation of them in the ſecond Septenary; when on all Hands it is agreed their Underſtandings are open, and capable of receiving more important Impreſſions.

Now if we view the Generality of Children from ſeven to fourteen, I am afraid we ſhall be obliged to confeſs, that however far they advance in what is commonly called Learning, they gain but very little in the Science of Manners. In *William* of *Wickham*'s famous School at *Winchester* there is this Motto, MANNERS MAKETH MAN: Whereby we are reminded, that all Learning which does not improve our Manners, is vain and unprofitable; the Perfection of Manners being the End, which Learning is only deſign'd as a Means to conduct us to. Yet ſo it happens, that Parents are frequently miſ-

led

led by confounding Names, by taking one thing for another, and concluding their Children have Manners becaufe they have Learning. Whereas in reality, a Child may, from want of proper Care, have a great deal of Learning, and no Manners at all: or, on the other hand, by timely and proper Tuition, advance greatly in the Improvement of genuine Manners, with little or no School Learning: which is all that is generally underftood by the Word Learning, with regard to Children in the fecond Septenary.

When a Man becomes Father of a Family, he ufually applies the Boys, as foon as he deems them of an Age for it, to School Learning; different according to the Rank he bears in Life: while the Girls, by a fhameful Indolence or Contempt, are often neglected in this Particular, and fuffered to become alternate Plagues and Play-things at home: at leaft with ftricteft Truth we may fay, too little Care is taken to form either the Mind or Heart of thefe to any great Advantage. The Boys, if dull, return Blockheads, and fo remain; if fmart, grow boifterous, audacious, conceited, and ungovernable; tyrannical to their Sifters; difobedient to their Mother; and fcarce are awed by their Father's ſeverer Brow. The Girls remain uncultivated in almoſt every thing but Vanity and a Love of fine Cloaths. Indeed they can work a little, (and perhaps but little) or they can dance, and ſo they ought; but ſhall ſcarcely be able to ſpell a Word right beyond a Monoſyllable; or write the Direction on a Letter with any Propriety. Is it an Exaggeration to ſay this is the uſual Education till fourteen? Surely Experience convinces us it is not; and tho' ſome Exceptions may doubtleſs be found, yet they are few in Compariſon with the whole.

Now let me aſk the Parents of ſuch Children, what real Comfort do they find in them? Do they not often with Sorrow, nay almoſt with bleeding Hearts, ſee them running counter to their Expectations and Wiſhes? Do they not daily ſee, and muſt they not therefore daily lament (unleſs they are ſelf-blind) that all their other Profuſion of Kindneſs ſo laviſhly poured on their Children, yields neither Profit to them, nor Comfort to themſelves? And whence the Cauſe of all this Diſappointment? Alas! 'tis too viſible, too apparent! It ariſes from a Neglect, or at leaſt an Abuſe of that early Authority they ought to exerciſe over them: from a Neglect, in not correcting in time

their

their Irregularities and Humours; from an Abuſe, in correcting them without Judgment and Diſcretion. Nor does this happen to People in inferior Stations only; no, 'tis every Day to be met with, not merely from the Peaſant to the Tradeſman, but from the Tradeſman to the Nobleman; and even among thoſe of the fineſt Underſtanding. But whence the Cauſe of this ſtrange Miſconduct and Omiſſion? It ſprings, as I take it, from Ignorance, or Inconſiderateneſs, or Partiality, or Paſſion, or from all together; but the moſt frequently of any, from falſe Tenderneſs, and blind Indulgence.

Every Man has his own way of judging, and generally abides by it right or wrong. I knew a Gentleman of refined Underſtanding, who frequently forfeited it, by a boundleſs injudicious Fondneſs for his Children. He would ſay to his little Boy at Table, Well, my Dear, what ſhall I help you to? The Child, accuſtomed to have his own Will, unſkilled to make a proper Choice, and following the Gratification of his depraved Palate, was ſure to chooſe the moſt unfit Diſh, by chooſing the richeſt, becauſe the moſt ſavory. The Father indeed would fain ſet him right, by recommending ſome ſimpler Food; No, my Dear, he'd ſay, have ſome Mutton, Mutton is beſt for you; and ſo of any other plain wholſome Diſh; but this Advice proves too late, after having ſet him wrong; nor would he eat a Morſel of any thing but what he himſelf approved of. The ſame Gentleman, as a Proof of his Senſe, took abundance of Pains to inculcate ſtrict Notions of Honour to his Children, tho' he often degraded that Senſe in the Application of them. One Day, at the beginning of the Week, he ſays to his Son, My Dear, I know you are a Man of Honour, and what you once promiſe you'll punctually perform; you are one Day this Week to take Phyſic; tell me then, what Day will you fix on? The Boy pauſes a little, and replies, Saturday, Sir. Oh! fye my Dear, ſays the Father, why ſtay 'till Saturday? why not take it to-morrow, or next Day? No Sir, replies the Boy, with an unbecoming Pertneſs, I'm upon Honour; the Choice of the Day was left to me, and I'll not take it before. What an amazing Inverſion of Ideas! Honour with Diſobedience! Who in this Caſe could be ſaid to hold the Reins of Government, the Parent or the Child?

Thus too does many an affectionate and even

even ſenſible Mother both ſee and feel in a Daughter, whom Nature perhaps has endowed with all that might make her ſweet and amiable, an Untractableneſs ſhe knows not how to account for. But tho' it is her own Miſmanagement, or rather no Management at all, which makes the Girl's Deſires irregular and inordinate, ſtill the fond Parent remains blind to the Cauſe. If Miſs knows Mamma is to go out without her, ſhe'll eat no Dinner; if the Dreſs of the Day is not to her Fancy, ſhe is ſure to remain ſullen 'till Night; and if an accidental Difference is made to a Siſter, or any other of her own Age, ſhe ſhall redden, and ſwell, and pout, and fret, 'till ſhe has fretted her Mamma ſick, to ſee her untoward Behaviour; and poſſibly fretted herſelf ſick too. 'Tis eaſy to diſcern the Principles ſhe acts upon; they are Self-will, Vanity, and the Love of Pleaſure, which ſhe has been uſed to be indulged in. No wonder then, that when theſe are not gratified ſhe is miſerable; and while they are, is it likely that ſhe can long be happy?

There ought to be made a conſiderable Difference between the Children of inferior People, and thoſe of Rank, with regard to their Tuition; nothing is more reaſonable; ſince the latter have innumerable Advantages

 over,

over, and are to move in a very different Sphere from the former. Still the Miſtakes in all are too often eſſentially the ſame; and only conceal'd or varniſh'd over by the external Education. Now, what I contend for is, that Parents of all Ranks have the Power, and are equally bound in Duty, to be themſelves the Teachers of their Children, with regard to that Self-Knowledge, and the genuine Docility ariſing from it, which are neceſſary to conduct them thro' Life with Eaſe and Benefit to themſelves, with Honour and Pleaſure to their Parents, and with univerſal Advantage to Society in general. I ſay again, that all Parents have the Power of anſwering this Obligation in great meaſure; but thoſe of Rank, Fortune, and Education, have it in an eminent Degree; and are therefore utterly inexcuſable, when they give into that groſs Neglect of it; which we daily ſee, even in the ſecond and more improveable Stage of human Life.

Tho' it is allow'd by all, that Children, long before they attain the Age of fourteen, are in general capable of receiving very advantageous Impreſſions, and are full as ſuſceptible of the reverſe; yet 'tis pretty evident, that much the Majority to that Period,

riod, gain few or no good ones; and I wiſh it were not as evident, that their principal Stock are of the bad Kind. But let us proceed to conſider them in the third Septenary, which brings them to the Age of twenty-one; the Period which generally cloſes our Obligations to them; ſhuts out in great meaſure our Power over them; and ſets them looſe on the great Stage of the World, every one to act their Part juſt as we have taught them. If well, great is our Honour, great muſt be our Comfort; and great and laſting is their Happineſs likely to prove, to themſelves, and to Poſterity. If ill, no matter what their Station is, they diſgrace it; and the Diſgrace with double Force is reflected back on ourſelves.

'Tis a well-known Maxim, that the firſt Impreſſions ſtrike the deepeſt. Thus, a Boy, who before fourteen has never been convinced that it was neceſſary for him to obey, will afterwards laugh at it as ridiculous; and if his firſt Leſſons were Pride and Pleaſure, the only Uſe he will make of his Underſtanding when more at large, will be to ſtudy to continue in the Purſuit and Augmentation of thoſe his favourite Objects.

Whether we conſider the Heir of a Family

mily at the Univerſity, or his younger Brother in a Merchant's Compting-houſe; whether we conſider a young Stripling deſtin'd to the Law, to Phyſic, or view him behind a Counter; we cannot make a true Uſe of our Eyes, without ſeeing innumerable Diſorders during this third Stage of Life. For tho' heretofore he has been treated as a Child or School-boy, he will now pretend to judge for himſelf; and as his Reaſon is weak, and his Paſſions ſtrong, that will ſlaviſhly run in purſuit of every thing which will promote the Gratification of theſe. I have already obſerved, that the only Uſe he will make of his Underſtanding, will be to abuſe it. For Example, he wants fine Cloaths, ſuch, perhaps, as are very unbecoming his Station; he wants two or three Suits, where one ought to ſerve; he wants an encreaſe of Pocket-money, far beyond a reaſonable Allowance, and often beyond what his Father can afford; or finally, he has ſome more vicious End in view. Now without once employing his Reaſon, or reflecting how much he has abuſed the Indulgence of his Parents, his Paſſions urge him on to effect whatever they ſuggeſt. To gain his Point then, with Addreſs and Cunning he applies to his Mother; whoſe blind Fondneſs for her Boy, will not let the Father reſt,

reſt, till his prodigal Humour is gratify'd. The Father, as a good one, ſhall argue the Caſe. "What, my Dear, can I do with "this extravagant Boy? I have ſpar'd no "Pains nor Expence in his Education, be- "cauſe on that I grounded all my Hopes "of his future good Conduct and Proſpe- "rity; he don't want Senſe, and has im- "prov'd pretty well in his Learning: if "not quite ſo well as perhaps he might "have done with a little more Application, "yet allowing for the natural Thoughtleſſ- "neſs of his Age, at leaſt well enough to "know how to act better. Still I ſee little "Proſpect of Comfort from him; becauſe "I ſee no Diſpoſitions in him but to Idle- "neſs, Folly and Extravagance. In ſhort, "if he goes on thus, what better can I expect "than to ſee him daily plunge deeper and "deeper into Extravagance and Vice: "and what muſt the Conſequence be but "irrecoverable Deſtruction? Shall I then "by continuing to humour him hurry on "his Ruin, perhaps in my own and yours?" But the fond Mother ſtill perſuading him that every preſent Folly is to be the laſt, urges her Suit; and enforcing all that Influence which in an amiable Woman ſeldom fails to ſucceed with an indulgent Huſband and doating Father, is almoſt always ſure to carry

carry her Point. Is not this the genuine Situation of many a Parent? Is not this the reigning Practice of many a Son? Of too many indeed!—The Father here describ'd is such a one as most Men will acknowledge to be a tender one; and some will be apt to think a discreet one; in allowing for the Inconsiderateness of his Age, weighing like a prudent Man his real Good, and generously resolving to furnish him with every reasonable Means of being wise and happy: still is he disappointed; and still are his Expectations frustrated. But need we ask the Cause? Surely it is too plain. More Pains have been taken to pamper and humour him, than to make it unnecessary to do either: more Time and Care have been employ'd to furnish his Head, with perhaps merely ornamental Knowledge, than to correct and enrich his Heart with such Sentiments as might improve his Manners. Can we then wonder that he precipitates into Ruin? No surely; we may rather wonder if he escapes it. But admitting that Fortune still favours him, and that he keeps up his Dignity and Reputation; how does he possess his own Mind, as a rational Creature, or a Brute? Does he act so as to deserve the Esteem of Mankind? If not, Life is not worth enjoying.

Let

Let us now view the fairer part of our Species; thoſe tender Branches our Daughters. They (thank Heaven) are not naturally ſo liable to Vices and Extravagancies as our Sons; but I wiſh I could ſay they were all as good as they are capable of being made; as amiable in their interior Sentiments, as their Forms might make us hope to ſee them. But alas! too often thoſe choiceſt Charms of our Eyes are the chief Plagues of our Hearts; and it is we ourſelves are the principal Cauſes, that they whom Nature ſeem'd to have form'd to be our principal Comforts, ſhould thro' our Miſmanagement become the Diſturbers of the Peace of us their Parents, and of their own Happineſs.

A Girl enter'd into the third Septenary paſſes ſoon into a Woman; but commonly ſpeaking ſhe is much ſooner ſuch in her Perſon and Appetites than in her Underſtanding: whence ariſe many of thoſe glaring Miſtakes they daily commit. A Girl who is tall generally conceits ſhe is wiſe; and becauſe 'till now ſhe has liv'd without controul, ſhe thinks Subjection and Obedience to her Parents, mean and ſlaviſh. It would be a Reflection on young Ladies to ſay they have no Manners, but ſtill it is too generally true that

that their Manners are falſe ones; ſpringing from Pride, and influenc'd by it. A Girl (of any Figure in Life) ſoon knows that the World has it's Eyes upon her; and as there are certain Motives which induce her to exert all her Skill to ſeem well bred, ſo there are certain Times ſhe really appears to advantage: but let the Maſk be thrown off; let the Reſtraint be taken away by which ſhe is confin'd; and we ſhall ſoon ſee where her Manners lye: we ſhall (I am afraid) oftentimes diſcover that they are not the Dictates of a well-regulated Heart. But as my Tenderneſs for the Sex will not ſuffer me deſignedly to miſrepreſent things, let us examine fairly the Conduct of a young Lady according to the too general Mode of breeding.

It appears already that the firſt Stage of Life was wholly ſpent in gratifying her Humour; the ſecond was employ'd in a ſuperficial Education, reſembling in ſome meaſure a Building ornamented without, but ill contriv'd and uſeleſs within. Self-will, Vanity and Pleaſure have hitherto been her Guides; and theſe inſtead of being check'd, are in the third Stage, greatly ſtrengthen'd and augmented: and have beſides added to them a boundleſs Love of Power and Uncontroul.

controul. Now from ſuch a Source what Virtues can we expect to flow? What Miſeries may we not fear? Alas! too ſoon are we convinc'd that her whole Soul is abſorb'd in Pleaſures; her Head runs round with them; ſhe is continually contriving, plotting, ſcheming; and all Oppoſition of her Parents becomes too weak: ſhe has not, perhaps, a Spark of real Duty, nor the leaſt Senſe of her miſguided Steps: and happy is it for her if her miſtaken Conduct does not in the End plunge her into Sorrow too great to ſupport. Happy is it for her if the Stream of Pleaſure ſhe is borne down with does not inſenſibly carry away her Honour and Virtue; or at leaſt daſh her on the fatal Rock of a miſerable Marriage. Wherever this Portrait is found to be genuine, let it be remember'd, that the Painter who draws a real Likeneſs ought not to be blam'd for the Diſagreeableneſs of the Features.

Many, it is true, have Fortune to ſupport their Pleaſures, however expenſive or irregular; but where that fails, where Fortune is ſmall, and the Propenſity to Pleaſure great, Honour and Virtue ſtand ſo very tottering, that they are in perpetual Danger: and if with this unbridled Love of Pleaſure, there be a tolerable ſhare of Wit or Beauty,

or

or both; who that reflects, can help trembling even at the Apprehension of a Fall? But tho' a young Lady should escape those innumerable Calamities which her giddy Conduct has laid her open to, what Hopes are there, that she who has never borne Contradiction, will so demean herself as to become amiable in the Eyes of others, or be happy in herself?

I could with great facility delineate a variety of shapes hideous to behold, which young People of both Sexes shew themselves in, when guided only by their Passions; but, to avoid Prolixity, will content myself with the general View I have already presented; and proceed to lay down such Rules as appear to me to tend most directly and securely to the avoiding the various Evils our Children are subject to, and seem most conducive to their real Happiness. But before I lay down any Precepts let me premise, that all Laws in general give Parents the sole supreme Power of governing their Children: 'tis the Order of Nature; and if her Laws are inverted, nothing but Confusion follows. If then Parents do not govern their Children at all; or what is worse, let their Children govern them, which is often the Case, the almost

unavoidable

unavoidable Confequence will be, that Train of Irregularities and Diforders we daily fee them run into; in which Cafe, there are but two Ways of their becoming fenfible of their miftake: either from a natural Goodnefs of Heart awakened by Time and Experiencc; or from a load of Misfortunes crufhing them down for want of Power to fupport them: now the one we ought not to truft to; and the other we fhould bend all our Study to prevent.

AN

ESSAY

ON THE

Government of CHILDREN.

HEALTH.

THO' the principal Deſign of this Attempt be that of regulating the Manners of Children; yet as Health and Education are of vaſt Importance in the Government of them, and are cloſely connected

nected therewith; I think myſelf oblig'd to ſpeak of what may tend to preſerve the one, and, in a due Degree, promote the other. For the ſake of Method I ſhall divide my Subject into three Parts; that is, range it under the general Heads of Health, Manners, and Education; which to me appears to be the only natural Order of treating it. Mr. *Locke*, it is true, in his Treatiſe on this Subject, calls the whole, Thoughts on Education; but notwithſtanding that general Title to his Book, he ſpeaks likewiſe of Health and Manners, and ranges them all in the Order here propos'd.

As Health is the reverſe of Sickneſs, my Readers will eaſily diſcern that it is not the Buſineſs of this Undertaking to invade the Phyſician's Province, by entering on the Cure of Diſeaſes; but only to point out ſuch Means as ſeem to have the moſt rational tendency to prevent them.

Firſt then, I earneſtly recommend to both Father and Mother, that their Children ſuck the Mother's Breaſt. But why, you'll ſay, take pains to addreſs each Parent diſtinctly? The reaſon is obvious. A Man cannot be converſant in Life, and not ſee that many a ſenſible Woman, many a tender

der Mother, has her Heart yearning to ſuckle her Child, and is prevented by the miſplac'd Authority of a Huſband. Parents upon the whole are to be conſider'd as equally and mutually concern'd in the training up their Children; therefore when I addreſs them by that one common Epithet, I mean either, or both. But there are, both in Nature and Reaſon, certain Provinces aſſign'd to each; and a Man's attempting to overturn them, would be as abſurd and prepoſterous, as a Merchant's ſending his Wife to tranſact Buſineſs upon Change, while he ſtay'd at home to preſide over the Nurſery.

Providence, we ſee, without any Expence to us, kindly ſends Food into the World along with the Child, by giving to the Mother a Breaſt flowing with Milk. But to what purpoſe is this beſtow'd? To be neglected and render'd fruitleſs? No ſurely; we cannot think thus indignantly of ſo great a Bleſſing. But beſides this evident Deſign of Providence, there is another important Conſideration; which is, that Mothers by ſuckling their Children cheriſh that Tenderneſs which Nature has implanted in them towards their Offſpring. For Experience ſhews, that the Office of ſuckling conſiderably augments in them the Affection from whence

whence that Tendernefs flows; ferves as Fuel to keep their fond Breafts in one perpetual Glow; and by fweetening their Care, enables them likewife to bring the tender Infants thro' their helplefs Age?

Another Argument for fuckling, which is not fufficiently attended to, becaufe not fufficiently known, is, that the Anxiety and Fatigue is perhaps fully compenfated by the Pleafure. The provident Author of Nature has order'd in this, as in all, or moft other Things, right and natural, that the Inducement fhall more than balance the Difcouragement. All Mothers who have experienc'd it, whofe Minds are temper'd with natural Affection, affure us, that there is an inexpreffible Pleafure in giving Suck, which none but Mothers know; for befides that the Senfation itfelf is faid to be mighty pleafing; to behold the Innocence, the Cunning, the Tricks, and the various Whims of a Child; to obferve likewife the early Sentiments they difcover; muft doubtlefs give a Pleafure which no Words can defcribe. Now if thus much be granted (and furely no Arguments can reafon it away) I cannot help advifing in the ftrongeft Terms, that every Father confent, and even promote, that the Child be fuckled by it's Mother;

Mother; if the Mother be in a Condition for it. But then, this Compliance, this Leave, if I muſt call it ſuch, ſhould be cordial, and from the Heart; otherwiſe a Mother, tho' the beſt Nurſe in the World, may become the moſt improper one, by a Huſband's ſo far ſouring her Temper, as to render her Milk, not only good for nothing, but even pernicious.

The general Good of all being what I aim at, I mean to offer the ſame Advice to all, as far as it can be practiſed; and therefore ſpeak according to the Nature of Things. Still I am not inſenſible how little Probability there is that my Advice herein will be follow'd by Perſons in high Life. For what Room is there in general to hope, that a fine Lady will lay herſelf under any of the neceſſary Reſtraints towards acting the Part of a good Nurſe, and generouſly give up ſome of the vainer Pleaſures of Life, in order to ſtoop to this Part of domeſtic Care? It is true that there may ſometimes be important Reaſons which may make their doing ſo improper; but it is greatly to be fear'd that thoſe Reaſons are oftener affected than real; and as this is a Duty not ſo eaſily diſpenſed with as People are apt to imagine, it is incumbent on Parents of the higheſt

Rank to confider how far they are really juftifiable in deviating from the Laws of Nature. But there is another important Confequence attends the Neglect with which People of Rank treat their Offspring in this Particular; that it thereby becomes a national Evil. It is univerfally known that the Little imitate the Great, and moftly too in what is wrong; that is, they catch their Vices fooner than their Virtues. Hence it happens, that becaufe a Woman of the firft Rank does not deign to fuckle her Child, the Neglect defcends to almoft the loweft Rank; and many Men whofe Figure in Life is very inconfiderable, fcorn to bear the Noife of a Child, tho' their own Flefh and Blood, only becaufe it is a Practice among their Betters to remove them. And hence too the Great have two Reflections to make on this Point, the Duty they owe to their Children, and, (tho' perhaps it is not a proper Obfervation here) the Influence which a Neglect of this Duty has on all beneath them.

While I am enforcing to Mothers the Duty of fuckling their Children, I muft endeavour to omit no material Circumftance, either that will contribute to the Eafe of the one, or the Advantage of the other. The firft that naturally occurs, is, the Time when

when a Child ſhould be put to the Breaſt: and as this is a Matter variouſly thought of, and often erroneouſly managed, tho' I could ſay a good deal from my own Obſervation, I have endeavour'd to ſettle it upon a much ſtronger Baſis; *viz.* the Experience of competent Judges. Dr. *Hunter*, well known to the Public both by his Lectures in Anatomy, and his Practice in Midwifry, and one of the Men-Midwives of the Lying-in-Hoſpital in *Brownlow-Street*, informs me, that at the firſt opening of that Charity, they generally conducted the Buſineſs of ſuckling in the following Manner. The Child was not put to the Breaſt till the Milk came freely, or run out of itſelf; and as the Breaſts commonly began to fill in about eight and forty Hours after Delivery, ſooner or later, they were allowed to fill more and more, perhaps as much longer, 'till the Milk began to diſcharge itſelf: to forward this, the Breaſts were frequently embrocated with warm Oil; to invite the Milk both by the Softneſs of the Oil, and the Motion given the Breaſts by rubbing it in with the Hand. This Method was adhered to pretty generally, 'till they found by Experience that it was wrong. For beſides that the Child might probably ſuffer in ſome Degree, by being ſo long depriv'd of it's moſt natural Phyſic and Food, many grievous Effects often attend the Mother; *viz.* painful Swellings and Inflammations of the Breafts, Milk Fevers, and Milk Sores.

Thefe Inconveniences induced the Practitioners of that Hofpital to alter the Method, which for fome Time paft has been as follows. The Child is put to the Breaft commonly within twenty-four Hours after Delivery: and tho' at firft it fucks little or nothing, yet by this means the Milk comes gradually and kindly; and before the ufual Time of the Breafts hardening in the other Method, the Difficulty is conquered in this; the Milk flows freely, the Breafts are foft and eafy, and the Heat of the Body continues temperate: infomuch that Dr. *Hunter* farther affures me, that there has been much lefs of Inflammations of the Breafts and Milk Fevers, and but one Milk Sore among upwards of fourteen hundred Women that have been deliver'd there fince this Method has been purfued.

Here, tho' it is a Digreffion from my Subject, I cannot help reflecting with Pleafure on the Benefit arifing to many induftrious virtuous People from the Inftitution of this Hofpital. Every Charitable Foundation, every Contribution to relieve the Needy,

Needy, does Honour not only to thofe who give, but to the Nation where it is given; for when Individuals are known to be humane and benevolent, Strangers will conclude it as a national Virtue. It is certain, that all public Receptacles for the Comfort and Support of the Diftreffed Indigent argue a compaffionate Heart in thofe who fupport them, and a juft Senfe of others Woe; but the Lying-in-Hofpital has a Delicacy in it peculiar to itfelf. The Ladies who contribute to it's Support, prove, in Terms far more expreffive than Words, their Sympathy with the Sufferings of their Sex; and particularly with thofe whom Fortune has placed the fartheft from them. The Gentlemen who encourage it, and labour for it's Promotion, fhew a Tendernefs which can only dwell in manly Hearts: for he certainly comes neareft to the Dignity of a Man, who has the tendereft Senfe of the Sufferings of the oppofite Sex; and particularly of thofe, which his own Exiftence is the neceffary Caufe of. But farther, moft other Public Charities feem in their Nature limited; feem to extend no farther than the immediate Relief of thofe under their Care; whereas this is far more extenfive: the Mother is comforted, and with tendereft Care brought thro' her Child-bed; the Child (as far as

Skill can reach) is ſafely entered on the Stage of Life; and thus is Mankind not only preſerved, but perpetuated; and thus too is Society enlarged, and improved, to a boundleſs Degree. Thus much have I ſaid to do juſtice to an Undertaking in itſelf highly laudable, and infallibly productive of the greateſt Good. But there is another Effect, perhaps hitherto unthought of, which will neceſſarily attend this Hoſpital, and is no leſs than a general Concern; that of the Improvement of Midwifry: the ſeveral Gentlemen who attend it in that Capacity, cannot but have the beſt Foundation in their Art, that which is extended and ſtrengthened by the frequent Occurrence of the more nice and uncommon Caſes among ſuch Variety: and the Women whom they educate to Midwifry in that Hoſpital, muſt from their many Opportunities become valuable Practitioners for ſuch of their Sex as are inclined to employ them rather than a Man.

But to return to the Matter in hand. This Method of putting Children to the Breaſt much ſooner than uſual, correſponds with the Opinion of Dr. *Cadogan*, who in a ſmall Pamphlet on the Management of Children, has ſaid a great many ſenſible uſeful Things; and among the reſt, he propoſes, that

that a Child be put to the Breaſt in ſeven or eight Hours after it is born; whereby, ſays he, "It would not only provide for itſelf "the beſt of Nouriſhment, but by opening "a free Paſſage for it, take off the Mother's "Load as it increaſed, before it could oppreſs or hurt her; and therefore effectually prevent the Fever; which is caus'd "only by the painful Diſtention of the lacteal Veſſels of the Breaſts, when the Milk "is injudiciouſly ſuffer'd to accumulate." To this I have two Things to add; Firſt, to recommend to Parents that the Advice here given be reduced to Practice, unleſs ſome extraordinary Circumſtances intervene; in which Caſe, their own Judgment muſt direct them to ſeek an Opinion ſuitable to the Exigence. Secondly, that all Precautions be taken to prevent the Mother's catching Cold, or being too much fatigued in the firſt Days after Delivery. It is here meant, beſides the Child's having it's moſt proper Nouriſhment, the Breaſt, as ſoon as poſſible; that the Mother be ſecured not only from the Danger of ſore Breaſts, but even from Inflammations and Fevers ſo common to the Sex in Childbed. But while we are guarding againſt Miſchief one way, it is no leſs our Duty to prevent it, if poſſible, every way; therefore do I again caution that the utmoſt Care be taken to prevent the Mother's catching Cold, or ſitting up in Bed too long for her Strength in the firſt Attempts to ſuckle her Child. It is common for a Child, when firſt put to the Breaſt, to be unapt; the Mother, eſpecially if a young one, is often awkward; and if the Nurſe be unhandy or careleſs, the Conſequences may be fatal; and indeed frequently are ſo: the Reaſon is plain. The Perſpiration which uſually follows Delivery is neceſſary; and where Nature is defective, Art is employ'd to keep it up: if then theſe Sweats are ſalutary, whatever obſtructs or checks them muſt be dangerous; and nothing ſooner or more certainly effects this than the being injudiciouſly uncover'd. But beſides catching Cold, there is great Danger to be apprehended from Fatigue. That too much Fatigue in theſe early Days after Delivery may be very pernicious, every body knows who is experienced. Nothing ſo common as a Woman's having had a good Labour, and being ſo extremely well, that on the ſecond, third, or fourth Day ſhe indulges herſelf with the Converſation of a Friend, or ſits up in Bed for ſome time for Refreſhment; in Conſequence of which ſhe grows hot, has a reſtleſs Night, and before Morning is in a raging Fever; perhaps delirious.

The

The precife Time of a Child's fucking is a Point much controverted, particularly among Ladies, but nothing afcertain'd. The prefent Fafhion 'tis true, is to let Children fuck only three or four Months; but furely this is too important an affair for Fafhion to take place of Reafon. From my Acquaintance with the Learned on this Head, I gather, that generally fpeaking a Child fhould not fuck lefs than fix Months, nor more than twelve; but that the Medium, that is, nine Months, is for the moft part the beft. Still there may be Reafons for varying thefe ftated Times; if fo, Reafon in that as well as in other things fhould be our Guide. And farther, there may be Circumftances which impede the Mother's fuckling her Child at all; the want of Health is a principal one; but then it fhould be a real want of Health, not an imaginary one. Where then a Doubt arifes, I advife Parents not rafhly and haftily to refolve for themfelves, but to confult proper Judges, and always, where it is in their Power, be determined by their Phyfician.

But here, as an Encouragement to Mothers to fuckle their Children, I muft obferve, that it is the Opinion of Phyficians that many Women would mend their Health by it; and very few, if any, hurt a good

Conſtitution, unleſs thro' Imprudence or Ignorance: now to obviate theſe, let Mothers be careful to ſet out right, and then they have very little to fear.

Hunger, Fatigue, and Fretting, are the three moſt obvious things that impair a Mother's Health in Nurſing. I ſay nothing of groſs Intemperance, violent Paſſions, and the like, for they are always to be baniſh'd; nay we are not once to ſuppoſe they exiſt in the Sex. Hunger is carefully to be avoided: while the Mother gives ſuck, ſhe ſhould never let the Keenneſs of her Appetite go off by waiting long for her Meals; for that often repeated will ſink the Spirits, fill her with Wind, impair her Strength, and conſequently not only hurt herſelf, but prejudice her Milk alſo.

I confeſs it is my Opinion that a very nice regard to a Nurſe's Diet is not ſo generally neceſſary as is imagined. Temperance is univerſally to be held as a Rule; but under the appearance of avoiding one Error, they run into a greater; they often eat of very rich Diſhes, and ſhun the uſe of Vegetables: whereas to People who are young and healthy, nothing is more wholſome than Vegetables blended with Meat: and the only Caution that is material to be given, is, that they guard them with Pepper; whereby they will keep under the Effect they ſometimes have, of producing Wind. But ſhould Garden Stuff, after all this, diſagree, Prudence will certainly direct the Mother to diſuſe it; tho' at the ſame time it muſt be own'd, that where this is the Caſe, her Digeſtion is not what it ought to be to conſtitute perfect Health. To this Head I will add, that where a Woman has been accuſtom'd to drink a glaſs or two of Wine or Ale at Meals, ſhe ſhould not debar herſelf from it now; as her waſte of Strength and Spirits certainly demand at leaſt her uſual way of Life; tho' it does not ſeem needful for her to go far beyond it.

By Fatigue I mean ſo much Exerciſe as manifeſtly impairs the Strength, or brings on various Pains, ſo as to render a Mother incapable of executing what ſhe has begun; or at leaſt makes the Office extremely ſlaviſh to her. Exerciſe is good, but Fatigue is bad. There are ſo many different Conditions in this great Family of the World, and ſo many different Circumſtances in each Station, that it is impoſſible to lay down Rules for every Individual, or preſcribe an univerſal one for all; in general I recommend on this occaſion the joint Attention of both Father and Mother. If a Man reflects

that

that while his Wife is ſuckling her Child, ſhe is labouring to compleat the principal Work for which they came together, he cannot ſurely ſuffer her to endure Fatigue beyond her Power to bear; nor can he feel for her that Tenderneſs he ought, if he impoſes any Hardſhip on her that can be diſpens'd with. On the other hand, the Mother is to remember, that beſides being chearful and keeping her Mind at reſt, ſhe muſt keep her Limbs at reſt too; that is, ſhe muſt often forego other Exerciſe, that ſhe may be enabled to beſtow a larger Portion of Kindneſs on her Child.

But there are ſeveral ways a Woman may be fatigued with Nurſing without the leaſt neceſſity. The firſt thing a Mother has to do, is, to uſe her Child to ſuch Poſitions in ſuckling as ſhe likes beſt, and is moſt convenient to herſelf. When up, the Mother ſhould by all means ſit upright, and the Child be rais'd to the Breaſt: the Child ſhould yield to the Mother, and not the Mother to the Child. That diſtorted Poſture ſo commonly ſeen in ſuckling gives great Pain to the Back, and cramps all the Limbs; and this without any other effect on the Child than indulging a manifeſt Wilfulneſs. When in Bed, the Child ſhould take the Breaſt as it lyes; and not incommode the

Mother

Mother by making her ſit up in Bed by the Hour, purely to humour it, as is too common: for this too, without any Benefit to the Child, greatly increaſes the Mother's Fatigue, by robbing her of her Sleep, and by expoſing her to catch Cold from the various Seaſons it happens in. But theſe Inconveniences may farther be obviated, by letting the Child lye in a Cradle without the Breaſt the Night thro', or with a Maid in another Room; for it is certain, that neither Breaſt, Drink, nor Feeding are ſo abſolutely neceſſary in the Night as is commonly imagin'd. Some of my fair Readers will, I doubt, reject my Counſel in this particular; but I urge it on the double Motive of Benefit to the Child, and Eaſe to the Mother. Yet not to be too rigorous in this Point, not to affect too ſenſibly a Mother's Tenderneſs, ſuppoſe a Child be ſometimes allow'd the Breaſt in the Night, it certainly ſhould be only ſometimes; for the Practice of letting it drag at it the Night thro' is a grievous Error: it hurts both Child and Mother; the Child by this Means is continually wrangling, fretting, and diſſatisfy'd, and the Mother is often ſo ſenſibly affected by it, as even to be thrown into Hyſteric Fits.

Difficult as I acknowledge it is to lay down an univerſal Rule, I will here attempt what

what appears to me to be generally practicable. According to the usual Management of Children at the Breast it may be averr'd, that they have too little Sleep, and too much Food: that is, their Sleep is short and broken thro' Mismanagement, and they are suckled or fed oftener than is conducive to Health. Now to remove this Error, I will not offer any Restraint in the Day-time, (tho' that in the opinion of an ingenious Writer [a] requires it) but endeavour to effect it by regulating the Night. To this End let a Child be undress'd, it's Night things put on, and be fed or suckled at seven o'Clock, and then put into it's Cradle; where without rocking (if used to it and in Health) it will fall asleep. Supposing the Mother to go to Bed at ten or eleven, if the Child should happen to be awake, let it be turn'd dry (as the Nurses term it) and suckled again; and it will sleep soundly for six or seven Hours: perhaps now and then it will whimper a little, but if it is not touch'd it will fall asleep again immediately. But supposing it is not awake when the Mother goes to Bed, let it not by any means be disturb'd, for that breaking of Childrens Rest so common with Parents makes them vastly tiresome; all that the Mother has to do in this Case is, to keep a warm Cloth in Bed with her, and when the Child awakes

[a] Dr. *Cadogan*.

take

take away the wet one as ſoon as poſſible, that it may not be too much diſturb'd by the Senſe of Cold; that done, let it have the Breaſt, and it will commonly ſleep again till it is time for the Family to riſe. The Child ſhould not have its Cloth ſhifted again; for frequently opening it when it ought to ſleep is a great Impediment to it's Reſt; and while wrapt up warm, and it lies ſtill, it receives no Harm from being wet: to this muſt be added, that the Mother be very huſh; no talking, no ſhewing the Candle, the Day-light, or any thing that may awaken it thoroughly. If this Method be adher'd to, I am perſuaded it will have many good Effects; it will give a longer reſpite than uſual from feeding or ſuckling; it will obtain what is of great Conſequence to a Child's Health, Sleep; and it will facilitate the Mother's Taſk by leſſening her Fatigue.

To ſuffer by Hunger or Fatigue does great injury to the Mother principally, but Fretting has always a double Conſequence; it hurts the Child too. A fretful Temper turns even Pleaſure into Pain; well then may it make a neceſſary Care a Fatigue. One Diſtinction however I would make that I think deſerves Attention; whether the Fretfulneſs be in Nature, be fixt and incurable; or whether it be owing to external

Accidents,

Accidents, the Occurrences of Things; ſuch as frequent Provocations from a Huſband, untoward Children, waſteful Servants, vexatious Law Suits, and many other Evils Life is fraught with. In the firſt Caſe, Women would do well to let ſuckling alone; for warm as I am in recommending this Practice, it is certain there are ſome few Exceptions, and this is one. But in the other, I urge ſuckling in great meaſure as a Remedy. For let the naturally good-temper'd Mother but once reflect that Fretting hurts her Child, and ſhe will avoid it for her Infant's ſake: beſides, the Love created in her for it by the Exerciſe of this natural Duty, will make her forget many other Cares; at leaſt it will counterpoiſe her Troubles, by mingling Pleaſure with Pain.

There is a Claſs of Women who are lifeleſs and ſluggiſh, an inſipid Race that do neither good nor harm; theſe ſhould by all means ſuckle their Children, for by ſo doing they would be enliven'd, and animated with a Deſire to become uſeful. If too they reflect, that the Intention of Nature is, that they ſhould rear their Children as well as bear them, they will ſoon be aſhamed of doing their Work by halves: and thus become much happier in themſelves, and of much more Conſequence to Society.

By the Obſervance of theſe few Rules, Mothers in general may ſuckle their Children, not only without Pain or Injury, but even with Pleaſure and Profit. They may ſometimes improve their Health; often leſſen their Cares, and mend their Temper and Diſpoſitions; and will always have a pleaſing Conſciouſneſs that they have obey'd the Laws of Nature, by having done all that was incumbent on them.

If after all that has been ſaid it is not thought expedient that a Child ſhould ſuck it's Mother; a Breaſt is certainly the beſt Subſtitute: but great Care ſhould here be taken, in the Choice of a Nurſe. She ſhould be young, healthy, good-humour'd, ſprightly, and temperate. The newer her Milk the better; it is beſt not to be above three Months old; and ſhould never exceed ſix Months, when the Child is firſt put to her Breaſt; if beyond that, either the Child muſt be wean'd too ſoon, or ſuck a ſtaler Milk than perhaps it ought. Some are of Opinion, that Breaſt-milk begins to loſe of it's nutritious Quality after the Expiration of a Year; but let us here obſerve the Operations of Nature. The younger Breaſt-Milk is, the thinner and lighter it is; fitted by Nature for the tender Stomachs of new-

born

born Babes: as it grows older, it becomes thicker, richer, and more ſtubborn of Digeſtion; by which gradual Change it is ſuited to the relative riſing Powers of Digeſtion in the Child. Hence it would ſeem, that Breaſt-milk, does not at this ſtated Time become poorer, but richer; rich perhaps to a degree of Rancidity; which, like groſs Food to others, is ſometimes ſtronger than Children can bear: and on this Principle it is I recommend where a Breaſt is to be ſought, that either the Milk be young, or the Child wean'd ſoon.

But ſuppoſing a Child to have no Breaſt (as Arguments whether good or bad will often be brought againſt it) the want of it muſt be ſupply'd by coming as near to Nature as we can. In order thereto, it is the Opinion of a Phyſician * in the Practice of Midwifry, whoſe Judgment in this Matter ought to have weight, that Cows-milk be diluted with Water, 'till it becomes as thin as Breaſt-milk, and given warm ſeveral times in the Day; that is, as often as a Child would have the Breaſt were it to be ſuckled: beſides this, it ſhould ſometimes be fed with other Milk Diet; viz. Bread and

* Dr. *Parſons.*

and Water boil'd lightly together, and Milk added to it.

When a Child ſucks it is uſual to feed it with nothing but Water Pap, that is, Bread and Water boil'd together, without the Addition of Milk; from a Notion that it ſhould not have two ſorts of Milk; but this Treatment is ſurely erroneous. Nay, there are ſome who improve upon this Error, and give their Children (at leaſt for the firſt Month) Water Pap only, even tho' they have no Breaſt.

It is both natural and commendable in Parents to inform themſelves what Diſtempers Children are ſubject to, and uſually dye of; and if we farther refer them to the Bills of Mortality, they will conſtantly find, that Gripes, Looſeneſs, and Convulſions make a great Part of the Account. Now beſides the latent Cauſes of theſe Diſeaſes, they have a very obvious one, *viz.* improper Food. For my own part I am convinc'd, even to Demonſtration, that many Infants owe their Death to the Miſtakes committed in this Point; and often to the falſe Practice of giving them Bread and Water only, and omitting that moſt ſalutary part the Milk. Milk (again I repeat it) is the Food of of Nature; with that alone, to an Infant, we may do almoſt every thing; without it, nothing.

Tho' theſe firſt Rules here laid down ſhould meet with general Approbation, and Parents from ſeeing how natural and reaſonable this Doctrine is, be induced to follow it; they have ſtill many things both to do and avoid, that are greatly conducive to their Childrens Health; and therefore demand their Attention and Regard.

As we have urg'd that Milk is the Food of Nature, ſo we may with equal Propriety call Bread the Staff of Life. Breaſt-milk my Readers will obſerve, is preferr'd to every other; but where that cannot be obtain'd, then Cows-milk, made thinner and lighter by the Addition of Water, is to ſupply its place; and, between whiles, the Child is to be fed with Milk-victuals; from which, as it is thicken'd with Bread, it will receive great Nouriſhment. But here great care muſt be taken to keep up its Appetite for this Food at firſt ſetting out; as it is of all others the moſt proper; and not ſpoil its Reliſh for it by the Admixture or Intervention of any thing elſe while in Health, 'till a more advanc'd Age.

The

The firſt Error uſually run into, is, the immoderate uſe of Spice and Sugar; which Phyſicians who have conſider'd theſe matters poſitively condemn: and if a Child is well, putting either of theſe in it's Victuals, anſwers not the leaſt good End. Spice and Sugar are certainly fine natural Productions, and of vaſt Uſe to Mankind; but the Food of Infants ſhould be as ſimple as poſſible; and if it is made otherwiſe by the early uſe of theſe, the Effects will always be very troubleſome, and oftentimes miſchievous. What is more common than to give young Children Lumps of Sugar to eat; yet what more erroneous? Every Day's Experience ſhews us how wrong the Practice is: it vitiates their Taſte; creates in them an unconquerable Fondneſs for it, even to a Degree of Vulgarneſs; and manifeſtly clogs their Stomachs.

The Error next in rank to theſe, or rather a part of the ſame, as Sugar is greatly concern'd in it, is, the Cuſtom Parents have of giving Children Tea. Tea, to a young Child, if we omit the Milk, has not a ſingle Ingredient to recommend it: the Sugar in it has already been treated of; the Water, (as Tea is uſually drank too hot,) ſerves to ſcald it's Mouth and Throat, or at

beſt

beſt to relax the Stomach and weaken the Tone of it; and the Plant or Shrub it ſelf has Qualities, which, to ſay the leaſt of it, ſeldom contributes to promote it's Health.

That this Herb of which our Tea is made has had many Tongues to ſpeak it's Praiſe, I am convinc'd; or it would not have obtain'd that univerſal uſe we now ſee made of it: and ſome likewiſe have taken up their Pen, and with great Labour deſcrib'd its Virtues and Utility to Mankind: but all this is too weak to ſtand againſt that infallible Guide, Experience. To inſiſt that Tea has no good Qualities would be offering an Affront to the Judgment and Experience of many wiſe People, and is very far from being my Deſign; on the contrary, I am convinc'd it has. Bohea Tea is eſteem'd balſamic, and Green is allow'd to be an aſtringent Stomachic. Still theſe or any other particular Qualities, do not juſtify it's general uſe; for while the ſame Experience proves that for one who receives Benefit by drinking it, ten receive Harm, it muſt upon the Whole be condemned.

Tea may be conſider'd like ſome certain Drugs, which in ſkilful hands are ſafe and uſeful, but in ignorant ones, poiſonous. That

That the intemperate and indiſcriminate uſe of Tea is hurtful, is too well known to be diſputed; ſome it is true are manifeſtly refreſh'd, comforted and enliven'd by it; others feel not the leaſt ſenſible effect from the longeſt uſe of it, and drink it purely thro' Cuſtom; but again there are othets, and thoſe much the Majority, who impair their Health ſo viſibly by this pernicious Practice, that they ſhorten their Lives, or at leaſt render them comfortleſs, if not miſerable. Now who that conſiders theſe things well, or but once reflects that 'tis at leaſt ten to one that their Children are Sufferers by it, can reaſonably ſpeaking be haſty in bringing them to it; eſpecially too if we farther reflect, that by a ſeeming magic Power it often enſlaves People even to Infatuation. Infants then have nothing to do with this darling deluding Liquor; and when at a more advanc'd Age, Parents ſhould ſtill give it them very ſparingly, if at all; and be careful to keep them if poſſible from ever being attach'd to it.

Before I take my leave of this Article, let me recommend to Parents ſome Obſervations for their farther guidance herein. Thoſe Children who have weak Nerves ſhould not by any means drink Tea at all. Tea ſhould never

ver be made ſtrong; nor drank in large quantities, nor hot, nor without Milk, nor very ſweet. Tea ſhould not be drank in a Morning by thoſe who cannot eat; nor can it in general be drank in the Afternoon with Safety, but by thoſe who have eat a hearty Dinner, and drink it ſoon. Bohea Tea is found to affect the Nerves the moſt ſenſibly; and Green, from its Aſtringency, is not only the moſt grateful, but its Effects prove it to be leaſt hurtful.

Many are the Errors which Parents fall into in the Management of Children, eſpecially at firſt ſetting out. I have often ſeen Children waſh'd away with the watry Gripes, when upon inquiry it appear'd they had no other Food but Water Pap: others reject this, and fall into the Error of giving Children Broth; which alone, is in it's Nature too laxative for Infants. But Water Pap muſt be condemn'd as far the moſt improper; for it is manifeſt that Bread, of which it is made, beſides the Fermentation it undergoes in the Hands of the Baker, has, according to the Juices it meets with, a farther Power of fermenting in the Stomach: therefore, ſhould Nature by chance be thwarted, ſhould univerſal Obſervation be for once contradicted, by ſhewing a Child whom Milk is unfit for;

in

in that cafe I recommend, that Broth be added to the Pap; which will bring the Food neareft to the Quality of that animal Fluid, Milk, the natural Nourifhment. And as watry Gripes are often owing to ill-digefted Pap, Broth, tho' laxative, would certainly from its Smoothnefs prevent or leffen the Stimulation in the Bowels; as we find in the Cure of fuch Gripes great Service from Glyfters of Oil, Chickens-guts, and other things of the like Kind.

But farther; I am clearly of Opinion, that the firft Change in Childrens Diet fhould be from Milk to Broth, and not from Milk to Meat: their tender Stomachs ought not to be put too early upon the Office of digefting the flefhy Fibres of Meat; but they may, as they approach to a Year old, by way of Introduction to eating Flefh, and by way of changing Diet, fometimes have Broth; but by no means for conftant ufe, to the neglect of Milk.

It is univerfally confefs'd, that in *England* we eat too much Flefh; and were I to urge all that might be faid on that Head, it would be dwelling too long on a fingle Point. But fince this Error of our Country is acknowledg'd by many of the wifeft Men in it, let it ſerve as a general Caution to Parents; let them turn it to the Advantage of the riſing Generation; by being neither haſty in giving Fleſh Meat to their Children, nor even permitting them to be intemperate in the Uſe of it.

To enforce this Precept, and prove the Reaſonableneſs of not giving Children Meat ſo ſoon as is uſual, I will here obſerve, that Phyſicians ſay the firſt Digeſtion ſhould be in the Mouth, the ſecond in the Stomach; whence it appears that Children have no Buſineſs with Meat 'till they have Teeth to chew it; nay, not 'till they have their Mouths almoſt full of Teeth; for they have not the Power of grinding down their Meat ſufficiently 'till they have got ſome of their ſtrongeſt Teeth, and thoſe every one is ſenſible do not come firſt. Hence we are furniſhed with an admirable Hint, which not to endeavour to reduce to Practice, would be injuring our Children, and baffling the Labours of learned Men, who make the Good of Mankind the Study of their Lives. Parents by the ſame Leſſon are inſtructed likewiſe, to make their Children accuſtom themſelves to chew their Meat well their whole Lives; for it is certain they would thereby

prevent

prevent many ill Effects arising from Indigestion.

Having thus, as near to Nature as I am able, led Parents into the first Steps of the Management of their Childrens Health, I shall now touch on Art; a little of which may, and will be necessary. It is plain that Children are born full of Foulness, full of Excrement; and Nature to remedy this, gives a purgative Quality to the Mother's first Milk; which Quality, as the Child cleanses, goes off. But if this first Milk be drawn away by another, as is frequent, in order to ease the Breasts; or the Child does not suck it's Mother, but an older Milk; in that Case it should most certainly be purged three or four times in the Month. For my own Part I have gone farther, and tho' my Children had the first Milk, I always began by giving them a little Syrup of Rhubarb and Oil of Almonds; which has constantly had a good Effect, not only on them, but on many others under my Care: the Rhubarb scours and cleanses them, and the Oil in some measure blunts its griping Quality, and prevents its leaving a Costiveness so common to that Drug. But tho' I have frequently given this, yet Rhubarb in Substance, corrected with a small Portion of

 Aromatic,

Aromatic, or mix'd with Gascoign's Powder, is found by Experience to agree very well: Syrup of Violets or Marshmallows, join'd with Oil of Almonds, are frequently given in order to cleanse the first Passages, and are very proper; tho' not so efficacious as Rhubarb. Nor are there any better Purges than these for new-born Infants, unless, (which very seldom happens) in great Costiveness, and then a little Manna. What farther relates to Physic and physical People, shall be spoken of hereafter.

In a Treatise of this Kind nothing must pass unobserved that is important; and nothing is more so, than the destructive Practice of drinking spirituous Liquors. For a Woman to have a Habit of Dram-drinking is always detestable; but for one who gives Suck, it is horrible beyond Expression: it is fraught with double Mischief, Destruction to herself, and Destruction to the Child. One would imagine, that so odious a Vice wanted not to be inveigh'd against; or at most that the Caution could no where be useful, but amongst Basket-women and Billingsgates. 'Tis true indeed, that the Illiterate and Vulgar are the most addicted to it; but melancholy Experience shews us, that Women every way happy in Life, Women of the best Understanding, and the best

beſt Education, are but too often tainted with it.

It is not my Deſign in general to write on the Foibles or Vices of Parents, but of Children; yet it muſt be owned, that where the Actions of the one have an Influence on the other, where the Connection is ſo cloſe that the Health or Morals of Children are affected by the Conduct of Parents, it is perfectly conſiſtent with the Plan I have laid down; and conſequently is within my Province. Thus then I obſerve, that there are many Women who never taſted ſpirituous Liquors 'till they gave Suck. A Child is kept lugging at the Breaſt 'till the Mother is ready to ſink, and a Friend recommends a Dram: the innocent Woman ſtarts at the Propoſition; but it being ſtrenuouſly urg'd that it will do her good and the Child too, ſhe follows the Counſel and drinks it. How reluctantly and with how much diſlike may be known by her ſhaking her Head at the very Smell of it, making Faces when it is down, and declaring it is naſty Stuff. Now for a while let me talk like an Apothecary. The Nerves give Senſation to our whole Frame whether of Pain or Pleaſure. This Dram acts immediately on the Nerves of the Stomach, and inſtantly communicates itſelf to thoſe of the Brain, which are exquiſitely fine; the Senſation is pleaſing, a general Glow is felt, and the temporary Relief it gives, perſuades her that Drams are not ſo pernicious as People pretend. But by and by the Languor returns, and ſhe has recourſe to her Dram again; tho' perhaps with this Difference, that inſtead of being perſuaded into it ſhe ſeeks it herſelf; and thus by a Return of Wants, ſhe finds a Return of Deſire; ſhe flies ſo often to her fancied Remedy, that at length ſhe is innocently and inſenſibly led into a Habit which infatuates her: even ſo far as often to rob her of the Power of getting rid of it. But the Habit contracted, what is the Effect? Why, that which at firſt was only a ſlight Injury, by this means becomes a mortal Wound.

The Human Frame, that Maſter-Piece of infinite Wiſdom, is compos'd of a great variety of Parts, of different Make, Texture and Quality; each of which has it's Uſe, and proper Office aſſign'd it. But that I may not confound any of my Readers by nice or obſcure Phyſical Diviſions, I will ſay it is compos'd of Solids and Fluids: the Fluids, that is, the Blood and other Juices, are allotted to nouriſh and preſerve the Solids; and the Solids, that is, the Fleſh and other

other hard Parts, ſerve as Pipes or Channels to convey in a due Courſe the ſeveral Fluids to their deſtin'd End. Now to preſerve Health, it is neceſſary that our whole Machine acts regularly; which it cannot do for any long Time with the pernicious Habit we have been ſpeaking of. Drams, which at firſt give only a ſlight Wound to the Nerves, by frequent Repetition enfeeble them; and in the End totally diſable them; as is evident by their bringing on Tremblings, weakening the Memory, and impairing the Underſtanding. To maintain Health, the Solids are to keep up their due Force or Spring, that they may propel the Fluids, and prevent their breaking them down by too great a Reſiſtance. The Fluids are to be kept in ſuch a ſtate, that they may neither run too rapidly, nor clog by the way for want of the circulating Power. Thus in Rivers, where the Banks and Fences are weak, the Preſſure of the Water will break them down; or if the Water be clogg'd and render'd foul by any Mixture foreign to it's Nature, or is otherwiſe obſtructed in it's Courſe, it cannot reach thoſe various Meanders, thoſe ſmall Canals it was allotted to fill.

Hence every Eye may ſee how deſtructive this unnatural Habit muſt be to our Frame. The Tone of the Stomach is weaken'd, and with it, the Power of Digeſtion; Obſtructions of the Liver and other Parts enſue; the Solids are broke, and the Fluids forſake their proper Channels: hence Jaundice, Dropſies, Palſies, and various other Diſtempers, fatal in their Conſequences, and doubly acute to thoſe who reflect, that they have brought them on themſelves: for however thoughtleſs or indifferent they may be while in Health, when bitter Remembrance accompanies the ſevere Effects, the Situation muſt be dreadful.

I have obſerv'd that many are innocently led into this grievous Habit: and they are the more liable to it, as the Goodneſs of their Conſtitution preſerves ſome longer than others, from being ſenſible of it's ill Effects. But they muſt beware of Illuſions, and convince themſelves of one Truth at leaſt; that inſtead of that Nutrition which proper Food yields, the Blood and other Juices are by this means vitiated; and with them that moſt ſalutary Fluid the Milk. It is true indeed that all Drams are not alike pernicious; nor do they, as I have juſt hinted, act alike on all Conſtitutions. Yet thus much is certain; that they all contain fiery Particles, a Pora Portion of cauſtic inflammable Matter, in general very injurious to our whole Frame; very unfit to circulate in our Blood and Juices; and above all, extremely prejudicial to thoſe Infants who imbibe the Infection by ſucking at a Breaſt thus unhappily tainted.

But beſides this dreadful Habit in the Mother or Nurſe, there is a Practice among the Vulgar ſtill more ſhocking; and which muſt make every reaſonable Creature ſhrink with Horror; that of giving Drams to the Children themſelves, even while Infants. Nothing is more ſtrongly urg'd by all moral Writers than the Force of Example; and when they mean to paint a bad Parent, they deſcribe a Child imitating thoſe Vices his Father acts before him. But here Deſcription is too weak; no Language has Force enough to expreſs the Horror of this Vice! Theſe unhappy wretched Parents foreſtall Imitation; they ſtay not 'till the Child has Power to follow their Example; but pour the deadly Poiſon down the poor Babe's Throat, even before it can ſpeak! What, I ſay again, what Language can deſcribe the Horror of this Vice? Surely none.

All wiſe Men agree, that Virtues flow,

or ought to flow, from the Head; that the Inferior receive their Influence from the Superior; and moſt act by Imitation of their Betters: but Experience ſhews us, that the Little can ſometimes teach the Great Virtues they were before Strangers to; and by a ſtill ſtrange Inverſion of the natural Order of Things, it often happens, that the Great imitate the Vices of the Little. But here I cannot refrain from exhorting Parents of every Rank never to ſuffer themſelves to fall into ſo dreadful an Error as that juſt hinted at. Thoſe who are already tainted with it are perhaps too abandon'd to be reclaim'd; or have it not in their Power to remove the Miſchief they have cauſed: but thoſe who are happily Strangers to it, muſt keep their Attention awake; muſt live in a conſtant Reſolution never to let a Child ſo much as touch ſo dangerous a Weapon; unleſs they chooſe to be their Childrens Murderers; chooſe to have them fall a Sacrifice to ſome dire Diſeaſe; or become Cripples, Idiots, or Brutes.

Before I quit this Head, I muſt take Notice of an inferior Degree of the ſame Error; leſs a Vice indeed, becauſe there is an Intention of Good in it, tho' generally a miſtaken one; I mean that of putting Brandy and other ſpirituous Liquors into Childrens Victuals. How this Practice came to be introduced is amazing! But tho' the general Pretence is preventing or curing Wind and Gripes, it is highly erroneous: for where theſe Diſorders really exiſt they ſhould be treated in another Manner; and by People whoſe Judgment can be depended on.

The next Degree of Error to this, is the early Cuſtom Parents have of giving their Children Wine. Grown People, even among the Temperate, often drink much more of it than is either needful or beneficial; but Children want it not at all. To give Wine to Infants is a groſs Error; and even to thoſe who have paſs'd that Stage, the Practice is very wrong.

Wine, tho' a general Term for the Juice produced from Grapes, is undoubtedly a very different Liquor, not only in Colour and Flavour, but in Quality, according to the Country it grows in; as is manifeſt by the different Effects of it on the Human Body. One Sort is found to conſtringe too much; another is loaded with Tartar; a third abounds with a large Portion of inflammable Spirit; and ſo on. But not to enter into a phyſical Analyſis of Wine, we will

will ſay it is allow'd to aſſiſt the Digeſtion, to warm the Blood, and give a certain Sprightlineſs, which, in other Words, we call a Flow of Spirits. Now in the Caſe of Children we injure them if we give them groſs Food, ſuch as requires Wine to digeſt; and if Wine be added to it, we put Fuel to Fire, Flame to Flame; nor does the Blood and Spirits need this foreign Aſſiſtance while young: the one is by Nature ſufficiently warm'd; and the other are beſt ſupported by Temperance and a chearful Diſpoſition.

I will not take upon me to fix preciſe Rules on this Head, both becauſe it is very difficult, and in general they would not be adher'd to: but thus much I ſeriouſly recommend, that Children in the firſt Septenary taſte no Wine at all; in the ſecond be vaſtly ſparing; and in the third fix a Temperance built on ſolid Principles of Reaſon and Virtue; ſuch as will beſt ſecure to them Health and Happineſs for their whole Lives.

I am here naturally led to ſpeak of Malt Liquor, the native Produce of our Country: but on this, as well as the two foregoing Heads, we muſt keep Temperance in in View, from the double Motive of Health and Virtue. Experience teaches us, that Malt Liquor can be rais'd to any Degree of Strength; that it is capable of inflaming the Blood and intoxicating the Brain; consequently it is capable of weakening and destroying our Frame when intemperately used. But besides these Effects, it has others often very hurtful, but less regarded, because less sensible. One, from a natural Weakness of the Bowels, it throws into habitual Purgings; another it oppresses with Wind; and in a third, from its glutinous Quality, it obstructs some of the Viscera, and has a peculiar Tendency to clog the Vessels of the Lungs, and thereby hinder Respiration, produce Coughs, and those fatal Circumstances frequently attending them. Hence it is easy to see how necessary the Parents Attention is, to guide their Children herein. Infants, at least for the first Year, have no Business with Malt Liquor at all; they ought not to taste it: Milk, or Water, or both together, is their proper Drink; and if after this Age, these were made the Liquor to drink with their Food, it would be no worse for them. However, not to be too rigorous in this respect, let Children after the first Year, wash down their Victuals with light clear Small-beer;

and

and nothing beyond that for the firſt ſeven Years. In the ſecond and third Septenary, the ſame Rule which has been laid down concerning Wine, ſhould be obſerv'd in all ſtrong Malt Liquors; they ſhould be very ſparingly uſed. Nothing is more dangerous than the Indulgence of Parents in this Point; for beſides the many ill Effects already mentioned, 'tis coarſe and vulgar; it clouds the Underſtanding, and renders young People unfit for Study. Beſides theſe, it gives them an early Bloatedneſs; and greatly endangers the laying the Foundation of a Sot for Life: or at leaſt gives them ſuch a Hankering, as cannot but be a great Impediment to their Happineſs.

Nothing is more talk'd of for the Good of Children, and yet nothing more unſettled, than the neceſſary Degree of Warmth; and while ſome Parents are ſanguine in maintaining the Neceſſity of much Cloathing, there are others as obſtinately prone to freeze their tender Babes: even ſkilful and ingenious Phyſians diſagree in this Particular.

It is a Maxim in Philoſophy, that Heat is a Principle of Life: and indeed, without the Aſſiſtance of the Schools, every one knows the Truth of it. All know, that Life

Life is warm, Death is cold; and therefore to ſupport Life, there muſt always be a Degree of Warmth. This premiſed, it appears that Warmth is natural to us; but where to begin, or how to maintain ſuch a Degree of it in our Children as will keep us from either Extreme, is not eaſy to determine. However, to keep as wide of Error as we can, we muſt keep cloſe to Nature's Laws.

Nature then, I think, points out to us, that new-born Children want more Cloaths in Proportion than others. When we conſider how warm a Bed they have long been wrapp'd in before their Birth; when we conſider too how tender all their Fibres muſt be; and ſee them ſhivering, trembling and cold as ſoon as the external Air ſurrounds them; we cannot but conclude that they are greatly cheriſhed and comforted by the Addition of Cloaths.

It is true that the ſame Philoſophy which teaches us that Heat is a Principle of Life, teaches alſo, that Action is the Cauſe of Heat: but new-born Infants being incapable of Action to any Degree, it appears to me, that for the Reaſons already given, they ſtand in need of an additional, or rather, an adventi-

adventitious Warmth, from Cloaths, Fire, Sun, or all, in their proper Time and Place.

Should any one urge that thin Cloathing of Children is the rational Way to make them hardy, and inure them to Cold, I am ready to grant it; but I cannot help being of Opinion, that it ought not to be begun with. In moſt other Things relating to Children we ſucceed beſt by beginning at once; but here I think we ſhould proceed by Degrees. Let Parents then at the Birth give Children all the Comfort Cloaths can afford them; and when ſome Months Time has hardened their Fibres, and thereby ſtrengthened their Solids, let them be thinned gradually. One ſenſible Diſtinction may be made that ſhould be univerſally regarded: that is, the Difference of Climate and Seaſons. A Child born in the midſt of Summer, or where the Air is incapable of affecting it very ſenſibly, need not to have ſo much cloathing as one born in the Depth of Winter, or in a colder Climate.

It is eaſy for my Readers to ſee that I am an Advocate for Warmth; and that I do not only recommend it as yielding great Comfort to Infants, but eſteem it highly neceſſary ceffary and ufeful to them: and fhould any farther Proof be required to fupport this Opinion, we may refer to all created Nature, animate and inanimate.

In this View of Nature we fhall find the Birds not only provide Nefts for their young, but cover them with their Wings, to guard them from the chilly Air, 'till Time has encreafed their Feathers. The Beafts with amazing Tendernefs, cherifh their young, 'till Nature has lengthened the Hair, the Wool, or whatever covers them; or Time has given them the Power of Action. Farther we fhall find, that Infects, and all the vegetable Creation, fhoot out into Life, and receive Vigor, Comfort, and Support, from that glorious Body the Sun: fo indifpenfably neceffary is Warmth; and fo effential to the raifing and preferving of All.

Such of my Readers as agree with me on this Head, muft ftill be cautious not to overact their Part. This Preceps fuits fo well the tender Nature of Mothers, that if heedlefs, they will eafiy flide into Error; and I fhould be wanting in the Duty of a faithful Guide, or an honeft Advifer, if I did not endeavour to prevent it.

Dr.

Dr. *James Douglas*, deservedly eminent in his Profession, once (within my own Knowledge) gave it as his Opinion of a Child he attended, that it perished with Cold. The Doctor had laid a Woman of Rank of her first, nay her only Child, a Son too, and Heir to a large Estate. The Season was cold; the Child was dry-nurs'd; and a small four-post Bed was, by the Advice of some ignorant People, made on purpose for it to lye in alone. In this neglected starving Way the Child was kept 'till ready to expire, and when too late to help it, they sought Advice. All Means were try'd in vain, the poor Babe sunk into the Grave: and, as I have already observ'd, the Doctor, upon examining every Circumstance, pronounc'd it starv'd to Death. Here we have an Instance of one Extreme of Error; and I have introduc'd it as a Hint to Parents that all Extremes are to be avoided; and that while they shrink at the one, they must be careful not to plunge into the other.

It has already been agreed, that Children at the Birth should have all the Comfort Cloaths can give them. I will now observe, that it is every Way advantageous, that for the first Year at least, they lye in a Cradle, or in a small Crib by the Bed-side of the Parents,

rents, or whoever has the Care of them. To put an Infant in a Bed by itſelf for ſeveral Hours before the Bed-time of the Mother or Nurſe, is in general too cold a Situation; and afterwards, if it is not then too hot, which with ſome is a doubt, it is attended with ſeveral Inconveniences. Firſt, it is pretty ſure to diſturb the Child; a Matter of real Conſequence: ſecondly, when once diſturb'd, it will very likely have no Sleep again but lying at the Breaſt, a Circumſtance attended with great Trouble and Anxiety to thoſe who ſuckle it: thirdly, there is always Danger more or leſs of the Child being overlaid; which is a Conſideration that ought juſtly to alarm every Parent, as many Children have by this means been kill'd in one Night's time. I am very ſenſible how watchful a tender Mother uſually is, but there are Times that the beſt are unguarded; and it is ſurely right for them to put it out of their own Power to hazard ſo dreadful an Accident. Nay this Danger has been thought ſo great, however common the Practice is, that the moſt ſenſible People have ſpoke and wrote againſt it. To obviate therefore this Evil, Parents need only let Infants lye in a Cradle or Crib; which will keep them in a regular equal Warmth, ſecure them from all unneceſſary Diſturbance,

Disturbance, and effectually prevent any fatal Accident.

By what has already been advanc'd, it appears, that tho' due Care is recommended, yet it is not design'd to cherish that false Delicacy which Parents, especially Mothers, are but too apt to keep up in their Children, whether Boys or Girls; on the contrary I have advis'd, that their Cloathing be thinn'd by Degrees. Let them too be wash'd every Day with cold Water, the Head and Limbs at least, if not all over; and be carried out as much as can be into the open Air.

To breathe in a free, open, pure Air, is undoubtedly of great Use; by giving that Spring to the Solids so conducive to the establishing and preserving Health. Children therefore, especially if born in *London*, stand in need of this Assistance; they should often have the Freedom of tasting a sweeter Air, than that which usually surrounds their Habitation. Here I am aware, that this Advice, instead of being properly relish'd, will be swallow'd greedily; instead of its serving to rouse the Care of Parents, it will endanger the banishing the Child, which under the Pretext that Air is good, will be sent to a Place, where perhaps every thing else

elſe is bad. Parents, eſpecially the Fathers, who do not love the Noiſe or any other of the Inconveniences attending the Care of Children, have a ſhort Way of doing Buſineſs by ſending them at once into the Country; and to ſupport the Reaſonableneſs of their Conduct, readily tell their Friends, that thoſe who write about theſe Matters recommend Air, and ſay that Children thrive beſt in it. But ſurely they have never ſtudy'd the Duty of Parents, or they muſt know, that it is always incumbent on them, unleſs Neceſſity prevent it, to rear their Children themſelves. But to prove farther that it is not always a Child's Good which they ſeek, ſo much as their own Eaſe, it is often ſent to be nurs'd even in *London*; ſometimes too in a part much worſe than they themſelves live in; perhaps where noxious Effluvia are continually ſurrounding it; or in ſome narrow Lane or cloſe Alley.

Where real Neceſſity pleads, no Arguments can be brought againſt it: otherwiſe I would univerſally recommend, that Children be brought up under the Eye of the Parents. Let the Methods propos'd have a fair Tryal; if thoſe are ineffectual, and the Child does not thrive, by all means remove it into the Country; but ſtill, if practicable, accom-

accompany'd with the Mother, and under her Care; if that cannot be comply'd with, ſend it to a Nurſe. Still I have one Objection that has great Weight with me, whatever it may have with my Readers. The common Country People (ſuch as we may ſuppoſe take Children to nurſe) tho' uſually very innocent, have nevertheleſs that Innocence intermixt with a large Portion of Obſtinacy; in ſhort, they will always do their own Way. Now it is well known that almoſt the only Fleſh Meat theſe People eat the Year thro', is Bacon and Pork; with this Meat, which of all others is the worſt in the World for Children, the Nurſes cram them unmercifully. To tell them that they give Children Meat too young, avails nothing; to urge that it is a groſs kind of Food, capable of creating bad Humours in the Blood, and thereby accumulating Diſorders, which like a ſmother'd Fire, will ſome time or other burſt out with Violence, is like encountering the Winds; Don't you ſee, they cry, how fat and jolly the little Rogue is? They are not aware, that to be fat is one thing, and to be healthy another: for bad Fat may be compared to ill-gotten Wealth, they both prey upon the Vitals. Thus then while I maintain the Advantages ariſing from Childrens Breathing in a pure Air, I

cannot

cannot help condemning the Practice of exposing them to many other Dangers.

Besides the Food, Warmth and Air, necessary for preserving the Health of Children, there is another Mean of great Importance, but much neglected, to the Detriment of many; viz. Exercise. When some Months Time, as I observed before, has strengthened their Solids, they are then fitted for Action; without which there is but little chance for Health: the Laws of Nature demand it; and it is almost incredible, the Mischief that attends the want of it. Exercise affords the most natural and the most comfortable Warmth to our whole Frame that can be. Exercise makes the Blood and other Juices circulate with Freedom; prevents the Mischief too often arising from Stagnation, and throws off the redundant Matter through the Pores of the Skin by insensible Perspiration. And Exercise too, greatly contributes to that Flow of Spirits, that lively pleasing Air and chearful Countenance so essential to our Happiness.

The first half Year of a Child's Life is far the least troublesome to a Mother or Nurse; for after that time Children begin to take Notice, shew they love Action, and where

where they are well nurſed, never are ſo happy as when they are exerciſed; and indeed it is ſcarcely poſſible to give them too much of it. There ſhould be no Sluggards about a Child, no body that wants either Will or Power to toſs it about continually; and from ſix Months, to a Year and half, or two Years old, it is really a great Fatigue to give it due Attendance. But Parents muſt remember it is an indiſpenſible Duty; and their faithful Diſcharge of it will, generally ſpeaking, be amply rewarded by a more ſolid Health in their Children than can be expected without it; and by having their future Trouble greatly leſſened: for how often does it happen that Children for want of due Exerciſe grow ricketty, become Cripples, or are puny all their Childhood, perhaps their whole Lives; to their own great Sorrow, and to the inexpreſſible Trouble, Pain, and Expence of the Parents.

Rickets is a Diſtemper extremely common in *London*; but if the Rules already laid down be obſerved, I dare affirm, it will very rarely be ſeen. It is not indeed the Deſign of this Treatiſe to cure Diſeaſes, but to prevent them; yet as thouſands of Children fall into the Rickets in a manner inſenſibly, often without it's being once apprehended;

hended; I would here not only keep the Attention of Parents awake, but propoſe a Remedy.

Let us then obſerve, that many Children have all the appearance imaginable of Health, Strength, and Vigor, till about nine Months old; after that Age they begin to dwindle, grow liſtleſs, heavy and inactive, which to account for, Parents find a thouſand Cauſes, perhaps all wide of the real. One aſcribes it to cutting the Teeth, another to a Fever, a third to loſs of Appetite, and ſo on; when after a Time it proves the Rickets: the Cauſe whereof is, generally ſpeaking, bad Nurſing. But whether this, or any other Weakneſs produces the Diſtemper, I earneſtly recommend, that it be not ſuffered to paſs unregarded, ſince much depends upon our early Care.

The great and noble Remedy for this Diſorder is a Cold Bath; and tho' the Tenderneſs of Mothers may make them ſhrink at the Propoſal, yet neither their own Weakneſs, nor the Child's Reluctance, muſt in this Caſe prevail, eſpecially when I aſſure them that a very ſhort Time will make the uſe of it not only eaſy but pleaſant.

If a Child along with this Diſorder has a Fever, a full quick Pulſe and ſhort Breath (as is very common) Parents ſhould certainly aſk proper Advice before they begin to uſe the Bath. But as ſome may be careleſs in this Matter, or at leaſt unwilling to ſubmit; and as many ill Conſequences may follow from ſetting out wrong, I will in that Caſe recommend, that two or three Ounces of Blood be taken away at the Arm or Neck; next Day purge it with Rhubarb, and repeat it to three or four times, at a Day or two's diſtance between each Doſe: and even where there is no Fever, and the Lungs play freely, it ſhould ſtill be purged as above directed.

The more Water and the colder the Bath the better. At firſt uſe it only two or three times a Week, afterwards every Day; and continue it (unleſs other Accidents intervene) 'till every appearance of Weakneſs be vaniſhed, even though it ſhould laſt long, or come on in the coldeſt Seaſon.

To obviate as much as poſſible all groundleſs Fears, I will on this Head add, that as Cold Baths act very powerfully on the whole Frame, they are frequently obſerved to give Cold at firſt uſing; and ſometimes affect the Limbs and other Parts very ſenſibly; all which goes off on repeating it. And indeed, where a Cold Bath is judged proper, the only Circumſtance which juſtifies the Diſuſe of it, is, it's leaving a Shivering and Coldneſs all over, inſtead of that pleaſing comfortable Glow, which generally follows the uſe of it.

The proper Cloathing of Children is a Conſideration of great Importance; and indeed the Opinions of different Men in the Learned World, and of different Women in the Converſable World, are ſo very many, as to render it next to impoſſible to fix a Standard for Dreſs with regard to Health only, that would in any manner ſquare with the various Notions ſubſiſting. Arguing on Principles of Philoſophy, from Reaſons founded on the Knowledge of Anatomy, and the Animal Oeconomy, will not go down with the Croud. Nor will Examples produced from Practice, prevail on the Learned to think the general Practice right. It is not enough to ſay, that different Nations act with more or leſs Propriety on this Head; for even our own Country is herein much divided in itſelf.

What I have before obſerved on cloathing Children, relates only to the keeping up a due Degree of Warmth, 'till Time ſtrengthens their Solids; but the grand Controverſy is,

 what

what kind of Cloaths they ſhould wear, and how they muſt be put on; how Boys ſhould be cloathed, and how Girls; what Cloathing conduces to Health, and what impairs it: with many other Things much diſputed, but ſtill unſettled.

Nothing is more certain than that Nature in general is our beſt, our ſureſt Guide, for the Conduct of Life; yet if we make the Law univerſal, we ſhall undoubtedly ſometimes err. Two things all Mankind inherit in conſequence of our firſt Parents Diſobedience, viz. the Turbulence of our Paſſions, and our bodily Defects and Infirmities: all are ſenſible of this; all ſee and feel them, more or leſs. How ſmall is the number of thoſe, whoſe Paſſions are by Nature ſo happily calm, as to keep them free from Irregularities! How few are thoſe, to whom Nature has given a perfect Form: whoſe Stature, Limbs, and Features, bear exact Proportion and Symmetry, free from Blemiſhes and Defects; ſuch as conſtitutes a finiſh'd Beauty: or whoſe Conſtitution is ſo happily temper'd as to have no Bias, no weak Side, no redundant Humours to diſturb Life and Health. This I ſay is evidently the Lot of very few. Still Providence, ever kind, has furniſhed us with Means to turn all things to our Advantage. To regulate our Paſſions we

are

are endowed with Reafon ; to rectify, as far as Nature will permit, our bodily Defects, we are fupplied with Judgment : but as in the firft Cafe we are apt to let Paffion get the Mastery of Reafon ; fo in the other, we often let our Judgment err, or fuffer Fancy to take place of it. Hence arife many of thofe Miftakes Mankind daily run into ; and hence too the Judgment of one will fometimes be perverted into Fancy, and the Fancy of another be falfly efteemed Judgment. From this view it is eafy to fee, how vaft a Field is open to Mankind to exercife their Judgment in ; but where that is weak, Errors will certainly make their Way ; which from the Propenfity we have to do wrong, are fometimes fo prevailing and fwift, as to become almoft univerfal ; even fo far as utterly to overturn fuperior Judgment. Now though we grant that every one is poffeffed not only of a Power, but of a Right of judging ; yet we do not agree, that the Judgment of the Weak, or of thofe who have neglected to exercife and improve their natural Faculties, fhould be abided by, and made our Rule of Conduct : for as our Law-givers fhould be wife, and as from them we feek to be fecured in our Property and our Peace ; fo from thofe who have fearched into Nature, who have ftudied the Animal Oeconomy, and are acquainted with the Structure of our Frame, from thoſe only can we rationally learn how to preſerve Health. To apply then theſe Arguments to the Matter in hand, I would recommend to Parents with regard to Cloathing their Children, to be attentive themſelves; to exerciſe and improve their own Judgment, as far as they have opportunity; not ſuddenly to run with the Croud, leſt it prove a vulgar Error; but endeavour to learn what is the Opinion of Judges: and by comparing that with the general Practice, they may draw ſuch Concluſions as will profit them moſt.

Dreſs, in the common Acceptation of the Word, is not my Province; thoſe People whoſe Buſineſs it is to promote it, know that the World is fickle and inconſtant; they know that Men will change, even though it be for the worſe, purely from a Love of Novelty: therefore is it that at one Time a Man has his Hips almoſt up to his Arm-pits, another Time he muſt ſtoop to get his Hand into his Coat Pocket; therefore is it that one Year a Woman is (at the Will of the Staymaker) to be ſhort-waiſted, another Year long-waiſted; with many more Abſurdities, that ought at leaſt to be laughed at. But where Dreſs is capable of affecting our Health,

Health, it both deſerves and demands Attention and Regard: And to that End, I will for the Inſtruction of my Readers, give the Sentiments of the Learned on this Head.

It is the Opinion of many, that every kind of Bandage is an Error in Practice; even Garters, Wriſt-bands, and Collars; that they impede the Circulation of the Blood, or at leaſt render it unequal and irregular, and prevent the proper Growth of the Solids; nay more, that they are a frequent though latent Cauſe of Apoplexies, and other dreadful Diſeaſes. It is farther their Opinion, that whatever compreſſes the Frame, (particularly the tender one of a Child) is dangerous; as Rollers, ſtiff Stays, and the like: that as the Trunk of the Body contains, what Phyſicians call the *Viſcera*, in which are the chief Functions of Life, whatever external Methods are uſed to bind or cramp them up, is prejudicial to Health. That the Lungs particularly are to have free room to play; and that if the Cheſt be externally preſs'd, whether by Rollers, Stays, Waiſtcoats, or any thing elſe, it lays the Foundation of many future Evils. To theſe general Opinions, let me add that of an eminent Writer. Mr. *Locke*, in his Treatiſe of Education, ſays, " Narrow

" Breaſts, ſhort and ſtinking Breath, ill
" Lungs and Crookedneſs, are the natural and
" almoſt conſtant Effects of *hard Bodice* and
" *Cloaths* that pinch. That way of making
" ſlender Waiſts and fine Shapes, ſerves but
" the more effectually to ſpoil them. Nor
" can there indeed but be Diſproportion in
" the Parts, when the Nouriſhment pre-
" par'd in the ſeveral Offices of the Body,
" cannot be diſtributed as Nature deſigns.
" And therefore what wonder is it, if being
" laid where it can on ſome Part not ſo
" braced, it often makes a Shoulder or Hip
" higher or bigger than it's juſt Proportion."
He then produces the Example of the *Chineſe* Women, who of all People on Earth, have the ſmalleſt Feet, not naturally, but made ſo by cramping them; from a notion that it is beautiful; by which Practice, ſays he, it is believed they impede their Growth and ſhorten their Lives. Now to confirm and ſtrengthen what is here advanced, we muſt obſerve, that beſides the univerſal Reputation Mr. *Locke* ſo juſtly obtain'd as a Man of Science, he was deſign'd for a Phyſician: and though he never practiſed Phyſic, he had ſtudied it. To theſe Opinions may be added the general Conſent of Mankind, that in thoſe Countries where Stays are not worn at

all,

all, the People are ſeldom or never known to be crooked.

Now let us examine the general Practice, and the Motives which influence it; that no Injuſtice may be done in a Treatiſe that aims at the general Good of Mankind. Mothers and Nurſes obſerve, that a new-born Child has no Support of itſelf; the Head leans on one ſide or the other; and the Body ſinks as it were into a Heap: to remedy which, and to prop up the helpleſs Babe, they put what is call'd a Stay to its Neck, they roll a Flannel many times round its Body, and at the Expiration of a Month it is uſually coated: that is, it continues when undreſs'd with the Roller; and in the Day Time when dreſs'd, it wears a Stay about the Waiſt. The Stay to the Neck is left off in ſome Months, and the Roller in about a Year; ſome ſooner, ſome later: but the ſame Method is uſed both to Boys and Girls. The firſt, ſecond and third Stays are uſually very ſoft and plyable; but after that, when a Child approaches to two Years old, they are then made ſtronger, that is, ſtiffer to the Feel; and theſe Sort are worn by Boys 'till they are breech'd, and by Girls their whole Lives. Nurſes urge, that Children are helpleſs, cannot ſit upright, nor be toſs'd about without them. And I re-

 member

member an eminent Surgeon, late of one of our Hoſpitals, once told me, that a Child was brought to him with ſeveral of its Ribs cruſh'd inward by the Hand of the Perſon who had been toſſing it about without its Stays.

But as I have juſt obſerved, it is not in Infancy only that Stays are uſed; but in one Sex, 'till four, five, or ſix, Years old; and in the other for Life. The Solicitude of Parents about Shape, is chiefly confin'd to the Girls; Boys, when breech'd, like Eels, twiſt themſelves into a thouſand Forms, and prove ſtrait at laſt; while the Girls, with leſs Freedom and more Anxiety, ſeldom come off ſo well. Still Mothers contend for the Neceſſity of Stays; and maintain from Experience, that the Shape, inſtead of being hurt with them, is ſpoil'd without them. Here then is the grand Point, whether Nature requires theſe Props or not; the Learned ſay they don't; general Practice ſays they do: the Learned recommend that Nature be left to Faſhion the Parts herſelf; but general Practice contradicts this: and who will take upon them to decide ſo important a Matter? for me, I confeſs it is too much.

When I read or hear the Opinion of ſkilful Men, and weigh their Reaſoning, I heartily concur

concur with them; and when I fee an exquifite Shape under a judicious Mother's Management, I am inclin'd to applaud her Judgment, and commend the Choice of her Staymaker. However, that I might not leave this Head and determine nothing, I have already recommended to Parents to exercife their own Judgment, and to feek that of others; whereby many of the Errors, become general thro' Ignorance and Time, will be removed. The Learned, unlefs dogmatical, will be brought to allow, that Stays may often be worn without the leaft Injury; that as Girls are by Nature more tender and delicate than Boys, many of them would have been deformed either thro' bad nurfing, or fome inbred Infirmity, tho' they never had worn a Stay in their Lives: and Parents will be convinc'd, that while Nature is labouring to compleat their Children's Growth, both Health and Beauty greatly depend on their not being braced injudicioufly.

As I am fpeaking of Health and Beauty, it will not be improper to obferve, that with regard to the outward Form, what is moft agreeable to fee, is often moft conducive to Health and Strength. Thus the Dancingmafter has Power to confer many Advantages on his Scholars. That Command and free Play

Play of the Joints of the Knees, with the Habit of keeping them unbent but when neceſſary, and the proper turning out of the Toes, add great Firmneſs and Grace both to ſtanding and walking: that graceful Power of the Arms, the eaſy Fall, and the dropping of the Shoulders from the Neck, gives a pleaſing Diſtinction of the bred from the unbred: and the keeping the Body upright, and throwing forward the Cheſt, are beſides being great Beauties, vaſtly conducive to the free Exerciſe of the Lungs, and to the proper Action of the whole *Viſcera*.

But while this Part of Education is juſtly commended as conducive to Health, and pleaſing to behold, what ſhall we ſay of thoſe, who under the Appearance of increaſing their Beauty deſtroy it; and who, while aiming at Health, often deprive themſelves of Life. I have ſhewn that bodily Defects are more or leſs the Lot of all Mankind; but where Judgment free from Error can rectify them, we have Power to do it. If we can find a Cure for Diſeaſes born with us, we certainly may and ought; if we can increaſe our Strength, and add Graces to Nature, we undoubtedly ſhould; we may curl our Hair, increaſe its Growth, or cut it off; we may and ought to comb or ſhave our Head, pare our Nails, and

and ſcour off all that Foulneſs which Nature throws out upon the Surface of our Body, and maintain a conſtant Cleanlineſs: But all this does not imply that we may give ourſelves a new Face; and yet little leſs is frequently attempted. When Nature is oppreſſed within us, ſhe often, for our Relief, throws out the Malady upon the Skin; if it happen to be on the Face, we grow reſtleſs and impatient; we are ignorant of the Kindneſs done to us; and to remove the Blemiſh to our Beauty, we unadviſedly drive back the redundant Humour; perhaps on our Vitals; and thus fall a Sacrifice to our Pride or Ignorance.

There is a Practice, particularly among the Great, ſhocking to Nature and to Reflection; that of uſing Paint. Paint is to the Face, what Affectation is to the Mind: as the one is a ridiculous Mimic of amiable Qualities we are Strangers to, ſo the other is a ridiculous Affectation of Beauty we cannot reach. But while Paint diſappoints thoſe who are attach'd to it, by conferring falſe Beauty, it is attended with the Miſchief of impairing real; and many who by Nature alone would be comely in the Decline of Life, are, by this odious Practice, hagged even in Youth. Temperance, Exercise, good Hours, and a chearful

ful Mind, will best preserve the Bloom of Life; but such is the present Age, such the prevailing false Taste, that Error is confounded with Error, and our corrupt Judgment is still farther corrupted. There was a Time that Paint was designed to give a false Bloom when the real was declining; but now it is used to hide even the natural Bloom: it is made an Instrument to destroy that Beauty which Providence has bestowed; and instead of being grateful for the Blessing, it is shamefully hid under a pale Enamel, or a dead White! What an Indignity, what an Affront is this to the Author of all Nature, to the Bestower of all Blessings!

Lord *Hallifax*, in his Advice to a Daughter, goes so far as to dissuade her even from the Use of Sweets. "Those Ladies (says he) "who perfume themselves, will be strongly "suspected of doing it to conceal some other "Stink." Cleanliness is to be preferred to every foreign Aid; for tho' it is certain, that Nature throws off some offensive Matter, whether perceptible or not, by the several Organs given for those Purposes, yet daily washing the Mouth, combing the Head, and using every other Means of Cleanliness, bids much fairer for rendering us inoffensive to others, than the general and immoderate Use

of

of Perfumes. And therefore I cannot but concur with this noble Writer, in diſſuading Parents from introducing among their Children the Cuſtom of ſeeking foreign Aſſiſtance in order to be ſweet. Should I add to this, that continually ſtriking on thoſe Nerves which convey the Senſe of Smelling to us, is prejudicial to our Health, I ſhould advance no more than what many learned Men hold as a Truth.

But there is another Pretext for uſing Sweets, which muſt not paſs unobſerved; that of keeping us from being ſenſible of the various Smells around us. It is true that thoſe are ſometimes ſo groſsly offenſive, as to juſtify, and even demand, our ſhutting them out: but in general, there is too much falſe Delicacy, too ſtrong a Tincture of Pride, and too little Senſe of our own Infirmities in this Practice. On theſe laſt Heads then I muſt beg Leave to admoniſh Parents, even of the higheſt Rank (ſhould this little Work ever fall into their Hands) to be greatly circumſpect with regard to their Children; that they be careful to give them a due Senſe of the Bleſſings Nature has beſtowed on them; that they point out to them the moſt rational Way of correcting natural Defects; and above all, to imprint on them a juſt Deteſta-

tion

tion of every Practice which has a Tendency to raiſe their Vanity, and add Fuel to their Pride. To this end, Parents ſhould convince their Children, that the faſhionable Coſmetics greatly endanger Health; Paint debaſes both the Face and the Mind; the wanton Uſe of Perfumes is an Error in Principle, and all are fraught with miſchievous Effects.

It may be urged, that Children are not ſubject to the Uſe of theſe things, at leaſt while Children: I grant it. But my Readers muſt obſerve, that when I enter on a Topic, I am naturally led thro' it; and as we never ſtand ſtill in Life, ſo Parents muſt bring their Ideas forward, and conſider their Children as always advancing. Nay I may without Impropriety ſay farther, that Vanity is one of the firſt things that Children learn; and it demands the early Attention of Parents to keep it under, by diſcountenancing the Practice of every thing which tends to ſupport or cheriſh it.

Parents are naturally anxious to have this firſt Entrance on the Stage of Life got thro' with Succeſs; and I flatter myſelf, that the Rules already laid down will conquer, or at leaſt leſſen the Difficulty attending it. How eager are all good Parents to ſee their Children weaned; to have them firm on their Feet; to find their Mouths full of Teeth; and

and to hear tham prattle: nay there are many, particularly Fathers, who think their Children of no Importance, at leaſt they have no Pleaſure in them, 'till theſe are effected. That nothing therefore may obſtruct this Progreſs, I will here add a Word or two more.

It is a Point much diſputed, whether a young Child is better or worſe for wearing Shoes and Stockings; for my own Part, I think they are both: but, as this may ſeem a Paradox, I will explain myſelf. The Diſuſe of Shoes and Stockings is to make Children hardy; but my Readers will remember, that unleſs Regard be had to Time and Seaſon, they may cramp their tender Limbs, and do them great Harm. Stockings therefore cannot with Prudence be totally neglected, leſt it prove a Neglect to the Child; and Shoes, when they are put on it's Feet, are, beſides being not ſo diſagreeable to ſee, much ſafer to walk about in; as nobody can anſwer that Pins, Splinters, Stones, and various other things will not ſometimes fall in their Way, even on the ſmootheſt Floor, or a Carpet. Thus much in their Favour: but what I have to ſay againſt them is not leſs ſignificant. According to the uſual Method of managing Children, they wear no Cloth in in the Day-time after five or six Months old; and then, if they are not carefully watched, they will frequently wet themselves, and thereby make Shoes and Stockings an Impediment to their thriving, by soaking them, as it were, in Wet, Cold, and Nastiness. Either then let a Child be kept clean with them, or intirely go without them; for of two Evils, it is always most eligible to chuse the least.

But a little Judgment and Attention would obviate this Inconvenience; for as even Infants are not without various Ways of shewing their Wants, an Attention to these, and a Method of putting them regularly into their Chair, would be very convenient both to Mother and Child: and if notwithstanding this, it should by chance wet itself, having dry Shoes and Stockings always ready to put on, would prevent any ill Effect.

I am of Opinion, that Parents are often too eager to have their Children walk; by which, they take such Means as serve to retard it. Two things much in use manifestly keep Children back, viz. much sitting, especially with their Cloaths up, and much standing. They should never sit long in their Chair, nor be left to support the Weight of their Bodies; while their Joints and

and Limbs are tender. Let them by all means feel that they have Feet, but let them not be left alone, 'till Time, Air, and Exercife have ftrengthened their Solids, and given them a lafting Firmnefs.

But we will now fuppofe that thefe firft Difficulties are all furmounted. Parents have ftill many things to do, which require indeed Attention, but neither need, nor ought to be accompanied with any confiderable Degree of Difficulty or Pain.

Notwithftanding a Child is advancing, I ftill recommend, that Milk and Water with Bread, or Milk-porridge, or Rice-milk, be it's conftant Breakfaft. Parents may fometimes alter their Courfe, may eafily contrive little Changes in a Child's Diet, that will be very pleafing, without either feeming to humour it, or varying it fo fenfibly, as to hurt the Quality. For Example, in Summer, pour warm Water on Milk to take off its Rawnefs, and let the Child with a Piece of Bread bite and fup: in Winter let it have Milk-porridge, or Rice-milk. Milk is accounted to lofe of its natural Sweetnefs by boiling; therefore in general it fhould be avoided.

But

But there is another Principle Parents are to act by, viz. a Child's Habit of Body. Nothing is more certain than that our Food may be made our Physic; and if our Judgment went Hand in Hand with Nature, we should happily escape many bodily Infirmities, many grievous Evils: for it would then be easy to see when she is regular, when not; whether she wants a Curb or a Spur; whether she is robust or delicate; or, in fine, whether she has any Bias, and where. To familiarize this, let me observe, that where a Child is hot, dry, and costive, Parents should sometimes desist from the Use of Milk, and give it Water-gruel, either with or without Currants; or very small Broth, or Milk-porridge, which last is rendered opening by the Oat-meal. So likewise, where the Bowels are weak, and there is an habitual purging, the Child should be kept more closely to Milk; have Rice-milk, Rice-gruel, or Broth thickened with Rice; or thick Milk, or hasty Pudding made with Milk and Flour. Of one or other of these things, as Occasion serves, a Child may properly breakfast as long as the Guidance of Parents will be necessary: and when it is no longer a Child, but comes to act for itself, it will not be easy to find more whole-

some

ſome Food. Tea, Coffee, and Chocolate are the moſt uſual Breakfaſts in lieu of theſe. Tea has been ſpoken of already. Coffee is hot and dry; it is rather fit for a Medicine than a Meal, and ſhould be uſed with Judgment; it is manifeſtly a Cephalic, and ſometimes removes a Head-ach inſtantaneouſly as if it were by Magic; but intemperately uſed, it is very apt to ſink the Spirits, and bring on Tremblings. Chocolate has a nutritious, balſamic Quality, yet it diſagrees with many People; it does not ſit eaſy on every Stomach; either from the natural Property of the Nuts, or from its being made too thick, and ſometimes drank with Milk, which renders it ſtill heavier. But, generally ſpeaking, Tea is the Breakfaſt for Children, which is often made worſe, by being accompanied with hot Bread. I have ſeen a Mother ſo cruelly kind, for ſo with Truth we may call it, as to give a young Child all the Crum of a hot Roll for its Breakfaſt; and this repeated every Day, till it had loſt not only it's Appetite, but almoſt it's Breath.

There is nothing Parents ſhould more promote in their Children than the Love of Bread; they ſhould be taught to eat a great deal of it with their Meat; be taught to eat

it

it ſometimes alone; but not be ſuffered to eat it quite new: for the Cuſtom of cramming Children with hot Bread, is one of the Ways that make them unhealthy, without Parents being aware of it.

Butter is allowed to yield great Nouriſhment, but there are Objections which Parents muſt not diſregard. It often riſes in the Stomach, is apt to give that Pain which People call the Heart-burn, and is judged to be frequently the Occaſion of Childrens breaking out, by obſtructing ſome of the Glands. Butter therefore ſhould be eat much more ſparingly than uſual, and great Care ſhould be taken that it is never rancid.

Cheeſe is a kind of Food which Children are naturally very fond of; and, if left to themſelves, will eat it to an immoderate Degree. I have obſerved before, that little Changes in a Child's Diet are at times very right; particularly to prevent any Diſlike to certain things, either from Diſuſe or Affectation; but when Cheeſe comes in turn to be the Meal, it ſhould be under great Reſtraint. Suppoſe, for Example, a Child's Supper is to be Bread and Cheeſe, the Bread ſhould moſt certainly be conſidered as the Meal; a very ſmall Quantity of Cheeſe to give it a Reliſh,

Relifh, and convey it down, is all it ought to have. Cheefe, tho' nutritious, fhould never be eat in large Quantity; it gives Children a reftlefs painful Fondnefs for what is relifhing, and takes off their Appetite from more wholefome fimple Diet; it is found to difagree with many Stomachs; toafted, it is particularly bad, and difficult to digeft; and it has often a Pungency, which creates Heat, Thirft, and Coftivenefs.

Flefh Meat has already been touched upon; I will here add, that befides the Parents Care that Children do not begin too foon with it, nor eat it intemperately, they muft pay a due Regard not only to the Quality of the Meat they give them, but to the Time and Manner of eating it.

Phyficians are of Opinion, that Animal-food is not in Perfection 'till full grown; for, like unripe Fruit, their Juices are crude, and always more or lefs improper to mix with our Blood, 'till they are in a State of Maturity: hence it appears, that Beef and Mutton are more wholefome than Veal and Lamb. Nor fhould Beef, as the Fibres of it are very ftrong, be eat too freely by thofe whofe Digeftion is weak; and when rendered harder

harder by lying long in Brine, it is ſtill more improper. Pork, tho' a favourite kind of Food, is in ſeveral Reſpects improper to be eat frequently; it is extremely apt to offend the Stomach; it has a remarkable Tendency to bring on Purgings; and it is ſuſpected not to form ſo pure a Chyle, and to be more diſpoſed to load the Blood with thoſe Particles which create ſcorbutic Diſorders than any other Meat. Upon the whole, no Meat is ſo univerſally ſuited to our Nature as Mutton. For after all our Labour and Expence to obtain greater Rarities, after we have fatigued ourſelves with Sport, hunted down defenceleſs Creatures, brought to the Ground the moſt wary Birds, and cloyed ourſelves with the choiceſt Viands, we find perhaps a truer Reliſh, and a better Appetite for a Mutton-chop. So Topers, after ſpending the Night in ſearch of the richeſt Wine, after rioting in Exceſs, and wearying the Tavern-waiters to pleaſe their Palates, ſeek Comfort and Refreſhment in a Glaſs of Water.

Fiſh is a ſort of Diet extremely improper for Children. I would recommend to Parents never to let a Child ſo much as taſte it for the firſt ſeven Years at leaſt. If it were nothing more than the Danger of Bones ſticking

ſticking in it's Throat, it is enough to alarm prudent People; but moſt kinds of Fiſh are naturally flabby, cold, and watry; are very unfit for young Stomachs, and uſually made more ſo, by being accompanied with rich Sauce.

Children ſhould not be debarred Fruit; but the Uſe of it requires ſome Attention; 1ſt, It ſhould always be good in its Kind, and ripe. 2dly, Regard is to be had what Sort agrees, and what diſagrees. 3dly, Some Limitation as to Quantity. It is a diſputed Point whether we may eat Fruit in a Morning; other Nations do frequently, we ſeldom. In *France*, *Germany*, *Switzerland*, and many other Places, the People always eat Bread with their Fruit; and it appears ſo rational that I believe it were better that we did too. Fruit gives ſome a Pain at the Stomach, others not; Apples, Currants, and thoſe Kinds, which, tho' ripe, have ſtill a Degree of grateful Acidity in them, uſually agree beſt. Pears and Plumbs, eſpecially the *Orleans* Plumb, have a Tendency to bring on Purgings, which ſometimes terminate in a Bloody Flux and Death; and therefore ſhould be given to Children with great Caution: but, in fine, Experience here, as in many other things, is to be our Guide. One general Rule I would recommend, which is, that the Skin or Rind of all Fruit that is in any manner tough, be not eat. It is the Pulp and juicy Part of the Fruit which refreſhes us; and Nature, to preſerve theſe, has wrapped them up in a tough kind of Coat, which is judged by many to be very unfit to take into the Stomach. I muſt not omit to ſpeak of Nuts. I obſerved before, that merely from the Danger of Bones Children ſhould be kept from Fiſh; ſo, had Nuts no other Effect than looſening the Teeth by frequent cracking them, which they do manifeſtly, they ſhould never be meddled with; but in Fact they have. I have ſeen People eat Walnuts 'till they could ſcarcely breathe; the famous *Barcelona* Nuts, beſides the Subſtance or fibrous Part of them, often abound with a rank kind of Oil; and even our own Hazel Nuts and Filberds, when eaten in any Quantity, are apt to create Thirſt, cord up, as it were, the whole Cheſt, and produce Coughs.

Self-gratification on one hand, and Self-intereſt on the other, have introduced ſeveral Trades the World in general might diſpenſe with; two of which demand my Obſervation, viz. the Confectioner and the Paſtry cook. That theſe Trades have their Uſe I do not deny. A Nobleman, according to the Rules of Politeneſs, cannot make an Entertainment without a Desert; thus the Confectioner becomes necessary: in inferior Life, the Coarseness of the Entertainment is taken off by the Assistance of the Pastry-cook: all which may be reasonable, if reasonably used. But when I consider the general Misapplication of these luscious Dainties to Children, I cannot but condemn it.

If a Child is sent to visit a Relation or Friend, the grand Compliment is, to apply to the Confectioner or the Pastry-cook; and 'till the little Visitor be crammed with Biskets, or Cakes, or Tarts, or Sweetmeats, or all in their Turn, and that even to a Surfeit, the welcome is not thought compleat. Still there is some Excuse to palliate this Mistake; the Child is considered as a Visitor; and these Excesses are the mistaken Effects of Good-Nature and Respect; both which are apt grievously to err against Judgment. But my Principals here are the Parents; for from them alone must come the Habit of doing right, and by them alone must the Error be prevented or corrected.

I have no Objection to a Child's having a Tart or Bisket by Chance, but I am a profess'd Enemy to the daily Abuses commited with them. If we view the Loads of Wigs, Tarts, and Cakes, every Day made at the Paſtry-cooks, we muſt be aſtoniſhed at their Conſumption. The Truth is, People give theſe Things to their Children 'till they have made them ſick, and then give them becauſe they are ſick. If a Perſon happens to call on a Friend where there is a Child indiſpoſed, it is ten to one but they find a Tart in it's Hands; Ah! poor thing, ſays Mamma, it has eat nothing to-day, ſo I ſent for a Tart for it. That the Hands, the Face, the Apparel and Bedding of Children, imprudently indulg'd with this kind of Food, be conſtantly daub'd and beſmear'd, is the leaſt bad Conſequence attending ſuch Indiſcretion; it has ſeveral other Effects, particularly on their Health; by vitiating their Appetites, engendering Crudities, and alienating them from more wholeſome Diet.

But let us go lower into Common Life; and view the various Outlets from *London*. What Swarms, what Multitudes of Children are there not in the Fields on every fine Sunday! And what is their Entertaiment? Why, generally ſpeaking, they are ſtuffed with a coarſe kind of Paſtry-ware made coarſe on purpoſe for Children, who of all the

the human Species ought not to touch it: then to compleat the Mifchief, they are to wafh it down with a foul, naufeous, heady kind of Ale, or other Malt Liquor. Yet when one oppofes this Practice, as every one muft with Hand and Heart, who has but a Head to guide them; Poor Things! cry the miftaken Parents, what! take Children into the Fields, and not give them a Bun! But how grievoufly does their dotard Fondnefs miflead them! Good Bread, with a very little Sweet Butter, wafh'd down with Water, or clear well-brew'd Small Beer, would preferve their Health; while the only ufe of this Trafh, is to impair or deftroy it.

To reduce to Method what has been here faid concerning Diet, I muft obferve, that next to the proper kind of Food, nothing is more conducive to Health than a Habit of eating Meals regularly. Children accuftomed to eat all Day long are feldom healthy; befides, that it makes them diforderly, and often throws a Family into Confufion to gratify all their little Humours. The proper Breakfaft has been already pointed out; their Dinner fhould be made of one Difh, only, unlefs by great Chance a paffing Tafte of a fecond; they fhould either eat a great deal of Bread, or blend their Meat with Greens, Turnips, or other Garden Stuff; Pickles and all high Sauces ſhould not be touch'd by them; and their Meal ſhould be waſhed down with Water or light Small Beer. Their Supper may, like their Breakfaſt, ſometimes be vary'd, as to the Auxiliary; Bread is to be the Repaſt; yet a ſmall Portion of Butter, Cheeſe, Fruit, or Tart, may in their Turn accompany it: the Vehicle the ſame as at Dinner. But ſhould a Child at intermediate Times, eſpecially before Dinner, complain of Hunger, and faſting long might make it's Stomach ach; in that Caſe nothing ſo good as a bit of Bread; and if uſed to it, it will eat it as eagerly as the greateſt Dainty; but to ſee Children walk about a Houſe with Tarts or Bread and Butter in their Hands, daubing every thing and every body they touch, is certainly wrong; being not only detrimental to their Health, but to their Manners too, as it is inexpreſſibly vulgar.

The Ideas of Parents may perhaps confine theſe Rules to the firſt Septenary of a Child's Life; but I muſt here obſerve, that no eſſential Difference, no very material Changes can be made from this, even in the ſecond and third Stages, without ſome De-

gree

gree of Error. Eating and Drinking are made too much the Bufinefs and the Pleafure of Life, to be confiftent with either our Health or our Reafon: Parents therefore who aim at acting on right Principles, muft for the fake of thefe, teach their Children to be regular and temperate in the ufe of thofe. It is right that they begin early, that they fet out well; but it is doubly fo, that they keep them in the fame Road; and as their Childrens Reafon gathers Strength, convince them that they muft never quit it, if they wifh to live a long or happy Life: and that, of all human Gratifications, an inordinate Attachment to Eating and Drinking is the meaneft, and moft unworthy a Man.

Mr. *Locke* propofes, as a great Means of preferving Health, that Boys (for it is for them only that he writes) have Holes made in their Shoes on purpofe to let in the Wet; which (fays he) being rendered familiar to them, will prevent their catching Cold. It is certain this Gentleman acts here upon a right Principle; but whether the Practice be altogether eligible, is a Doubt. Nothing is fo hurtful to the Head, the Eyes, and the Breaft, as catching Cold in the Feet; and therefore I cannot but concur with this ingenious Writer, in recommending the Ufe of

 cold

cold Water in order to make Children hardy. I have before advifed, that young Children have their Limbs wafhed daily with cold Water; now as many things may be rendered familiar and eafy by Cuftom, if, as they advance, their Feet were daily immerfed in cold Water too, it would undoubtedly be of vaft Service, and greatly tend to confirm their Health. But if this be never practifed, or the Practice fet afide, which is nearly the fame thing, it demands double Care of the Parents to prevent their being liable to Colds.

To this End, Children's Feet fhould be wafhed in Water a little warm'd; for it is extremely dangerous to make a fudden Derivation of the Blood up to the Lungs or Head, which is the natural Effect of cold Water. And it is for this Reafon that People are never fuffered to walk into a cold Bath, but are thrown forwards, that the Immerfion may be total at the fame inftant. Nay, Mr. *Locke* himfelf was fo fenfible of this, that tho' he advifes wafhing the Feet daily in cold Water, he would have it begun with in the Spring, and the Water lukewarm, and made colder and colder by Degrees: "For (fays he) it is to be obferv'd "in this, as in all other Alterations from "our

" our ordinary Way of living, the Changes " muſt be made by gentle and inſenſible " Degrees."

The next Mean is, that Children have always dry Shoes. There is a great deal of Miſchief attends the miſtaken Delicacy of Shoes. Thoſe who always tread on Carpets, who never go abroad without a Coach or a Chair, may perhaps wear with Safety the thinneſt that can be made; but to ſee People in inferior Life, or thoſe engaged in real Buſineſs, trampling thro' dirty Streets, and ſoaking their Paper-ſoals in continual Puddles, is ſurely every way abſurd: but as this Practice is evidently detrimental to Health, as it frequently occaſions Coughs, ſore Eyes, Head-ach, Rheumatiſm, and other Diſorders, it is highly incumbent on Parents to keep Children free from theſe Dangers by uſing them, in Winter eſpecially, to ſuch Shoes as will keep them dry. On this Head it will not be amiſs to give a Caution againſt Shoes that pinch. Parents muſt be attentive to this both in Boys and Girls, for many by this Means are made ſo tender-footed, and have ſuch painful Corns, that they are a kind of Cripples their whole Lives: and are not only very uncomfortable to themſelves, but are often thereby greatly disabled from doing their necessary Business.

I must not here omit, so far as relates to Health, to mention Sleeping, and the Circumstances attending it. "Of all (says Mr. "*Locke*) which looks soft and effeminate, "nothing is more to be indulged Children "than Sleep. In this alone they are to be "permitted to have their full Satisfaction, "nothing contributing more to the Growth "and Health of Children than Sleep." I have already with regard to Infants shewn, that they ought not to be disturbed from their Rest; and even past that Age Sleep affords them great Nourishment. Nothing certainly is more injudicious and unnatural than the Custom many Parents have of keeping their Children up late. If they wish them to be healthy, temperate, or wise, they must create in them a Habit of early going to Bed and early rising. As the many Conditions in Life oblige, or at least lead People to act differently, so it is extremely hard to fix precise Rules herein; but in general, 'till Children approach nearly to Men and Women, they would do best not to sit up to see, much less to eat, a Family-supper at nine o'Clock.

Lying

Lying on ſoft Beds is undoubtedly wrong; the *French* have a good Cuſtom of putting a Matraſs above the Feather-bed, which prevents their ſinking into a Softneſs very prejudicial to Health. Soft Beds abſorb too much of our Juices, cauſe a greater Waſte than we can ſpare, enfeeble our whole Frame, and have a remarkable Tendency to give a Pain or Weakneſs in the Small of the Back, by heating the Reins.

Mr. *Locke*, amidſt great good Senſe, has ſome Notions a little rigorous, which probably are never followed, nor do they ſeem altogether needful. He propoſes that a Child's Bed be deſignedly ill made; that is, ſometimes high, ſometimes low, ſometimes rough, ſometimes ſmooth; for my part, I am deſirous to baniſh every ill-judged Tenderneſs, every falſe Fondneſs; but as I write for the Uſe of both Sexes, and all Conditions, I cannot confine my Ideas to a Tent or a Cabin. Let Children by all Means lie on Matraſſes inſtead of Beds, for the Reaſons already given; let them lie with a Bolſter only, and no Pillow, for it is not good for them to have the Head high; let them lie either on one Side or the other, and not on the Back; and let them lie pretty

ſtraight

ſtraight in the Bed, yet not fully ſtretched out, for that would impede the due Action of the animal Functions, and render Sleep leſs profitable to them. With regard to the Form of their Beds, I think, Decency requires that they be orderly and regular; nor is there any Fear that a Change of Bed will affect them, for moſt young People ſleep ſound wherever they are laid.

It has been generally ſaid, that we ſhould keep our Heads cool; and many on that Principle, even tho' their Heads are ſhaved, lie without a Night-cap. I will not take upon me to determine the Matter, but obſerve, that the Night-air ſeems to require ſome Guard; and many are of Opinion, that lying with the Head warm is moſt healthful; and particularly good for the Hair, the Eyes, and the Teeth.

Another Obſervation I ſhall here make, is, the Error of ſleeping in ſmall Rooms, and by Choice in the lower Part of a Houſe; it is certainly right that we ſhould have Space for a due Circulation of Air, that it may not become thick and foul, which is very common in cloſe Bed-chambers; nor ſhould we lie ſurrounded with Curtains, for that is confining ourſelves to the Air within the

the small Compass of our Beds. Parents would do well to let Children lie with the Curtains undrawn; and even where they have tender Constitutions, drawn only at the Sides of the Bed; but never all round, unless really sick: for this Practice, however common, is highly erroneous.

Notwithstanding the general Rules laid down concerning Exercise, I must here observe, that as Children advance in Life, that is, when they approach to Men and Women, great Regard should be had to the Exercise suitable to their Circumstances and Constitution; but these are too many to admit of enlarging upon here. I will in brief observe, that those who are hale receive the greatest Advantage from walking; the tender, especially the Hectical, and those who have weak Nerves, cannot bear this Exercise to any Degree, but gain Strength and Vigor from riding on Horseback; and indeed it often happens, where walking cannot be borne without great Fatigue, and waste of Strength and Spirits, riding, on the contrary, not only gives Pleasure, but increases both. Where Infirmity is so great, which doubtless will sometimes happen, that neither of these Exercises can be pursued, then a Coach, or some other Vehicle, should supply

ſupply their Place; for it is of great Conſequence not totally to diſuſe Exerciſe: but Parents muſt remember this is too indolent in a State of Health; and is not by any Means to be encouraged by Choice. Beſides theſe, there are many others under the Name of Sports and Paſtimes, which if well regulated, and Care be taken that thoſe engaged in them do not injudiciouſly drink cold Liquors, or otherwiſe expoſe themſelves to inclement Seaſons, are very ſalutary; ſuch as Fencing, Dancing, Bowling, Digging, Gardening, and many others; all in their Nature good, and at times not to be ſhunned, eſpecially by thoſe whoſe Life would otherwiſe be inactive, thoſe particularly who are devoted to Study.

There are yet ſome farther things relative to Health, which Parents muſt not diſregard. Conſtitutions are ſo variouſly formed, that the ſame Employment which ſuits one Child, will not another. If one is cloſely confined to Study it will impair his Health, and either ſhorten his Days, or make him miſerable: if another is engaged in a laborious Buſineſs, his tender Frame, perhaps, ſinks under it: if a third is indulged in an eaſy Occupation, where Action would have ſuited his Frame, he becomes indolent,

indolent, inſipid, and infirm, a Burden to himſelf and others. Laſtly, there are Occupations in Life whoſe Fumes are known to affect us; and ſome Regard ſhould be had even to theſe, ſince the Health of our Children is concerned: not that I here recommend the Obſervance of each Nicety, or would have Children afraid of every Vapour that riſes around them, or of every Employment that is accompanied with Labour: no; that would be making Life too painful, and fix in our Children an unmanly Timorouſneſs, which would make them puny, frivolous or hurtful; and would be ſwerving from the Opinion of the greateſt Men that have ſtudied and wrote on theſe Subjects: For *Hippocrates*, *Celſus*, and all thoſe who were beſt acquainted with what Phyſicians call the Non-naturals, maintain, that, beſides Temperance and Air, Exerciſe, and that too of the moſt laborious Kind, particularly Huſbandry, is indiſpenſably neceſſary for Health. What then in general I here adviſe, is, that Parents, in ſettling their Children, have an Eye to their Health, at the ſame time that they ſtudy their Intereſt and Proſperity.

Having thus with real Pains, and an unfeigned Deſire to promote the Welfare of Mankind,

Mankind, pointed out the general Means of preſerving Health, and, I hope, ſet in a true Light thoſe Errors which uſually tend to impair or deſtroy it; if Parents ſeriouſly adhere to the one, and avoid the other, their Children will receive many and great Advantages therefrom. It may be urged, that the Treatment which ſuits one Child will not another; and that general Rules are always ſubject to particular Exceptions: I grant it. Still this does not juſtify thoſe Parents who ſubmit to no Rules at all. I have ſaid before, that all Laws give Parents the ſole Power of governing their Children; I may alſo maintain that the ſame Laws oblige them to do every thing to promote their Welfare. Thoſe who are unacquainted with the Duty of a Parent, muſt learn; thoſe who know, muſt practiſe. Let this Admonition then rouſe the Attention of Parents; and let theſe Precepts ſerve as the Foundation, whereon to build the ſolid Health of their Children. The Conſtitution is like the Countenance, ſomewhat different in every one; where therefore any Deviations from Rule are the Effect of Judgment, I ſincerely applaud them; and where any Principle here laid down proves erroneous, I chearfully ſubmit to the Removal of it.

Many of my Readers will ſtill perhaps expect, that ſomething ſhould be ſaid concerning the manner of treating Children in Sickneſs; but they muſt remember, that I ſet out with no farther View than the preſerving Health, by avoiding every Irregularity and Exceſs: and when Diſeaſes happen, which cannot be obviated, nor even foreſeen, it is not the reading a ſingle Volume that will qualify Parents to undertake the Cure of them: no; they muſt apply to thoſe who make it their Study and their Profeſſion; to thoſe whoſe Judgment, whoſe Integrity, and whoſe Diligence they can confide in. To this End I will here endeavour to point out to Parents the moſt rational Way of proceeding.

One would imagine, that nothing was eaſier to determine than this Matter; for what can be more natural in Sickneſs, than ſending for a Phyſician? He who from his Youth has laboured to acquire Knowledge, who has devoted his Life to Study, who has ſearched into Nature, and diſcovered the moſt hidden Cauſes; who has ſacrificed many even of the innocent Pleaſures of Life, that he might become uſeful to Mankind; and who, to accompliſh this, has ſpent perhaps a good younger Son's Portion. Can

any

any thing, I ſay, be more natural or more rational than this Proceeding? And yet, who is there that has any Knowledge of the World, that is acquainted with *London* particularly, that does not daily ſee a very different Practice? Who is there that does not know, that the Apothecary, the Nurſe, the Quack, and many others, oftentimes baffle the Phyſician, or keep him out of Play.

Every Nation is diſtinguiſhed for ſome Peculiarities of it's own. In *France* the Phyſicians have but little Dignity, and their Fees are low; yet nobody in Sickneſs preſumes to act without them; they are always call'd firſt: in *England*, the Reputation of Phyſicians is deſervedly great; but their Fees are high, and they are uſually call'd in laſt. As Sickneſs is in it's Nature every Way expenſive, as the Doctor's Fee is always Gold, we cannot but be ſenſible, that there are many People in the Nation, who either from a Deſire to contract the Expence, or from a Want of Ability to give the cuſtomary Fees, do not, at leaſt 'till Danger threatens, ſend for a Phyſician. And it is for theſe, and other Reaſons, that ſome Medium between the Patient and the Phyſician ſeems neceſſary: which Medium is no where to be found, but in the Apothecary.

Let

Let us now enquire a little into the Nature of the Apothecary's Bufinefs, and fee of what Ufe he is to Mankind. Pharmacy, the Apothecary's Art, is branch'd out of Phyfic; for as now the Apothecary fometimes prefcribes, fo originally the Phyfician was Apothecary too. An Apothecary's Education is not fo deep, nor his Application to Study ufually fo clofe, as the Phyfician's: yet as Genius is not confined to the Phyfician, but is by Nature as capable of refiding in the Apothecary; fome Degree of Learning, an Acquaintance with proper Books, which are equally open to both, and conftant Obfervation on Difeafes, will certainly furnifh him with a confiderable Stock of ufeful Knowledge. Experience is the Mother of Wifdom. While the Phyfician is labouring at Theories, the Apothecary is perhaps deeply immers'd in Practice: and as all allow that nice Obfervation is of vaft Ufe in Phyfic, while the one is fearching into Caufes, the other, if he improves as he ought the Opportunities he is furnifhed with, gains a Knowledge of Effects. Hence it appears, that an Apothecary is capable of being, not merely an ufeful, but a valuable Man to Society; and perhaps equally fo, both to Patient and Phyfician. Phyficians could

could not keep up their Dignity, nor act with Safety without this Medium. Who is it they confide in that the Drugs are good, and the Letter of the Prescription faithfully adhered to, but the Apothecary? Who is it that gives the Patient that close Attendance he frequently wants, but the Apothecary? Who is it that has the Trouble of applying Leeches, of applying and dressing Blisters, of adminstering Vomits, &c. of watching the various Changes that arise, and of running in Pursuit of the Doctor to check some threatening Symptom, but the Apothecary? And who is it, in fine, that on every Emergency, in every real or fancied Danger, is called out of his Bed to administer some speedy Relief, or appease some groundless Fears of the Patient, or their Friends, but the Apothecary? Still all this, tho' literally true, tho' it proves the Apothecary (where a good one) to have some real Importance, yet it does not put him upon a Level with the Physician, much less justify the shutting him out from Practice. Those who deny that Apothecaries can sometimes cure Diseases, flatly contradict what every Day's Experience proves; and those, who, to magnify them, depreciate the Physicians, are guilty of an Injustice, which can have no other Source than Ignorace, or an evil Mind: for,

for, to put Things upon a fair Footing, the Apothecary ſhould be conſidered as an Auxiliary; or, as I have before expreſſed it, a neceſſary Medium between Phyſician and Patient.

Health is a nice Affair; and Life precious to every Individual. The beſt Advice then I can give to Parents is, that they do not, where theſe are at Stake, hazard either one or the other by Indolence, or an ill-tim'd Frugality. Thoſe who are rich, let them at once ſend for the Phyſician, eſpecially if it be a Matter of Moment; and ſurely Prudence points out this to us: ſo thoſe who cannot reach the beſt, let them take the next beſt; that is, where calling in a Phyſician would too ſenſibly affect their Circumſtances, Prudence demands, that they employ a good Apothecary. And even theſe, tho' they conſult their Apothecary firſt, ſhould ſtrain a Point where Danger threatens; and neither attach themſelves too cloſely to the Man who is fond of his own Judgment; nor condemn another's Tenderneſs in propoſing farther Advice. But I may on this Point ſay farther, that it is ſometimes the greateſt Proof of Wiſdom in an Apothecary to deſire the Advice of a Phyſician; for tho' Diligence, Integrity, and many other Qualifications are highly neceſſary

necessary in this Profession, yet none is equal to that Penetration, which gives him the Power of seeing Danger before it is too late to apply a Remedy.

As for the Calumnies, the Sneers, and the Misrepresentations of ignorant or designing People, such as Apothecaries and Physicians being in league together, and playing into one another's Hands; the Eleven-pence in the Shilling; the cramming People with Physic they do not want; and much more of the like Nature; these are things that scarcely deserve any Notice. I have now been full thirty Years in the Business; have seen and done far from an inconsiderable Share; have attended with Physicians of every Rank, from those who first enter'd into Practice up to those who have reach'd the Summit; yet cannot charge either any single Physician, or myself, with even an Attempt to enter into an Association to the Prejudice of Mankind. On the contrary, I have seen some who have laboured with disinterested Zeal for their Benefit; not merely because they could not have their Fees, but because they would not take them. Here I cannot help observing how much the World is misled by Appearances; because People see an Apothecary with a good Suit of Cloaths on, they conclude he is above Want; and because caufe they fee another in a Chariot, they pronounce him rich: fo too becaufe a very few Phyficians make Fortunes, they conclude, that all of the Profeffion are Wealthy. But how fallacious is all this! There is no Profeffion, no Trade in the Kingdom which we call genteel, that has fo few rich Men in it as the different Branches of Phyfic. Many a Man in it, fenfible that the World would have no Opinion of his Skill, if he appeared to Difadvantage, keeps up a Port with aching Heart; many a Chariot is in daily Danger of breaking down; and many owe their Stability more to their own Patrimony, to their Wives Portion, or fome other fortunate Event, than to the Produce of their Bufinefs.

Two Things with refpect to Sicknefs Parents are to guard againft; one is, the Neglect of calling for Help in time; the other, that amazing Attachment to Nurfes, and what they call good old Women. I efteem it a Misfortune in a Family, where a Phyfician or an Apothecary appears as regularly as the Baker; and to prove that I do fo, I have faid before, that our Food may often be made our Phyfic; and have pointed out many Ways to prevent Difeafes: ftill it is a Fact, that all Errors are beft rectified at the Beginning; and the fooner a Diftemper is attacked, the ſooner, in all Probability, will it be conquered. Good Women are extremely apt to treat phyſical People with Contempt; and this chiefly to magnify their own Skill. If they have any Knowledge, as ſome of them doubtleſs have, to whom principally do they owe it? Is it not from converſing with phyſical People, and ſeeing how they proceed? moſt certainly. And yet theſe ſame good Women ſhall wonder that any body ſends for a Doctor or an Apothecary to a ſick Child! What, they cry, do theſe People know about Children? A good old Woman is better than all of them. She muſt be a very good old Woman indeed, that knows more than Men who have made the Knowledge of Diſeaſes the whole Study of their Lives. But ſuppoſing that Reaſon and Reſolution get the better of this Weakneſs; Parents have ſtill more to do; it is not enough that Medicines are preſcribed, they muſt be ſure that they are taken. For beſides the Repugnance in the Child, there is a Difficulty perhaps in the Nurſe; and if ſhe thinks it wrong, it will be hard to ſet her right; and harder ſtill, to prevail on her to give them to the Patient. Parents, in this Caſe, muſt either reſolve not to aſk Advice, or reſolve to ſee the Medicines taken.

Nurſes

Nurſes have a Province of their own, in which they are very valuable, that is, a diligent attentive Care; for in vain do Parents ſeek Advice, in vain do Phyſicians preſcribe, if Nurſes are negligent, unwatchful, or careleſs. But while I do them the Juſtiee they deſerve, while I acknowledge the Merit of their Station, and recommend that it be rewarded, I cannot help repeating to Parents, not to ſuffer them to baffle ſuperior Knowledge. If any Change happens to the Patient, or a Difficulty ariſes unforeſeen, let them ſuſpend for a Time the Execution of the Orders given them; but let them not fruſtrate the Phyſician's Intention, by throwing Medicines away, giving them by Halves, or giving ſomething of their own added to it, or in it's ſtead; and then concealing what they have done: all theſe things are grievouſly wrong, and every way unjuſtifiable, as they frequently diſappoint the Patient, or diſgrace the Phyſician. If a Nurſe has made any uſeful Obſervation on the Patient (which all good Nurſes ſometimes will) there is not a Doctor in the Kingdom, if a Man of Senſe, but will hear her, and turn it to Advantage; but if her Conceit leads her to ſet aſide or overturn what is propoſed, however merry it may make herſelf, every

G thinking

thinking Perſon in the World muſt condemn ſo capital an Error.

The laſt Caution I ſhall give to Parents relative to Health, is, the Danger of Noſtrums and Quack-Medicines. I believe there is not a Phyſician nor an Apothecary in the Kingdom but what has ſeen the Lives of People, particularly of Children, ſacrificed to this Practice. What is it that conſtitutes the Phyſician, that proves the Man of Judgment, but the varying his Preſcriptions, not only according to different Diſeaſes, but according to the different Circumſtances of the ſame Diſeaſe? And yet theſe Noſtrum-Mongers, with unparalell'd Boldneſs, often attempt to conquer all Diſeaſes with one Arcanum, one pretended Remedy. Who that hears theſe Boaſters, or that reads their printed Accounts, but muſt diſcover many Abſurdities on the very Face of them. The Man that promiſes what is repugnant to common Senſe, argues himſelf either a Knave or a Fool; and yet People are often ſo little attentive, or ſo regardleſs of Health, that they do not diſcover their Error, 'till it is ſometimes too late to remedy it. That I may do ſtrict Juſtice to every one, I am ready to grant, that many Diſcoveries have been made in Medicine by mere Accident; and

and that ſome of the Noſtrums in Vogue are in themſelves good; nay ſome of them were the Diſcoveries of able Phyſicians; Diſcoveries ſince ſeiz'd on by deſigning People, and pirated into a kind of Property. But what does all this avail in the Hands of ignorant People? What is a Man the wiſer for being placed in a Repoſitory of the fineſt Drugs, if he knows not how to apply them? Or wherein does he differ from one ſet in a Library of the choiceſt Books, without being able to read? Yet are People every Day vending Things, which they know not the Nature nor Uſe of; and ſo far impoſe on the weak and credulous, as often to make a Fortune at others Coſt.

Opium, Mercury, and all the powerful Drugs, are every Day ſcattered about the Kingdom, and indiſcriminately offered to all, whether they want them or not, whether they are good for them or not; and the ſpecious Terms they are recommended in are apt to miſlead, not merely innocent, but very ſenſible People. Since then Things are ſo, Parents muſt be very wary how they touch ſuch dangerous Weapons. 'Tis great Odds but they miſtake their Child's Diſorder; 'tis great Odds that the random Medicine they give is not ſuited to it; and how will they reconcile it to themſelves if any fatal Conſequence enſues? Upon the Whole, as a Friend to Mankind, independent of any private Intereſt, as one who aims at the Benefit of Society, and wiſhes to preſerve the riſing Generation, I cannot but adviſe Parents to be tender, circumſpect, and judicious, in ſo important a Matter as their Children's Health. When they are well, let them uſe every prudent Means to keep them ſo; if they are ill, let them aſk good Advice; by which Means they will often ſave their Children's Lives: and even where a Miſcarriage happens, their Prudence and Juſtice will be attended with this Conſolation, that they have done their beſt.

MANNERS.

MANNERS comes next under my Confideration: it implies fuch a Government of our Children as tends to regulate their Conduct, by making their Actions what they ought to be. And though Health has been treated firft, from it's being generally thought the moft immediately neceffary, yet if this Regulation, this due Government does not accompany every Endeavour to preferve their Children's Health, Parents will often be difappointed, and find their Labour fruitlefs.

The Bafis of Government is Authority: without that, in vain do we expect any Order in our Children, any Happinefs to ourfelves. Cities, Armies, Kingdoms, all are fuftain'd by it: and fo too muft private Families be. By Authority I do not mean that ftern Brow, that trembling awful Diftance, nor that Bafhaw-like Behaviour, which favours more of the Tyrant than of the Parent; no: I mean a rational, yet abſolute Exerciſe of a Degree of Power, neceſſary for the regulating the Actions and Diſpoſitions of Children, 'till they become wiſe enough to govern themſelves. But becauſe ſome Children attain this neceſſary Knowledge ſooner than others, and one Child will be better able to conduct itſelf at fifteen, than another at twenty, or even thirty; there is but one general way of aſcertaining the length of Time our Authority ſhould be exerciſed in it's full Force; which is that ſettled by the Laws of our Kingdom; viz. 'till the Age of twenty-one. And if we can once ſeriouſly reſolve to employ this Term ſo critical to Children, ſolely to their Advantage, Authority will thenceforward become uſeleſs: it's Terrors will vaniſh, and be wholly abſorbed in the united Conſiderations of the Parent, the Friend, and the Companion: in a Word, our Children well conducted to this Age will afterwards take as much Pains to make us happy, as we have done to make them wiſe. But to proceed.

As ſoon as a Child diſcovers the firſt Diſpoſitions to Perverſity and Self-will (which as ſure as it is born it will too ſoon begin to do) I adviſe moſt earneſtly that it be attended to; for much depends upon it. Here I muſt

muſt caution my Fair Readers in particular, not to ſuſpect me of Cruelty; ſince the Pains I am taking is intended to prevent the Neceſſity of uſing any Severity during our whole Lives. But what! you'll ſay, ſhould a Child be corrected before it can ſpeak? I anſwer, that the firſt Principle in human Nature is Self-love; Reaſon, the ſecond Principle, opens only by degrees. Now as ſoon as the Paſſions of Children ſhew themſelves, they ſhould certainly be checked: and as the Fear of Chaſtiſement is included in Self-love, it is eaſy to turn this to their Advantage, 'till Reaſon ſhall have gained ſo much Strength as to render it unneceſſary: no one can abſolutely fix the Time, but within the Year moſt Parents will find a Neceſſity to begin; and before half the firſt Septenary is paſt much may be done.

In the Government of Children Parents ſhould be obſtinately good; that is, ſet out upon right Principles, and then purſue them with Spirit and Reſolution: otherwiſe their Children will ſoon grow too cunning for them, and take the Advantage of their Weakneſs.

Severe and frequent Whipping is I think a very bad Practice; it inflames the Skin, it puts the Blood into a Ferment, and there is besides, a Meanness, a degree of Ignominy attending it, which makes it very unbecoming: still there may be Occasions which will render it necessary; but I earnestly advise that all the milder Methods be first try'd. A coarse clamorous manner of enforcing Obedience is also to be avoided; it is vulgar, and nothing vulgar should be seen in the Behaviour of Parents to their Children, because through the Eyes and Ears it taints their tender Minds: still, let Parents make their Children both see and feel the Power they have over them.

If a Child is passionate and wilful, a Look, or a little Tap on the Hand, will, without hurting it, sometimes suffice to convince it that it is doing wrong; and will often cure the Fault, or at least keep it under. A Child, in a perverse Mood, throws down it's Playthings; if they are taken up fifty times successively, they are still thrown down as long as the Spirit of Contradiction lasts: now the Remedy here should be to take them away; or by a serious Countenance shew you are displeased; and the Child will very probably not only soon be quiet, but be less prone to do the like another Time. I have seen Children that could not speak, distinguish perfectly

fectly thofe who were difpofed to fpoil them from thofe who were not; fcratch Faces, break China, and play the tyrant over all who humour'd them, and yet not offer to lift a Finger againft thofe who did not. By all means let Children be play'd with, and have every Amufement; but great care muft be taken to diftinguifh Play from Mifchief; innocent Freedom, from a growing Perverfity.

The Humours even of Infants are innumerably various. One Child will not fleep but on a Lap; another there is no Peace with unlefs rock'd in a Cradle; a third will cry when a Candle is taken away; and to fhew us why it cry'd, it is quiet the Moment it is brought back again; a fourth will fwill Tea or fome other improper Liquor out of meafure and out of time; and a fifth will eat Trafh 'till it can eat nothing elfe, nor that itfelf. In thefe Cafes I advife Parents to confider if their Children are acting for themfelves, or they for their Children: one Grain of Judgment will fet them right; one Minute's Reflection will fhew them their Error; but, when they once fee it they muft refolve to avoid it for the future. I call'd fome time ago on a Friend, and took a Family Dinner; when to my great Aftonifhment I ſaw little Maſter, not yet a Year old, drinking Porter. What, ſaid I, do you give the Child ſtrong Drink? Oh! Sir, reply'd Mamma, he'll drink nothing elſe. Now is not the Fault of ſuch Proceeding obvious? and is not the Remedy as obvious? Parents ſurely cannot be ſo blind as not to ſee their Children's Health impair'd, and their Humours ſtrengthen'd, by this miſplac'd Indulgence; and all for want of a little Reſolution, a gentle Correction, or a ſeaſonable Reprimand; nay perhaps only a Look; which given with an authoritative Air, would often have the deſired Effect. Conſtant Experience proves how wrong, nay how ineffectual, the oppoſite Practice to this is; thoſe who give a Child every thing it cries or aſks for, ſtrengthen indeed its Wilfulneſs, but are far from making it happy. How many improper Things are there which Parents give a Child becauſe they cannot quiet it? Who has not ſeen a Picture, a Book, a Watch, and other valuable things expoſed to be deſtroyed by it through this miſtaken Management? But ſurely it is right that even among the Baubles contrived on purpoſe, the Parents, not the Child, ſhould have the Command of them; that is, they ſhould be given or taken away at Diſcretion; and this without Paſſion or Ill-nature on one Side, and without

out Clamour or Fretfulneſs on the other. Parents ſhould every Day more and more convince their Children of their Power over them, by reſtraining their little Irregularities, and by weakening their Paſſions; now this they cannot do without an early Attention to their various Diſpoſitions and Tempers; that they may thence learn what Propenſity is ſtrongeſt, what Foible is moſt predominant.

Nature, 'tis true, is not alike bountiful to all; nor does ſhe give the ſame Propenſity, the ſame Temper to all. One Child is born with ſweet and mild Diſpoſitions; another more ſanguine, and full of Fire; a third has a Redundance of Acrimony; and ſo on: yet different Tempers are ſometimes a kindneſs beſtow'd on us by Nature, on purpoſe for us to act ſome certain Part on the great Stage of Life. It is therefore the Parents Buſineſs to watch the Temper of their Children; to check any evil Tendency, any ill Diſpoſitions, and prevent every Exceſs from growing into a Habit; nay more, to change the bad Humour into a good one; as Phyſicians adminiſter Medicines to alter the Blood and Juices. That famous Reply of *Socrates* to the Phiſiognomiſt was excellent: "Nature "(ſays he) intended me a Monſter; but Rea-"ſon

"son has made me what I am." Cardinal *Richlieu* (speaking of external Graces) says, "Every thing to a Gentleman should be natural." Now it cannot be supposed that he means, we should know how to speak, or move, or dance gracefully, without being taught; no, but these Things by Acquisition should so far enter into us as to seem interwoven in our Nature. Thus did Philosophy change the Vices of *Socrates* into Virtues; and thus should Parents correct and alter the irregular Dispositions of their Children: they must temper and moderate the Fire of one, lest it grow too impetuous; they must animate the Mildness of another with a Degree of Warmth, lest it become sluggish; and they must blunt and sweeten the Acrimony of a third, lest it degenerate into Rancour; which last Frame of Mind, as it is of all others the most detestable in itself, and the most dangerous to Society, so of all others it requires the nicest Care to manage; in short Parents, as I have already observed, are to let their Children see and feel their Affection for them, and their Power over them; and then regulate their Actions as they find necessary.

I have still my Eye on Children in the first Septenary, and with Concern view the Majority of them humour'd, and therefore humoursome;

mourſome; Boys audacious and impudent under the Name of courageous; and Girls pert and vain under the name of witty. It is my Opinion the Parents need not trouble themſelves much to reaſon with their Children in this Stage; firſt let them conſider what is proper for them to do, or avoid; then enforce their Compliance in ſoft and winning Terms; or, if not with a ſmiling Countenance, at leaſt with a ſmooth Brow and without harſhneſs: but whenever they attempt to diſobey, let them ſhew by a Word or a Look that they are abſolute: which Method I think ſhould be ſeriouſly adhered to. Though I have already obſerved that Children have Knowledge much earlier than is commonly imagined, they have yet no Judgment to guide their Actions, What they chiefly diſcover to us at this Age is Cunning; therefore if Parents neglect Reproof when neceſſary, they will ſoon get the better of them. For Example, a Child cries becauſe it is to go to School; ſhall Parents fondly to quiet it keep it at Home? by no means. A Doſe of Phyſic is to be taken; ſhall they, becauſe it is unpleaſant, humour the Child, and throw it away? no ſurely. There is no other Method here but being ſerious; you muſt go, you muſt take it; when Children thus ſee their Parents in ear-

neſt

neſt, Obedience very ſoon becomes familiar and eaſy.

Nor is an unreaſonable Compliance with the Humours of Children what Parents take it for; they falſely think it Tenderneſs and Love; but far from it; it is Love degenerated into Weakneſs and Folly. But it is eaſy to ſoften this ſeeming Rigour in the Behaviour of Parents, by their addreſſing the Underſtandings of Children at other Intervals, ſuppoſing it to be open. What more natural and reaſonable than to ſay to a Child, You know, my Dear, all good Children do as they are bid; all Children to become wiſe muſt go to School; you would not ſurely be rank'd among bad Children by being diſobedient? You would not, I hope, be a Blockhead? yet if you do not apply to your Learning you muſt be one. Thus too with Regard to Medicines: You know, my Love, Phyſic is to make you well; I am ſorry you have occaſion to take it; I am ſorry it is unpleaſant; but ſince it is neceſſary for you, prove yourſelf a good Child, and take it at once. Here I muſt beg leave to expoſtulate with Parents on the Errors uſually run into in this laſt Particular. How comes it that there is ſuch an univerſal Difficulty in getting Medicines down a ſick Child's Throat?

How

How comes it that the moſt ſprightly talkative Child cannot be prevailed on to ſhew its Tongue to the Doctor, yet the Moment his Back is turn'd he will loll it out twenty times? The Reaſon is plain; Parents do not teach their Children to obey. Inſtead of Compulſion or Reaſon, they uſe Flattery, Bribes and Deceit: but I am practically convinced that all this, however common, is wrong: and indeed where Obedience is not inſiſted on, and made a firſt Rule of Action, few things can be right. As Medicines are generally nauſeous, a Repugnance to take them is as natural as ſhrinking at Pain; notwithſtanding this, where they are really neceſſary, and unleſs they are ſo, nobody ought to be troubled with them, a Child at any Age, from the very Day it is born, till it is a Man or Woman, may, and ought to be made to take them. But to do this Parents muſt ſet out right; they muſt have the Child under Command. That every Parent is actuated by a Principle of preſerving the Life of their Child, I will take for granted; but this is not enough: they muſt go on to the Execution of the Means. The Infant of a Day ſhews its Repugnance to ſwallow a few Grains of Rhubarb; the Child of a Year will twiſt it's Head about every Way it can, that the

Spoon

Spoon or Cup which contains the Doſe may not reach it's Mouth; and by the time it is three or four Years old, it will probably daſh the Cup out of the Hand of thoſe who offer the Potion, or tell them in plain Terms it won't take it. Now, without mentioning the Conſequence this may be of to it's Health or Life, there is another of great Importance; namely, that a Child thus uſed to get the better of all about it, and convinced it can conquer it's Parents, is ſeldom diſpoſed to conquer itſelf; ſo that where Self-will is very ſtrong, Reaſon will doubtleſs be weak; and only ſerve to aggravate the Fault by fixing an Error, perhaps for Life. Yet great as all theſe Difficulties appear, they vaniſh at the Entrance of Reflection and Reſolution. If Parents conſider that they are bound by every Tye to make their Children obey, and then reſolve to fulfil this Obligation, the Buſineſs is done: therefore with regard to Medicines, what have they more to do? Nothing but the Execution, which may be effected with Eaſe. For Example, take a Child from it's Birth to the Age of twenty-one, and divide this Time into three, not equal parts, but States; call the firſt the unreſiſting State; the ſecond the State of Cunning; and the third the State of Reaſon. The firſt is extremely ſhort, we cannot count it it by Years, and ſcarcely by Months; nor is there any Trouble here with Medicines, but putting a Spoon or Cup to it's Mouth, and holding the Head back 'till the Doſe is ſwallowed. The ſecond State laſts long; and tho' ſoft and winning Words are always to be preferred, yet they ſeldom ſucceed here; a ſerious Countenance and a reſolute Air are the ſureſt Means to conquer; and theſe maintained, there is nothing to fear. The Difficulties of the third State, that of Reaſon, are greatly leſſened by the Succeſs of the preceding; for a Child habituated to obey, looks back with Pleaſure on it's Compliance with every reaſonable Command; and tho' it before obey'd and took Medicines, becauſe it muſt, it now takes them becauſe it ought.

I cannot but be of Opinion, that every Method in the Management of ſick Children contrary to this is erroneous; I think I have ſeen all tried that is in the Power of human Invention; and many who read this cannot but be convinced that their own Endeavours have often been fruitleſs. The firſt Rule Parents are to lay down to themſelves is, never to deceive their Children; for ſurely thoſe who are to teach them never to be deceitful, cannot but be very unfit Perſons

Perſons to deceive them themſelves: nor does this ſquare with the Practice of quibbling down a Doſe of Phyſic, under a thouſand Shifts and Turns, and even manifeſt Falſhoods. The next Rule is, to avoid the Practice of Bribes. Children ſhould be taught to know, that their greateſt Happineſs is their Parents Love; therefore the Cuſtom of giving them Sugar-Plumbs, Cakes, Toys, or Money for every thing they take, is grievouſly wrong: it gives them a Fondneſs for improper things; it gives them a reſtleſs Deſire for every new Bauble; and above all, it gives them an early Mean-ſpiritedneſs; an odious Selfiſhneſs; a Deſire of being paid for every thing they do.

At the ſame time that I recommend to Parents never to call things by wrong Names, never to attempt impoſing on a Child's Senſes or Underſtanding, or to force down Medicines with Bribes; ſo I alſo recommend, that they avoid Harſhneſs and Violence, unleſs preſſed to it by great Neceſſity; but this Caution is almoſt needleſs after what has been ſaid: for with the Method propoſed, it requires no more than to approach the ſick Bed with, Come, my Dear, take your Doſe; if the Child ſays, it is nauſeous, grant it: but at the ſame time ſay,

ſay, We do not take Medicines for Pleaſure; but to make us well: if it declines it, urge how wrong it is to dwell on what would be gone in a Minute; and if any Difficulty ſtill remains, inform it, that it is not for your Sake you urge it, but it's own; and that while you are doing all you can to reſtore it to Health, you muſt, and will be obeyed. At intermediate times, let Parents, by a fond, engaging Behaviour, convince their Children how tenderly they love them; let them frequently mingle with them in their little Plays and Sports; and let them ſometimes overlook Trifles, that they may have more Influence in Matters of Moment.

Lord *Hallifax* obſerves, that the firſt Impreſſions Children receive are in the Nurſery; whence he infers, that Mothers have not only the earlieſt, but the moſt laſting Influence over them.

That the firſt Care of Children, and many of the moſt tender Offices they require, are the Mother's Province, is an undoubted Truth; but when the forming their Manners is under Conſideration, the Influence of both Father and Mother ſhould, if poſſible, be equal; at leaſt it is neceſſary that Parents

go

go hand in hand, and not counteract one another in the Government of them.

Parents ſhould make it a Rule to themſelves, never to ſhew to their Children, both at once, the Marks of extreme Anger, or exceſſive Fondneſs; but when a Child has done ſuch a Fault as demands of the Father to affect great Severity, let the Mother put on an equal Share of Lenity and Compaſſion mixed with Grief: and ſo on the reverſe. Thus too on other Occaſions, when the Mother prudently expoſes all the motherly Fondneſs of her Heart, let the Father as prudently conceal a Part of his, and, with an Air of Steadineſs, inſinuate, that the Conduct which is approved is no more than Duty. But Parents will never be able to act with due Moderation in the Government of their Children, without firſt reſolving to govern, with the utmoſt Prudence, their own Paſſions and Tempers. And how will they be able to do this, unleſs they look inwardly, and ſtudy to find them out? If the Man be of a choleric or moroſe Diſpoſition, and the Woman of a phlegmatic, mild, and affable Temper, the Contraſt may prove ſovereignly beneficial to their Children, if the Parties, conſcious of it in themſelves, reſolve mutually

ally to apply it under the Direction of Prudence; and found the Government of their young Family's Passions on that of their own. Whereas, if ignorant of their respective Foibles, or heedless to turn them to Advantage, they give a full Loose to them, and agree in nothing but an unbridled Exertion of them as Occasion or Accident offers, the Contrast will probably prove fatal both to themselves and their Children: they will for the most part be pleased and displeased alike out of Time and out of Measure; their Severities and Lenities will often jar, and rob each other of their due Effect; their Punishments and Rewards, by being never, or but seldom, and that by mere Chance, proportioned to the Failings they mean to correct, or the Merit they wish to encourage, will prove fruitless, if not destructive: and what is still worse, they will seldom fail, in the midst of Correction, to strengthen the Misconduct they aim at reforming, by the Example they give of it in their own Persons; and as seldom miss, in the Extravagance of their false Fondnesses, of perverting the Minds of their Children from the noble Love of Virtue, to the reptil Hankerings after Rewards, Praises, and Caresses. If a Child is to be reformed of any peevish or passionate Behaviour, what Effect

Effect can Correction have on him, if given by a Parent delivered over by his own Passions to all the Fierceness of a Brute? It may make him hate the Correction, but can never make him hate Faults, the opposite Virtues to which he sees not the least Example of in his Corrector. If another is to be encouraged in some commendable Action, what Benefit will he receive from an Excess of Fondness, while the being humour'd in other Actions, perhaps highly discommendable, only teaches him to exchange Vice for Vice, or one Folly for another? Or finally, what Advantage can be produced to Children from Reprehension or Approbation, from Punishments or Rewards, however well proportioned, timed or placed, if there appear to them in the Parents a Dissention in the bestowing them; and that they are the Overflowings of Passion or Partiality, rather than the Result of Reason and Equity? Parents then should seriously acquaint themselves with their own Tempers, and mutually consent and agree on the Methods of regulating their Children; never to reward or punish, seem angry or pleas'd, but by Concert; and above all, never to correct while in a Passion, nor reward till the fond Fit be over.

There

There are many things in the Management of Children rather to be wiſhed than obtained; not ſo eaſily practiſed as deſired; among theſe, one Expedient, I think, might often prove ſucceſsful towards attaining this happy Medium I have been ſpeaking of. Where a Father is of a choleric, haſty, and ſevere Diſpoſition, and the Mother the reverſe, which is moſt generally the Caſe, it were greatly to be wiſhed, that, by mutual Conſent, they ſometimes exchanged Offices in the Government of their Children. Would the Father reſolve to make it his Study ſo to conquer his Temper, as ſeldom or never, but in extreme Neceſſity, to interfere in reprimanding and correcting his Children, but rather to take upon him the Office of Commendations and Rewards; and of treating them with all the Affability he is Maſter of: and would the Mother take an equal Reſolution to conquer the Softneſs of her Nature, to reprimand and puniſh them on proper Occaſions with all the Sternneſs ſhe can ſummon; remitting them for the Applauſe or Gratifications they may deſerve to their Father: would Parents, I ſay, with theſe Diſpoſitions, reſolve on the Practice, I cannot but think it would produce excellent Effects in the Government of Children:

Children: confidering the very little Danger there would be of the choleric, or naturally fevere Father fpoiling his Child by Excefs of Fondnefs; or the naturally tender Mother ruining it by extreme Severity.

I will here fuppofe, what is moft agreeable to good Senfe, that Parents in general have fuch good Difpofitions as to intend the real Benefit of their Children; but either that they have not thought on what was neceffary to be done, or thought on it but confufedly: I will fuppofe too that both Father and Mother agree in this general Intention. Still, as all have their feveral Ways of judging, the moft fenfible People will be liable to have different Notions of different Things, and even different Ways of doing the fame Thing; which, fo far from being wrong, if well attended to, may contribute to the great Emolument of both. Yet Parents muft be extremely cautious never to differ about the Government of Children in their Hearing; it does incredible Mifchief; but particularly, it alienates them from their Duty; and weakens the Authority of the Parents on one Side at leaft, if not on both.

If a Child is to be in the Hands of a Nurfery-maid, (which is general among People

People of Condition) great Care ſhould be taken in the Choice of her. I am an Advocate for Knowledge and Good-breeding, but they are not ſo much wanted here. The Requiſities are, Cleanlineſs, Good-temper, Docility, and Innocence. Every one allows, and is ſenſible of the Benefit of Cleanlineſs; and genuine Good-temper is no leſs advantageous; but if with theſe Parents find a tractable docile Mind, joined with a native Innocence, they have found a Treaſure; and ought to prize it accordingly. The Parents are to be their Children's Guides, and the ſole Judges what ought to be done for them; therefore I cannot but account it a ſingular Happineſs, when they find a Servant who will treat their Children in the Manner they require. But farther; a Servant with this Turn of Temper, will every Day improve in the Knowledge and Behaviour neceſſary to her Station: and from ſeeing the Reaſonableneſs of the Parents Injunctions, take pains to enforce them on the Child.

But as a Variety of Circumſtances in Life may alter our Views; ſo we are often obliged to vary our Mode of proceeding, tho' directed to the ſame Point. Thus it ſometimes happens, that a very young Couple become Parents, who are totally unacquainted with what ought to be done; in that Caſe, it is undoubtedly neceſſary that they ſeek a Perſon already ſkilled in this important Buſineſs; poſſeſſed too of all the Requiſites I have juſt pointed out: and ſuch an one with Care and Pains may be found. As Misfortunes are but too common, ſo there are Women who are not only well born, but whoſe Education and Manner of Life is truly virtuous; whoſe only Fault perhaps is, that they inconſiderately married too young; and whoſe Misfortune is, that Death by depriving them of their Huſbands, has deprived them of Support: whence they are glad to accept of a Service, which unexperienced Parents ought as gladly to engage them in, and reward them for.

It is not enough that Children have wiſe and diſcreet Parents, who employ too a faithful Deputy; no, they muſt alſo be guarded from the Interpoſition of Friends and Relations. They are dangerous Sharers in our Government, and dangerous Rivals in our Children's Affections. No body ſurely can miſtake me ſo far as to think I would exclude Relations from the Reſpect and Duty due to them; by no means: they may aſſiſt with their Counſel in the Abſence of of the Children, or they may encourage filial Duty in the Abſence of the Parents; but in general they ſhould not be allow'd to interfere in the Management, nor on any Account thwart the Parents Injunctions, or diſcover oppoſite Sentiments in the Children's hearing. What more common than for a Lady to have a Maiden Siſter live with her, who is pretty ſure to ſpoil the Children by a miſtaken Fondneſs. A Child grows ungovernable, and the Parents correct it; now as Children are cunning before they are wiſe, immediately it flies to it's Aunt; who, with eager Embraces, and pathetic Nonſenſe, ſeldom fails to pervert the Parents Correction with ill timed, and worſe judg'd Conſolations. Is it not eaſy to ſee that Children by this Party Management will be miſled; and that if it does not miſguide their Affection, it will at leaſt weaken their Duty?

That Children have Knowledge very early is plain to us a thouſand different Ways, but in none more evidently than their cloſe Attachment, their viſible Fondneſs, for ſome one Perſon, whether Father, Mother, Aunt, or Nurſe; though commonly it is the Mother or Nurſe, or whoever is moſt with them, or moſt humours them. This Fondneſs is perfectly natural, and we are not to be surprised at it; but my Readers must remember it is the Parents Business to regulate their Children's Desires; and this they cannot do, if they indulge and cherish a blind Fondness in them, though it should be even to themselves. Filial Affection in it's full Extent is undoubtedly an exalted Virtue; still to be rational, it must be just: and as there are many things which Parents cannot lawfully command their Children to do, so there are many things which Children ought not to comply with, even though commanded by a Parent. For Instance: if a Man dislikes his Wife, or a Woman her Husband (and melancholy Experience shews us these things do happen, and that there is sometimes a fix'd Aversion on one side or both) is it therefore lawful for a Man to teach his Children to hate their Mother; or the reverse? by no means: nor can a Child comply with so impious a Command. People who know but little of Life, may think such an Injunction impossible; but it is far from it. Many Incidents approaching very near to this are too frequently to be met with; and I have myself the Pleasure of being acquainted with a Gentleman, whose whole Deportment is such as renders him amiable in the Eyes of all who know him; yet this Gentleman, when a Student, was almost

almoſt totally abandon'd by his Father, for no other Reaſon than that of writing ſome Letters of Duty and Affection to his Mother. But to return to this firſt Fondneſs we diſcover in Children. The Cauſe of it is moſtly owing to their being too much confined to the Arms of one Perſon, or too much indulg'd by another: yet whatever it is owing to, the Effects are very diſagreeable, very inconvenient, and ſometimes very fatal.

When a Child is in the Arms of thoſe it is fond of, no body muſt meddle with it under pain of a Slap on the Face; and tho' this Behaviour is often put up with, and the Parents perſuade themſelves it is pretty, yet their Friends, when abſent, ſeldom fail to condemn them as the Cauſe of this Behaviour: but ſhould any one, regardleſs of the Slaps, take the Child into their Arms, the little Creature is immediately in a Rage, the whole Company is thrown into Diſorder, and nothing can quiet it, but returning to the Arms of the miſtaken Fondler. Here at one View is Error upon Error, Abſurdity upon Abſurdity; the Child by this miſtaken Fondneſs is made miſerable, and the Mother or Nurſe a Slave. Now to obviate this Inconvenience, my Advice is, that every

Child, after ſix Months old, be accuſtomed to various Faces; be put into the Arms of various People, young or old, fine or ordinary; ſo as to make every one they ſee in ſome Degree ſamiliar: Parents are to make their Children happy; keep them active, lively, and ſmiling; and this they cannot do, if they cheriſh or indulge in them a Diſlike of going to any other but themſelves. I know this Weakneſs in Mothers and Nurſes is attended with many Inconveniencies; it creates in Children an early Fear; often an unconquerable Shyneſs; it ſours their Temper, and ſtrengthens their natural Wilſulneſs; which laſt Effect is plain to every Eye; for to make the Child quiet they take it away from the Stranger; by which Treatment it ſoon ſees it can conquer it's Parents. But Parents encourage this partial Fondneſs in Children, for fear they ſhould not love them: this is a Miſtake; for even Infants ſoon know their Mother or Nurſe; and ſoon too do they both ſee and feel a Happineſs in them they do not find in others: like People who toil themſelves with Sights and Shows, they return to their own Home, and enjoy a Content ſuperior to every thing they felt abroad.

Children, while young, may be compared

to

to Machines; which are, or ſhould be, put in Motion, or ſtopped, at the Will of others: but here it muſt be confeſſed, that 'till they are able to conduct themſelves, they ſtand in need of good Conductors. For Example, Children have the Gift of Speech; but to how perverſe a Purpoſe, unleſs regulated? Their Wit, their Cunning, or their Knowledge, often ſerve but to miſlead them; ſerve but to ſtrengthen the natural Corruption of their Will. What is more common than for a Child to make no Anſwer when aſk'd a Queſtion? Or what more common than for another, or perhaps the ſame in a different Mood, to tire a whole Company with inceſſant Prating? Now nothing can regulate theſe but the Judgment of Parents; the whole Machine, that is, the Words and Actions of Children, are to be under their Guidance alone: to this End, they muſt ſet out with a Reſolution to conquer; and never quit the Field of Argument 'till they have. When a Queſtion is aſk'd a Child, no Matter by whom, whether by the Parents, a Viſitor, a Servant, or a Beggar, it muſt never be ſuffered to go unanſwered; all the Rules of Breeding and Civility demand it; and nothing can excuſe a Non-compliance: ſo, on the other hand, when a Child has a fluent, voluble Tongue, and is diſpoſed to talk out of Time and Place, and to ſay perhaps many improper or unbecoming things, it muſt certainly be reſtrained. But tho' I urge this, it is not merely becauſe Children ſhould ſpeak or be ſilent; do a thing, or let it alone, when bid; for however right or pleaſing all this is, it is far from being the only Motive; no, it is the Influence the oppoſite Behaviour will have on Children's future Lives that muſt be the Point in View. A Child accuſtomed not to anſwer when ſpoke to, will probably contract a moroſe, dogged, or, at leaſt, an uncivil Habit; another ſuffered to out-talk every body in the Houſe, will be in Danger of becoming an impertinent, if not an empty Prater; and if a third is never refuſed the thing it aſks for, it will be but ill prepared to bear Diſappointments. Parents I know are apt to think nothing of theſe Irregularities; but it is Inattention to the firſt Errors which lays the Foundation of Vices for Life. What is it diſtinguiſhes Mankind from all created Nature, but that ſuperior Power, Reaſon? Yet what is it makes this noble Faculty, this boaſted Power, ſo often uſeleſs, nay deſtructive, but the Corruption of the Will? Will is a diſtinct Power in the Soul; but as it is naturally corrupt, if Parents neglect an early Reſtraint of it in their Children, it is great

odds

odds that their Reaſon will never be able to conquer it: nay there are many who never attempt the ſubjecting it; who baniſh every thing which does not favour their Inclinations, however irregular; and even among thoſe who ſtruggle for Reaſon to gain the Aſcendant, the Combat is often unequal. Hence appears the Neceſſity of attending to the earlieſt Words and Actions of Children; of obſerving the Biaſs they take; and of moulding their tender Minds, that the firſt Dawn of Reaſon may be cheriſhed and improved in them.

Parents ſhould give their Children an early and an ardent Love of Truth; in order to this, it is not ſufficient that they give them Precepts, they muſt add Example too. There is no Vice more dangerous, none more odious, than a Habit of lying; and yet none more common. But what is ſtranger ſtill, Parents themſelves are often the Perſons who teach it them. It is very far from being my Deſign to charge Parents with an Intention of leading Children into this capital Error; but that they do it either thro' want of Thought, or want of Judgment, is evident. Firſt, they groſsly miſtake their Children's Capacity; and from a Notion that they know nothing, ſay a thouſand improper things in their hearing: then, when they find themſelves obſerved, are obliged to uſe many Shifts and Turns to get rid of their Curioſity and Importunity. The next Cauſe is, that Parents do not make Duty their Children's Rule of Conduct. A Child ſees ſomething in it's Father's Hand, and aſks, What is that? The Father anſwers, Nothing. But why make ſo abſurd a Reply? Will not the Child in Return act the ſame Part? *Jacky*, what have you got in your Hand? Nothing. A Child ſees it's Mother put Money, Fruit, or any thing elſe in her Pocket, and aſks for it; immediately ſhe replies ſhe has none: the Child taking the Conviction of it's Senſes, cries for what it has ſeen; and the Mother, after repeated Denials, has no other Way of pacifying it, than the giving what it cries for; and thus prove ſhe has been maintaining a Falſehood. I was once in Company with a Lady, who with a ſort of half Whiſper, ſaid her poor little Girl had Worms, and ſhe muſt give her ſome Phyſic; Miſs immediately cries out, What, you are talking of me now: No, no, Child, ſays Mamma: I know you are, replies Miſs; I heard you talk of Phyſic, but I'll not take any I am reſolved: No, my Dear, repeats Mamma, I'm not talking about you; I'm talking of

ſomebody

ſomebody that is in a Conſumption. Surely ſuch Behaviour reflects greatly on the Underſtanding or Conduct of Parents. Children ſhould be told their Duty without Diſguiſe; and it is certain they may often be won to it by ſoft and gentle Means; but Falſehoods, Prevarications, and puzzling the Truth, can never be the Way to lead them to it. Parents then, beſides animating their Children to a Love of Truth by daily Advice, muſt themſelves carefully avoid all obſcure ambiguous Language in their hearing; all Signs, Nods, and Winks, which can anſwer no other End than perplexing their Underſtandings, or raiſing in them a reſtleſs painful Curioſity. Sir *Roger L'Eſtrange* tells a Story that pleaſes me for it's thorough Honeſty. "A Man met an Acquaintance "in the Street: What, my Friend, ſays "he, have you got under your Coat? "Why, replies the other, what I have un- "der my Coat, I put there on purpoſe that "you might not know." Thus Parents without quibbling or evading, without Harſhneſs or Ill-nature, need only convince their Children that all things are not proper for them to have, nor all things fit for them to know.

There is a Propenſity in Nature which greatly

greatly deſerves the Attention of Parents, that is, Curioſity: and this when well regulated, may without Impropriety be called the Gate of Knowledge. How lifeleſs, ſpiritleſs, and inſipid, is a Child without it! How pleaſing, and how capable of daily Improvement with it! Parents then ought to cheriſh this Propenſity, as it's Uſe is boundleſs. But tho' Curioſity is in it's Nature a Means of Improvement, it is extremely apt to degenerate into Impertinence; and herein Parents cannot be too circumſpect. For as they are really two oppoſite Qualities, the one a Virtue, the other a Vice; great Care ſhould be taken to praiſe and reward the former, and diſcountenance and puniſh the latter. Parents, beſides the Inſtructions and Encouragement they give to Children in this Point, ſhould throw them in the way of exerciſing it, and attend to their Behaviour when unconſtrained. For Example; if I never lock up my Books, my Children will learn that they have the Liberty of reading them, unleſs expreſsly forbid; ſo likewiſe if I leave Letters or other Papers about without reſerve, they may with Freedom examine them; and if they did not, I ſhould think them incurious: but if they look over my Shoulder on purpoſe to ſee what I am writing, if they break a Seal to read the

Contents of a Letter, or pry into my Scrutore becauſe I have accidently left it open; it will be eaſy for me to determine that they are degenerating into Impertinence.

Uſeful Curioſity ſhews itſelf by innumerable Enquiries into the various Productions of Nature and Art; hence inſenſibly ariſes in Children, a Love of Knowledge, and a Love of Labour; hence too they learn to diſtinguiſh the Uſeleſs from the Uſeful; what they ſhould purſue from what they ſhould avoid. Impertinence ſhews itſelf by prying into the Affairs of others; employing their Thoughts and Time about what does not concern them, to the Detriment of all within their Reach. Hence ſprings that Neglect of real Knowledge we daily ſee in many; and that Croud of Trifles which waſte their Time, and tend only to hurt others, and do themſelves no good. For in proportion to the Time they ſpend in acting wrong, ſo much do they loſe of the Knowledge how to act right. But beſides it's being ſo detrimental and deſtructive to Society, Impertinence has ſomething in it ſo mean and hateful, that Parents cannot do too much to keep their Children free from it.

Parents ſhould encourage in their Children a lively

a lively chearful Diſpoſition; but quite pure, and unmixt with Vice, however diſtant. In order thereto, they ſhould never ſuffer them, for any conſideration, to utter an indecent Word, or commit any irregular Action which has the leaſt bad Tendency; but above all, Parents muſt be careful themſelves, never to ſay or do any thing in their Preſence that they ought not to hear or ſee. This Caution may ſeem unneceſſary, ſince all acknowledge how great the Force of Example is; yet if we view the general Conduct of Fathers particularly, we ſhall be obliged to own they ſtand greatly in need of it. For what more common than to hear Men ſwear and utter many indecent Expreſſions before their Children? And what more natural than their Imitation of them? which Poiſon, when once imbibed, cannot eaſily be expelled. As my Aim in writing is purely the Hopes of conveying Inſtruction, ſo I ſpeak my Thoughts with Freedom; and every one is at liberty to take or leave what they like, or what they find moſt neceſſary and applicable to themſelves: ſtill I cannot help urging in the ſtrongeſt Terms, a ſtrict Regard to Decency as an univerſal and indiſpenſable Obligation. For whoever conſiders how naturally propenſe we are to catch the Taint, and how very hard it is to wipe it off, will

ſurely

ſurely agree with me, that thoſe are much the happieſt who eſcape the Infection the longeſt.

But beſides the niceſt Care with regard to Words, Parents, as I have obſerved before, ſhould be greatly circumſpect in their Actions. Nothing groſs or indecent ſhould be done in their Sight; a Mother ſhould by no means appear too much undreſſed in the Preſence of her Son; nor a Father in that of his Daughter; for theſe and many other things, though in themſelves innocent, are not allowable; they give Boys a Boldneſs which borders on Impudence; and they are apt to wean Girls from ſome Degree of that Modeſty they ought ſo carefully to preſerve.

I cannot but recommend, what I doubt very few will comply with, that Boys and Girls, even when Infants, have not only ſeparate Beds, but, wherever it is practicable, always lie in ſeparate Rooms: nor ſhould they ever be expoſed naked to one another, or the leaſt wanton Curioſity be permitted: the Eyes and Ears convey Corruption to the Mind; and we cannot begin too ſoon to ſhut up every Avenue to Vice. I am ſenſible of the Singularity of this Doctrine; but I am firmly perſuaded many good Effects would flow

flow from the Practice of it. It is Matter of Astonishment to me, to see discreet and good People universally over-run with the false Notion, that Children do not observe; as if because they are Children, they neither hear, nor see, nor feel: whence they often lead them, or suffer them to be led very early into some kinds of Knowledge, which should be the last for them to learn. I grant indeed that such is the general reigning Corruption, that however carefully Parents avoid tainting their Children's Minds, they will still be exposed to the Contagion of others; but if they have the Happiness of seeing these things always discountenanced by their Parents, and are never suffered to copy the corrupt Manners of others, the odds are greatly in their Favour: but if after all they should still turn out vicious, Parents will have at least the consoling Reflection, that they did every thing on their Part to prevent it.

At the same time that Parents are industrious to make Children obedient to themselves, they must teach them to consider every one as an Individual of Society, and give them a deep Sense of the Necessity of good Behaviour to all, whatever be their Circumstances or Condition. In every Family there are particular Obligations which Children

Children muſt be taught to diſtinguiſh, and to reduce to Practice. Next to their Parents, Children owe to all ſenior Relations, Reſpect and Duty; to their Brothers and Siſters they owe not only a tender but an unalterable Affection; and all of more diſtant Kin have a Claim of Reſpect which cannot be refuſed them. Yet all this is but little, if compared with the univerſal Demand Mankind have on one another. We cannot without Injuſtice deny Virtue and Merit our Eſteem; old Age is venerable, and to refuſe the Honours due to it, is a Degree of Impiety; Obligations demand Gratitude; Misfortunes call for Friendſhip and Compaſſion; and even Vice and Folly demand our Pity and Concern, nay more, demand our Endeavours to remove them. But among the various Situations in Life, that which moſt requires the Care and Attention of Parents is, the teaching Children a due Regard to People in Poverty and Diſtreſs. It does not coſt much pains to give Children a proper and becoming Behaviour to their Betters and Equals; but to perſuade them to maintain a conſiderable Degree of Reſpect to Inferiors, or to thoſe in diſadvantageous Circumſtances, is an arduous Taſk; ſtill it may and ought to be done. Nothing ſo humanizes the Soul, nothing ſo ſtrongly proves the Man, as ſympathizing

pathizing with, and relieving the Diſtreſſes of our Fellow Creatures: 'tis then the Duty of Parents never to let their Children ſpeak or act with the leaſt Degree of Rudeneſs to the loweſt among Mankind; never to let them divert themſelves with their Rags or Miſfortunes; but on the contrary, they ſhould ſometimes furniſh them with Money or other Things, that the Relief they deſign to give the Needy may paſs through their Hands: and at the ſame time imprint this Truth on their Minds; that he who is thus reduced to aſk, is often far more deſerving than he who beſtows.

Another indiſpenſable Duty of Parents to their Children is, that they teach them never to dare to ſport with the natural Defects of others. As an ingenious Author ſays, "This Practice, though levelled at the Creature, reflects on the Creator; it mocks the "Architect, and burleſques the Creation." 'Tis ſtrange that Perſons of the beſt Underſtanding ſo ſeldom reflect on this Point. What can be more abſurd than to ridicule one Man for being too tall, and another for being too ſhort? one for having too little Noſe, another for having too much? The Degrees of Beauty and Deformity are infinite; and to be perfectly free from natural Defects

Defects and Blemishes is the Lot of very few: nor is it easy to fix the Standard of Beauty. We know by Anatomy, Sculpture and Painting, the general Rules of Symmetry and Proportion, and thus easily distinguish the gross Defects; but Beauty in the superlative Degree, in it's ultimate Perfection, is not so readily determined. But farther; what is beautiful in the Eye of one is not so in the Eye of another; what was accounted Beauty in some former Age or distant Country, is not esteemed such at present. Since then we see that 'tis our general Lot to be more or less defective, and that All are made by one Almighty Hand, how inhuman must it be to insult or despise another for what, if an Imperfection, it is not in his Power to avoid; and that perhaps while the Insulter himself is not free from other Blemishes, full as obvious and offensive to many.

But the Defects of the Body are not alone the Subject of our Ridicule; we sport too with those of the Mind. Providence for wise Reasons does not give to all alike; are we therefore to hold another in contempt for not knowing so much as ourselves? Are we to laugh at a Man for not knowing what he has had no opportunity to learn? no surely. A Neglect to improve, and the Abuse of

natural

natural Talents, are the only things that deſerve the Scourge; and even here it often happens, that he who exerciſes the Rod, deſerves it more than he who feels it. Such however is the Partiality, ſuch the falſe Practice of Mankind. Can Parents then be too careful to obviate theſe Errors in their Children? Can they take too much Pains to imprint on their Souls the Meanneſs and Folly of ſuch Miſtakes? ſurely they cannot.

Another Caution equally neceſſary is, that Parents utterly avoid all Diſtinction of Favourites among their Children. Sometimes the Father has his Darling, and the Mother her's; ſometimes they both doat on the ſame Child, and neglect the reſt. Again, it is frequently obſerved, that Mothers are extravagantly fond of the Boys, and either treat the Girls with a viſible Indifference, or groſsly neglect them, they know not why. It is true indeed that it may, and ſometimes does happen, that one Child in a Family is ſuperior in Parts to the reſt, or is particularly engaging, and may be ſaid to merit that partial Diſtinction Parents make; but to ſhew that Reaſon is not always their Guide, I appeal to general Obſervation, whether it does not often happen, that the greateſt Favourite is the greateſt Booby? Yet allowing that

that a Lady loves her Son beſt, becauſe he is really a ſmart Fellow; it is poſſible thoſe very Qualifications ſhe ſo much admires, and which attract her to him to the Prejudice of the other Children, are the things ſhe ought to be moſt diſpleaſed with; things, which if ſounded to the Bottom, would often prove Vice or Folly. But ſuppoſing that the favourite Son is really what he appears, more amiable than the Girls; may not this be owing to Accident or Deſign? May it not be the Effects of ſuperior Education, or a greater Knowledge of Men and Manners? moſt certainly. All young People are, what they are, in proportion to the Opportunities they have had of acquiring Knowledge, or the Uſe they have made of them; ſo ſhut them out from Opportunities, and they can never improve; becauſe they are deprived of the Means: thus it often happens in Families; the Boys are in the World, and gain a Knowledge of good Behaviour; the Girls are coop'd up, and Mamma wonders at their Ignorance! But what farther increaſes a Mother's Surprize is, that ſhe does not find her Girls improve in proportion to the Opinion ſhe entertains of her own Abilities: now allowing, what cannot be generally true, that ſhe has all that a Woman can be poſſeſſed of, if they are confined to the Company

of

of her chiefly, their Knowledge of the World will be very ſcanty. To be acquainted with the World, we muſt ſee it; to know Mankind, we muſt know their Faces, and mark their Deportment; and from ſeeing a Variety of Manners, muſt come the Power of poliſhing our own.

I ſay not this as an Intimation to Parents, that they ought to throw their Children wild and untaught into the World, far from it; on the contrary, I am convinced how much they want to be fortified againſt it's Snares; and how nicely they ought to be conducted: but with reference to the Matter in hand, I would fain make Parents ſenſible how irregular, nay how unjuſt their Partiality uſually is; particularly in baniſhing Children from their Affections for not knowing what they have had no Opportunity to learn. If then Parents really intend the Good of their Children, they muſt with the utmoſt Reſolution throw off all Partiality; if not, 'tis more than probable it may greatly injure, or even undo, a whole Family. The Darling is liable to be ruined thro' Indulgence; the reſt, thro' Neglect and Ignorance. Children, by this unequal Treatment, conceive a Hatred to one another, and often to the Parents themſelves, which perhaps laſts as long as their

their Lives. But beſides that this injurious Treatment debaſes their Minds, it is productive of many dreadful Evils; for hence proceed, not only inveterate Malice, but Confuſion, Law-ſuits and Poverty; and hence too proceed raſh, precipitate, and diſgraceful Marriages; with many other Calamities, which it would require a Volume to enumerate.

Parents ſhould by all Means conſider, that every Child is equally the Object of their Love and Care; and, by the Right of Nature, equally demands their Protection. The Laws indeed, for the Support of Families and Dignity, have, in ſome Caſes, made an Inequality in the Diſtribution of Fortune, which muſt be ſubmitted to: ſtill that does not take take off from the Obligation of Parents, nor juſtify a blind or whimſical Partiality. There is no Topic I would more enforce than this, yet none more difficult to preſcribe Rules for. It is certain, that rewarding the good, and puniſhing the bad, is both a Virtue, and a Duty; yet at the ſame time that I acknowledge how much the good Child deſerves, I cannot reſolve to abandon the bad: the Voice of Nature and Reaſon cry out loudly againſt it. I will for once ſuppoſe Parents entirely diveſted of Partiality, and that the Difference is really in the Children, and not in themſelves. Are they ſure there are no Faults in their Education? Are they conſcious that they have not expoſed them to be corrupted by others, tho' they have not done it themſelves? Are they convinced thoſe Acts of Diſobedience which their Children commit are the Effects of Malice prepenſe? or may they not be rather the Sallies of thoughtleſs, giddy Youth? All theſe things Parents muſt nicely weigh, before they carry their Reſentment againſt a Child to Extremes. Let Parents reflect, that a Boy whom they cannot now controul, and whom perhaps they are going to expoſe to the capricious Fury of the Seas, and deliver up to an Academy of Vice and Profaneneſs in order to reform him, may be much ſooner reclaimed by proper Pains and Remonſtrances, than by throwing him into the Jaws of Licentiouſneſs: for how often do we ſee a diſorderly Youth, touched, by a Parent's well-timed Clemency, with a Senſe of his Miſtakes; and when the native Fire of his Youth is abated, become truly wiſe and good; a Pattern of Virtue, and an Honour to the Age he lives in? Can Parents reflect on this, and not reſolve to try every Expedient before that of diſinheriting a Child, abandoning him to Miſery and Want, or giving him

up

up to that Nurfery of Immorality, the Sea? My ferious Advice in this Point is, that Parents be not hafty in driving things to Extremities. Let them with unwearied Patience try every gentle Means in their Power; and certainly by fuch Methods they will have the faireft Chance to fucceed. For if Children fee their Parents conftantly aiming at their general Good; if they find them hold the Scale of Juftice with an equal Hand; and experience their Affection and Tendernefs to be void of Partiality, even after repeated Provocations; if, I fay, they once become fo happy as to reflect on thefe Circumftances in their true Light, (as fooner or later undoubtedly they will) I cannot but hope the moft abandoned will be reclaimed, and the hardeft Heart foftened into Tendernefs, Refpect and Duty. But here lies our common Error; we grow impatient at a Child's Difobedience and Untowardnefs, and without ftriking at the Root of his Vices, without levelling at, and removing the Caufe, we dwell on the Effects; his Follies give us Pain, and we do not try fo much to cure him, as to eafe ourfelves; and therefore rafhly remove him from our Sight by fending him to Sea: in my Opinion, the laft Place in the Univerfe to make a bad Boy a good one. I heard a Story fome Years ago of a rich Citizen of *London*, which deferves to be remember'd with Honour. He had a Son, ſome Years paſt a Boy, addicted to every Extravagance, and who had almoſt worn out the Father's Patience and Indulgence by repeated Abuſes of them, and by continual Cravings. The Father at length conſulted a Friend, in order, if poſſible, to deviſe a Remedy: when he had poured out his Soul in Grief, and ſhewn that his Kindneſs had been almoſt boundleſs; the Friend replied, I have, Sir, a Remedy to propoſe, that I think deſerves the Experiment. The World calls you a hundred thouſand Pound Man; but tho' that may not be ſtrictly true, yet from my own Knowledge you are very rich: throw at once ten thouſand Pounds into your Son's Hands; that Sum cannot ruin you, and it is poſſible it may ſave him. The good old Man, with Heart full of Deſire to do whatever might convince his Son how much he wiſh'd his Happineſs, very readily came into the Propoſal: he ſent for him accordingly, and thus addreſſed him. "You "know, my Son, how dear I have always "held you; you know how much I have "deſired your Happineſs and Proſperity, by "the Pains I have taken to promote them; "but you do not conſider how much you "have abuſed my Indulgence: your boundleſs Love of expenſive Pleaſures has ſo far "blinded you, that you neither ſee my "Kindneſs,

" Kindneſs, nor your own Folly. But here, " take the utmoſt Proof of an afflicted Fa- " ther's Fondneſs; take this ten thouſand " Pound, and huſband it as you pleaſe. If " you uſe it well, it will not be the laſt Fa- " vour you may hope from my Tenderneſs: " but if you perſiſt in the Abuſe of my " Bounty, 'tis the ſole Proof of it you muſt " ever expect." The Son, ſtruck with A-mazement at ſo much Goodneſs, and touch-ed with a deep Senſe of his former Ingrati-tude, from that Hour became all he ought to be, and all his Father's Heart could wiſh. This genuine Relation may in great Mea-ſure ſerve as a Guide to Parents. It is true every one has not ten thouſand pound to give; but there are ten thouſand Parents who may, by exerting their ſeveral Capacities accord-ing to their Station, preſerve their Children from the Ruin they are threaten'd with: and thus turn them from Objects of Vexa-tion and Grief, into Inſtruments of Joy and Happineſs.

At the ſame time that the Authority of Parents is to be maintain'd above every other Conſideration, Children ſhould be taught to love them to a ſuperlative Degree. This Love in Children to their Parents, will naturally make them fly to them on every Emer-gence; and thus Obedience will become a

 Pleaſure:

Pleaſure: whereas if they are kept at a Diſtance by an auſtere Behaviour, or are treated in a cold, lifeleſs, inſipid Manner, they will be apt to doubt of their Parents Affection, and be induced to ſeek Comfort from others: and then no wonder if they fly to Aunts and Couſins, when even the Servants, from the Stable to the Kitchen, will have Power to engage their tender Hearts, and rob Parents of that ſuperior Affection they ought ſo jealouſly to engroſs to themſelves. Nothing requires more the Parents Attention, than the preſerving that golden Rule, a Medium in their whole Conduct to their Children; therefore while they are careful not to ſpoil them by too much Indulgence, they ſhould at the ſame time ſtudy to win their Hearts.

Parents ſhould be particularly careful not to diſpirit their Children; which undoubtedly will have a bad Influence on their whole future Conduct. There is a Degree of Courage to be maintained that is not only graceful, but abſolutely neceſſary to carry us thro' Life, which Parents therefore muſt not deſtroy. Some of my Readers may perhaps think, that while I am enforcing Obedience, I am myſelf undermining Courage; but let me aſk them whether a Soldier loſes his Courage by being under Diſcipline? by no Means. On the contrary, a Conſciouſneſs

of

of the Regularity of his Exercife, and of his Skill in the Ufe of Arms, always animates him in time of Danger: thus Children kept in Decorum, and under a Habit of doing right, will have far lefs Fear than thofe who are acting as their Paffions lead them: unlefs indeed they are quite abandoned.

Courage difcovers itfelf by a Command of Countenance, a dauntlefs Air and Behaviour, join'd with fuch a Degree of Refpect, Duty, and Self-knowledge, as fhews it to be free from Impudence and elf-conceit: it is a Firmnefs of Spirit that enables us to encounter every Danger when neceffary; and to demean ourfelves in a proper Manner under Trouble, Pain, and Difappointment. But here Parents muft be very careful to diftinguifh falfe Courage from true, imaginary Evils from real: let there be no trembling about Hobgoblins, or dark Holes; no Stories of Apparitions to raife Terror in the tender Minds of Children: Parents fhould never mention thefe things to them, nor, if poffible, fuffer any body elfe to do it; unlefs it be to laugh at, and expofe the Folly of them.

Nothing can be a greater Weaknefs than the creating or cherifhing thefe Fears in Children: nay how fenfelefs a thing is it to make them afraid of a dark Room, a Chimney-ſweeper, or whatever elſe can impreſs a groundleſs or an unjuſt Fear on them; for more or leſs they feel it their whole Lives, and by that Means are oftentimes made very miſerable. Children, as ſoon as they can diſtinguiſh, ſhould be taught to look, and move, and ſpeak with Courage; and, as they grow up, they ſhould be put frequently in the Way of exerciſing it, whereby many natural or acquired Weakneſſes will be conquered: ſuch as, a Fear of the Water, Riding, and innumerable other things, which Parents ſhould by every Means endeavour to prevent or remove: taking along with them this Caution, not to treat thoſe Children whoſe Spirits are naturally weak, with the ſame Freedom they do the more robuſt; nor ever raſhly expoſe them to real or imminent Dangers.

There is another Species of Fear, ſo far removed from Virtue and good Senſe, that Parents cannot do too much to baniſh it from their Children's Minds; I mean that which is the Offspring of Superſtition. What Pity is it that this heatheniſh Principle ſhould ever find a Place in a Chriſtian Breaſt: that People who are taught to rely on Providence alone, and who know that Happineſs is the infallible Reward of a virtuous Life, ſhould

never-

neverthelefs defert that Providence, and turn their Backs on the Comforts and Advantages annexed to it, to run in Search of Mifery. Fear is natural to the Soul of Man; but it is Reafon only that can fix it's juft Bounds. If I have a Child in the *Indies*, and dream he is dead, am I to be miferable till a Letter from him convinces me of my Folly? If I am about engaging in an Affair, of itfelf not only innocent but laudable, am I to put it off becaufe it is an unlucky Day? or becaufe a fenfelefs, withered Hag fhakes her Head over a Difh of Coffee-grounds, am I to fear that Deftruction is coming upon me? No, no; all thefe are Inftruments of Mifery, which nobody muft meddle with who claims being a rational Creature. Superftition and Happinefs are incompatible, as every Day's Experience proves. Parents then, effectually to avoid thefe Evils, muft teach their Children a juft Abhorrence of Superftition; they muft teach them too, that the only Fear confiftent with a Reliance on Providence, and confiftent with Virtue and good Senfe, is the Fear of doing wrong; that is, of being vicious.

The general Indulgence of Parents to their Children in gratifying their unreafonable Humours, is no fmall Obftacle to their Happinefs; but that is not all, it difturbs the Oeconomy of the Family, and every Day, perhaps every Hour, throws the Houſe into Diſorder; and thus turns that into Slavery and Vexation, which Providence deſigned as a Comfort and a Bleſſing. There is a well known pleaſant Story which ſeems not unſuitable here: A Lady gave her Daughter, about three Years old, to the Care of a Nurſery-maid, with poſitive Orders that Miſs ſhould never be ſuffered to cry; Whatever ſhe wants, ſays the Lady, be ſure let her have it; I will not have her cry. The Maid ſoon grew weary of her little Tyrant, and archly reſolved on a Method to convince Mamma of her Miſtake. Accordingly, one fine Evening, the Girl put Miſs into a Window; See, my Dear, ſays ſhe, ſee that pretty Moon; ſhall I give you that pretty Moon to play with? In a ſhort time ſhe work'd up the Child's Fancy ſo ſtrongly, that nothing would quiet her but the Moon. At length Mamma (upon hearing her Child cry) in great Rage entered the Room; How dare you, ſays ſhe, let my Child cry? Madam, replied the Maid, Miſs wants—Don't tell me ſhe wants; ſhe ſhall want nothing ſhe has a Mind to have. Madam, repeats the Maid, (as ſoon as ſhe could be heard) Miſs wants the Moon; and your Ladyſhip knows I can't give it her. The Lady was ſtruck dumb; Miſs ſtill cried

cried vehemently, and nothing could quiet her, but a ſevere Whipping from Mamma's own Hands.

There are but two Ways of ſubduing the Paſſions, *viz.* Force and Reaſon; but there are a thouſand Ways, and thoſe daily uſed, to inflame and ſtrengthen them. When a Child is accuſtomed to have all it aſks for, it ſoon becomes unreaſonable in it's Demands; and in the End expects Impoſſibilities. Now which is moſt eligible, to keep the Paſſions regulated, and prevent their making great Reſiſtance; or to ſuffer them to riſe to ſuch a Height, that all our After-care will not be ſufficient to check them? Parents then ſhould by all Means accuſtom themſelves to deny their Children ſome things, even ſuch as are innocent and reaſonable; not indeed to gratify a cruel Pleaſure, for that they ſhould abhor, but to familiarize them to Diſappointments, that they may brook them the better. Beſides, by this Method, every Grant from the Parents will be eſteemed a Favour, and received with Gratitude and Alacrity; whereas the granting every thing they aſk, deſtroys the very Life and Spirit of Compliance, and it ceaſes to be a Favour. A little Judgment and Experience will ſhew Parents how to vary theſe Grants and Denials, if they do but attend to them; and if

Children are under any Degree of Regulation, nothing is more eaſy.

Yet this by no means implies that Children are not ſometimes to have what they like; far from it: but the Regulation I have been ſpeaking of makes their own Lives comfortable and eaſy; and at the ſame time furniſhes Parents with frequent Opportunities of diſcovering their various Inclinations and Propenſities, and puts it in their Power to confer many little Favours on them, that otherwiſe they would not be ſenſible of. For Example; there are two Sorts of Meat at Table equally innocent; in that Caſe Parents may ſometimes, without Impropriety, give a Child it's Choice; this Indulgence, when allowed without Clamour or Rudeneſs in the Child, looks graceful, gives it Spirit, and a pleaſing Air: beſides, it affords Parents an Opportunity of diſcovering, if a Child has any natural Antipathy, any unconquerable Averſion, to certain Kinds of Food; or any thing in it's Conſtitution that has a Repugnancy to certain Meats, which, tho' it may like, always make it ſick; all which muſt be diſtinguiſhed from Humour and Daintineſs. But it will be impoſſible to arrive at this Knowledge, if my firſt Principle, Obedience, be neglected; for if a Child be ſuffered always

to

to have it's own Humour, what a fantaſtical Figure does it make at Table! I have ſeen a ſenſible well-bred Woman ſweat with Confuſion at the Behaviour of her Child, and able to eat no Dinner herſelf for attending to it's Humours. One Minute it would have one Meat, the next another; this was too fat, and that was cut in the wrong Place; by and by it would have ſomething elſe, and after all grow ſullen, and not eat half it's Dinner: but Obedience obviates this Confuſion, and makes all calm and regular; Children take whatever is given them, and eat it without Reluctance or Reſerve. Thus while they ſee they are not to be humoured, Parents will be at Leiſure to attend to them, and may eaſily obſerve what Food ſhould be generally given, and what avoided; and thus too Parents might have half a dozen Children at Dinner with Peace and Joy, while the oppoſite Behaviour makes one a Plague to the whole Table.

This Attention to Children will likewiſe diſcover what Companions they like, and often, why they like them; by which Means Parents will be able to judge if their Diſpoſitions are good or bad; vulgar or polite; tending to Vice or Virtue; all which will furniſh them with Hints for granting or denying certain Acquaintance.

The

The ſame Rule Parents ſhould obſerve, thro' the ſtated Actions of every Day; that is to ſay, at Riſing, Breakfaſt, Dreſſing, School, Dinner, Supper, and Bed-time; all are to be under ſuch Regulation, that no Oppoſition or Untowardneſs obſtruct the Order of their Deſigns: theſe I call the ſtated Actions, becauſe they are things that conſtantly and regularly return; and Parents ſhould by all Means habituate their Children to conſider them as Acts of Obedience and Duty that muſt be readily complied with. On this Head I earneſtly recommend, that Parents introduce Order and Method among their Children; by laying out their Time, and allotting different Hours in the Day for different Exerciſes; by which Means all will go ſmoothly on, and render their various Employments extremely eaſy. Here I cannot help obſerving, how ready People are to give opprobrious Names to what they diſlike or are Strangers to. A Man, becauſe he does not love Order, or does not underſtand it, endeavours to brand it with the Epithet of Formality; whereas in reality, nothing conſiderable or truly important can be carried on without it. How comes it, that, beſides the Artizans, and other Day-labouring Men, we ſo regularly ſee the Clerk in his Office, the Merchant upon Change, the Phyſician with his Patient, and the

the Judge on the Bench? but becaufe the Nature of our various Employments in Life require it, and becaufe Order is the Soul of Action. To be convinced of this, we need but view the firft Elements of Learning, where we find Letters and Figures always ranged in the fame exact Order. But we may go farther, by obferving, that Logicians teach us the Arrangement even of our Ideas; fo indifpenfably neceffary is Order and Method for the conducting us through Life. But while I urge the Ufefulnefs and Neceffity of Order, I would not be underftood to mean a rigorous and ftarch'd Precifenefs in all we do; on the contrary, I have already recommended, that Parents endeavour to give their Children an eafy and a graceful Air. I am very fenfible, that as in the Productions of Nature there is often difplayed a beautiful Irregularity, thus Order and ftated Times may be difpenfed with in fome of the greateft Actions the Soul of Man is capable of. And as in Wit the fudden Propriety of the Thought and Expreffion makes the Beauty of it; fo in the Exigencies of Life, an unpremeditated Act of Benevolence, doubly proves the Goodnefs of the Heart from which it flows: ftill as Judgment is fuperior to Wit, fo Order is fuperior to Irregularity.

I have already recommended that Parents

ftudy

ſtudy to win their Children's Hearts; and it is on this Principle, that Love be made to take the deepeſt Root in them. Love and Fear are two great Springs of human Actions; both which muſt be maintained, both ſhould by turns appear, but Love muſt be predominant. Would Parents make their Children good, let them daily inſtill into them that noble Motive, Love. Would they make their Children happy, let them prove they deſire it, by ſhewing their Love to them. Would they make Duty a Pleaſure, let them teach their Children to love it, by teaching them a chearful Obedience. In the whole Oeconomy of human Life nothing is ſo eſſential to Happineſs as this Principle; for as all Actions are, or ſhould be guided by ſome Principle or other, ſo thoſe which have a generous well-directed Love for their Motive, bid faireſt for attaining that genuine Happineſs, which all aſpire at, but ſo few find. Hence it is eaſy to ſee how neceſſary it is for Parents to cheriſh in their Children this great Principle of Virtue and Happineſs; 'tis this keeps their Duty awake, and turns that into Eaſe and Joy, which otherwiſe would be a Burthen and a Pain; 'tis this that ſtems the Torrent of irregular Actions, and checks the riſing Paſſions of our Children, by producing in them the oppoſite Effect, Fear; that is, a Fear of offend-

ing.

ing. Of all the important Steps neceſſary for forming the Minds of Children, and for conducting them thro' Life with Happineſs to themſelves and others, nothing is more truly ſo, than the animating their Actions with well-tempered Affection; it makes them open, generous, and noble; and it takes off that Narrowneſs of Mind and Heart, ſo diſadvantageous to themſelves, and ſo detrimental to Society: for in proportion to the Affection they prove for their Parents, ſo much will they increaſe in what in their future Lives they beſtow upon others. Children who love their Parents as they ought, will ſeldom fail to diffuſe in ſocial Life a general Affection around them; they will love their Huſbands, their Wives, their Children, and their Friends: nay they will love the whole human Race, by promoting, in ſome Degree or other, the Good of every one within their Reach. Such are the Benefits ariſing from a Love founded on juſt Principles; ſuch the Force of this Heaven-born Quality!

I have obſerved that Fear is another great Spring of human Actions; and were it only ſuch a Fear as Love creates, it would be truly laudable. But Experience too ſadly proves how much Mankind are actuated by a Fear of Pain, Diſgrace, and Poverty; a Fear

Fear which, in it's Nature, is servile, mean, and base; such as Parents should seriously endeavour to banish from their Children's Breasts. It may be reasonably asked, whether this Baseness, this unworthy Fear, so visible in the Majority of Men, be natural or acquired? When we view indeed our Children in some Individuals, and see them forsake every generous Offer of being happy, and cling immoveably to sordid Meanness, we may, in these Instances, conclude it is Nature; but when we consider them in the Lump, and take a general Survey of the Principles which guide their Actions, we must surely own it is in great Measure acquired: that is, the Dignity of Man is debased, in an almost constant Succession from Father to Son, by the false Estimation we make of Happiness; by forsaking Reason's purest Streams, to follow our corrupt Passions.

To evince this, let me here descend a little to Particulars. Parents desire their Children's Happiness, (I say nothing of those Monsters who neither feel nor act the Parent's Part) but how do they attempt to reach it? certainly in a Path the most remote from it. No sooner have Children a Place on the great Stage of the World, but their Will is irregularly cherished; before they know where they

they are, or know to what End they have a Being, their tender Minds are impreſſed with Principles as oppoſite to Happineſs as Light to Darkneſs. Who firſt awakens in them a Spirit of Reſentment and fierce Revenge, even before they can ſpeak? Thoſe who beat the Floor, the Chair, the Table, or whatever little Maſter has heedleſsly run againſt, and hurt himſelf with. Who firſt inflames their Vanity, by kindling in them Self-admiration, and a Paſſion for Dreſs? Thoſe who ſet out with teaching Miſs to admire herſelf only becauſe ſhe is fine. Who is it raiſes in them a Thirſt of Gain, an early, and a ſordid Love of Money? Thoſe who give a mean Reward the Preference to Virtue; or who, by direct or oblique Inſinuations, perſuade them that there is no Happineſs but in Riches. Who, in a Word, expoſes them to the Fury of every tempeſtuous Paſſion, by opening the Flood-gates of irregular Pleaſures? Thoſe who indulge them in every thing they aſk; who never contradict their Humour, however irregular; or who neglect to curb their Paſſions, and ſubject them to Reaſon. From this View of the too general Conduct of Parents, we may with Reaſon infer that Fear, the Spring which actuates the Majority of Mankind, is more acquired than natural: for where inordinate Deſires are cheriſhed, a

Fear

Fear of not obtaining what we wiſh, or of loſing what we poſſeſs, produces many Actions unworthy ourſelves: Actions not only unjuſtifiable, but which conſtitute certain Miſery under the Maſk of Happineſs.

To obviate then theſe Evils, to prevent the Acquiſition of a baſe, mean, unmanly Fear, and to lead Children into the Path to Happineſs, let Parents, as I have before recommended, make Love take the deepeſt Root in them; but as Fear will naturally by turns prevail, let them with the warmeſt Zeal labour to make it a Fear dictated by Love, and guided by Reaſon.

But how ſhall this be effected unleſs Parents act on right Principles? The grand Obligations of Parents to their Children conſiſt in teaching them a Knowledge of themſelves, a Love of Duty, and a Love of Virtue. Whence it is evident, that the Attention of Parents to conduct their Children as they ought, is indiſpenſably neceſſary, even to the third Stage of Life; but it is doubly ſo at the Beginning. It is a judicious Obſervation, that he who ſets out wrong is half undone; and tho' this holds good in the general Concerns of Life, yet it is no where more applicable than in the falſe Steps taken in the initiating our Children. For if Principles

ciples oppoſite to Self-knowledge, Duty and Virtue, are either created, inculcated, or cheriſhed, where is the Wonder that Children prove the reverſe of what was expected? or that while they ſeem to aim at Happineſs they find themſelves wretched?

Thoſe who build with Judgment, are always careful to lay a ſolid Foundation. I will now hope that Parents are ſenſible that the general Practice in the Management of Children is erroneous; and the general Neglect of them unjuſtifiable. I will hope too, that I have here ſhewn, however imperfectly, that Virtue alone is the Baſis on which their Happineſs is to be raiſed. An early Obedience, a Love of Truth, a ſpotleſs Innocence, and a becoming Courage, tempered with Self-knowledge, make the Groundwork of my Deſign; of that genuine Manners I mean to recommend. The Edifice however is ſtill to be rear'd; that is, other Virtues both general and particular are to be taught, and brought into Habit: the whole Frame of Mind and Heart muſt appear regular, orderly, and beautiful; not accidentally ſo, but reſulting from Reflection; they muſt be eager to embrace Virtue, and watchful to ſhun Vice: in a Word, be always diſpos'd to do what is right, and never, with Deſign, do what is wrong. Here perhaps I ſhould

I ſhould throw aſide my Pen: if I have been ſo happy as to convince Parents of their firſt Miſtakes in this important Work; thoſe once rectify'd, the reſt may be ſupply'd by abler Guides: for I neither have, nor pretend to have, the Power requiſite to diſplay or enforce thoſe Virtues, the Knowledge and Obſervance of which make up the Meaſure of our Duty.

But to awaken Parents ſtill farther, I muſt obſerve, that teaching their Children all the moral Duties is not only their Province, but more or leſs their Obligation. A learned and ingenious *French* Author ſays, that Parents are the beſt Inſtructors, if they themſelves are well inſtructed. For, ſays he, "A Father who has but two or three accuſtom'd "to reſpect him, finds no Difficulty in keeping them to their Duty. He has them "conſtantly at home with him; he can take "the Hours when they are moſt docible; "he knows their Capacity, their Genius, "and their Inclinations. He can inſtruct "them at leiſure, and allow the neceſſary "Time for it." And a little farther he adds; "What is here ſaid of Fathers muſt in Proportion be underſtood of Mothers, prin-"cipally in regard of their Daughters." Here then I recommend to Parents that they do not content themſelves with laying the

Foundation,

Foundation, but labour on till the Superſtructure is raiſed and the Deſign compleated. For as Men who juſtly aim at Reputation, and who deſire to fill with Honour ſome Poſt or Profeſſion, ſpare no Pains to qualify themſelves for it; ſo thoſe, who would fulfil the Deſign of Providence in making them Parents, muſt take care that they do not lead Children out upon the Stage of the World, and leave them to act their Part alone, till they have taught them thoſe Duties that will beſt ſecure Happineſs both to themſelves and others.

It will ſtill perhaps be expected that I ſhould treat of the farther Means to effect this great End; but my Readers muſt remember, that beſides my being unequal to the Taſk, beſides my being confined to the Compaſs of a ſmall Volume, theſe important Matters have already been handled by many abler Pens, to which I refer them. However, to anſwer in ſome meaſure a reaſonable Expectation, and farther to prove the Sincerity of my Intentions, I will here touch on thoſe Virtues which are univerſally allowed to be eſſentially neceſſary; and which all, who would be eſteemed wiſe and good, muſt both know and practiſe.

We are now to ſuppoſe, that Children are con-

considerably advanced; not only that their first Lessons were Obedience, but that their Minds have been tempered with Duty, and with such a Knowledge of Right and Wrong, as strongly to incline them to adhere to the one and avoid the other: we will suppose too, that their Reason, unblinded by Passion, has gained so much Strength as to be able to exert itself to advantage: that is, that those Perceptions and Distinctions, with many other things which natural Logic is capable of teaching, have so far improved their Understanding, and disposed their Will, that they are fitted to receive more important Lessons, and practise them when taught.

Prudence then comes first under Consideration: it implies such an orderly Conduct of our Words and Actions, as keeps us free from those Irregularities which hurt ourselves and offend others. Prudence is a Virtue attended with innumerable good Effects, but particularly as it frequently shuts the Door not only against Misfortunes, but against Injustice. It is not to be doubted but that the Prudent are sometimes unfortunate. A thousand Evils surround us, a thousand Darts threaten our Destruction, which cannot be obviated because they cannot be foreseen: still it is certain that Prudence keeps off many Calamities which would otherwise befall us. But

But befides the Advantages arifing from Prudence to ourfelves, it makes us pleafing and ufeful to others. Men naturally love to converfe with the Difcreet; from them they learn the Art of fhunning thofe Rocks which fo many others have fplit on? from them they difcover a fafer Path to tread in; and from them they often labour to model their own Actions. Farther, the Prudent are not only pleafing, but valuable to Society. A prudent Man is efteemed by all who have any Dealing with him. Mankind have naturally an Attachment to their Property; therefore are they with great Reafon inclined to truft it in the Hands of the Difcreet, rather than the Indifcreet. Hence appears the Neceffity of teaching Children the Nature and Advantages of Prudence; but as it is one of the graver Virtues, it feldom appears in young People, unlefs it be thofe who are fo happy as to have prudent Parents, that labour to implant an early Habit of it in them.

There is a natural Confcioufnefs in the Mind of Man of his own Significance; and where he takes Prudence for his Guide, fome real Advantage may always be made of it. No Man is fo high as not to require the Aid of thofe beneath him; no one fo low but he may be uſeful to his Betters. Parents therefore inſtead of inculcating on their Children a falſe Pride, or raiſing in them a vain-glorious Flame, ſhould give them a due Senſe of others Significance and their own; this, accompanied with Prudence, will ſhew them the true light they ſtand in; ſhew them their juſt Diſtance from thoſe above them, their Nearneſs to thoſe beneath them. From this View will ariſe not only that genuine Self-knowledge ſo eſſentially neceſſary for their Conduct in Life, but that becoming Pride, which at the ſame time that it proves to them the Obligation of acting in ſome certain Sphere, animates them with Reſolution to behave in it as they ought.

Prudence is a Check to Extravagance, Vice, and Folly; nay, it is often the Guide of virtuous Actions; for even Benevolence, Generoſity, and Charity, Actions greatly noble in themſelves, unleſs well directed, timed and placed, will often be the Cauſe of others Ruin and our own. Prudence therefore, of all Virtues, may juſtly be call'd the Balance that keeps us from Extremes.

I have elſewhere obſerved how dangerous it is for Parents to rate their Children too high; nor is it leſs ſo to ſink them too low: there is a certain Spirit to be maintained, without

without which our Children will degenerate into Meanneſs; there is a Degree of Dignity they muſt ſupport, without which they will become not merely uſeleſs, but burthenſome: Parents therefore muſt carefully attend to this, leſt in avoiding one Evil they fall into another: And no Means ſo likely to gain the Medium, as Self-knowledge under the Direction of Prudence. By this they are check'd in the Pride of towering too high; and by this they are lifted from that Meanneſs which Sloth, Ignorance, or falſe Humility is apt to plunge them into.

Here I might expatiate on the Cruelty of ſome Parents, who uſe every body well but their own Children; who act not only the Sovereign, but the Brute, the Tyrant, and the Monſter over thoſe whom Nature calls on them to cheriſh, comfort, and love: and often, under the Pretext of making their Children humble, harraſs them into Miſery, and fix a Hatred to themſelves. However, I will not purſue a Reflection ſo ſhocking to Nature; but rather hope that once to know it will be a ſufficient Motive for it's Baniſhment.

But of all the Advantages attending Prudence, there is none equal to the Bar it puts againſt the Raſhneſs of young People in plunging themselves into the Mistake of an inconsiderate Marriage: and indeed were it the sure Means of preventing this Evil alone, it would both demand and deserve all the Attention of Parents to lead their Children into the Knowledge and Practice of it. How few are those whose Passions never rise above the Mark of Reason; how few whose Duty never nods; what Grief does such a mistaken Step bring on the Parents; what Care, what Sorrow, what Misery on the Children! Here, in the strongest Light, we may view the necessity of Prudence. Suppose a Father (one of some Figure and Circumstances) educates his Son suitable to his Condition in Life; and then engages him in Business, either as a Clerk, an Apprentice, or whatever Station occurs: at this Age, and in this Situation, he is exposed to a thousand Dangers; but particularly to that of a rash and an unequal Marriage. The young Fellow, if unguarded by Prudence, is open to all the Arts, the Smiles, the Hypocrisy of some one at least of the opposite Sex, who thinks it her Business to make her Fortune; while he, a Stranger to his own Heart, and ignorant of the Consequences of such a Step, involves himself in Sorrow, if not in Destruction. The transient pleasing Dream once past, he looks around him with Amazement! but 'tis now too late! the Chain is link'd, the

the Fetters are tied, and nothing but Death can break them! After various Contrivances to conceal the raſh Deed, at length it reaches the Parents Ears. What a Scene of Affliction is here! Not the lively Picture of a Poet's Fancy; not the fabled Repreſentation of romantic Diſtreſs; but real Life overwhelmed with boundleſs Grief. A generous Father who has ſpared no Coſt to promote his Son's Felicity; a tender Mother, who with endleſs Anxiety has ſought the faireſt Proſpect for her favourite Boy; view them alternately ſtruggling with Love, and Rage, and Fear, and Reſentment! What muſt they feel to ſee their Expectations fruſtrated, their utmoſt Wiſhes vaniſhed, their darling Child undone! We ſay, it is dangerous to rouze a ſleeping Lion; nor is it leſs ſo, to kindle the Reſentment of Parents: for to be greatly exaſperated is to fall into a Frenzy, which we cannot ſtop at Will. Thus it often happens with thoſe whoſe Children precipitate themſelves into Miſery; their Rage becomes a continual Reſentment, or an unconquerable Hatred. And alas! how dreadful are the Effects! What more common than for a Child to be baniſhed from his Parents for a Step like this. I know not what Effect a Deſcription may have on thoſe who hear or read it, but, for my own Part, I think a Child, who thro' ſuch groſs Folly and Disobedience has shut himself out from the Doors, the Hearts, the Affection of his Parents, is in the most calamitous Situation upon Earth.

But let us change the Scene. Let us suppose the Parents Grief subsided, or that Love and Pity have got the better of Resentment. How fares it with the disproportioned Couple? Does a Reconciliation with the Parents secure Happiness to them? Alas, no; they know but little of Life who conclude so. There is always Danger in Disparity, especially where Vanity or Ambition predominates. The Woman who is suddenly lifted up from a very low Conditon, commonly makes but an aukward Figure; and what is worse, she is apt, in affecting to be like her Betters, to misuse the Dominion he is invested with; and, instead of demeaning herself like a good Wife, she becomes a Vixen, a Shrew or a Tyrant. Yet granting that none of these Evils happen, granting that a Woman has really Merit, and that she labours to improve her natural Talents, in order to suit them to her new Condition, there are still other Evils to fear. Reflection on past Folly naturally draws Resentment on the Object of it: and tho' when two Parties once become Man and Wife, they are obliged to maintain Fidelity, Tenderness and Love to one

one another; yet Experience unhappily ſhews us that this Obligation is often violated. He who is extravagantly fond without Regard to Merit, will often be unreaſonable without Provocation. Thus, when a Man, in his cooler Thoughts, compares what he is, with what he might have been; reflects on what he has loſt in graſping imaginary Happineſs, or views himſelf, thro' a Diſparity of Years, chained to faded Beauty, to declining Life, while himſelf is in his Bloom; not all the natural or acquired Merit of his Wife, not all the Tenderneſs that can flow from the ſincereſt Love will be able to balance his Diſappointment: he frets, and ſwears, and raves, he breaks out into Extravagancies, which frequently end in the Deſtruction of them both; Deſtruction to their Peace, and Deſtruction to their Fortune.

Nor is this Portrait of private Woe the only one that can be repreſented. A thouſand others might be produced, all eſſentially the ſame, all fraught with Miſery, and only different in Circumſtances or Degree. To ſee the Heir of a great Eſtate forſake his Father's Manſion, and marry the Dairy-maid; to ſee a young Lady trained up in all the Pomp and Pride of Wealth, throw herſelf into the Arms of a Man whoſe only Merit perhaps is a deceitful Tongue, or a borrowed lac'd Coat; or to ſee another ſteal to the *Fleet* and marry her Father's Footman; are things ſo prepoſterous in their Nature, that one cannot reflect on them without ſhuddering.

Certain it is, that great Merit ſometimes lies cover'd in Obſcurity; and it is but juſtice to render it conſpicuous, by raiſing the Poſſeſſors of it to an exalted Station. And farther, a young Man, who has with great Pains and Expence qualified himſelf to act in a genteel Profeſſion, tho' he ſhould not have a Shilling in the World, has a Title to expect a Fortune with a Wife; nor does he know his own Significance if he neglects it: for allowing that the Woman he marries has Perſonal Merit, if they are balanced by the ſame good Qualities on his Side, the Proſpect he has from his Trade or Profeſſion is often more than an Equivalent for the Advantages he reaps by her Fortune. Nor is it theſe things I mean to inveigh againſt; what I condemn is in general far otherwiſe: we ſee a wild Flame ſeize our Youth, Inclination cheriſhes it, and they fall a Sacrifice to their Imprudence. How happy then are they whom Prudence guides; how conſoling the Reflection, that by ſteering with this Pilot they eſcape the common Wreck.

Among

Among the moral Virtues neceſſary to be inculcated, among the Obligations of Parents to their Children, nothing ſo much demands their Diligence, Attention and Regard, as the teaching them a Knowledge and a Love of Juſtice. How noble is this Virtue! how vaſt in it's Extent! and, alas! how little is it practiſed! Some Virtues ſtand as it were alone, and may be ſeparated from every other; but this, when underſtood and practiſed in it's utmoſt Latitude, ſeems to unite almoſt every Virtue to itſelf. Juſtice teaches us all the Obligations we are bound to maintain in Society; now it is certain that theſe are many more than are generally underſtood. Men ſoon learn thoſe things which the Laws take Cognizance of; and therefore, unleſs quite wretched or abandoned, avoid them; but what are theſe, if compared to many others which Nature, Reaſon and Reflection make us conſcious of? What are theſe to the many Injuſtices which ſpring from Pride, Sloth, Luſt, Avarice, Slander and Revenge? Surely nothing. But without enquiring what Actions evade the Law, or triumph over it, I will endeavour to give my Readers a true Idea of Juſtice; and point out to them the proper Steps for leading Children into the Exerciſe of it.

Here I cannot avoid returning back to the

Infancy of Children, nor help reminding Parents of the Neceſſity of an early Care. Virtuous Principles are the beſt Foundation of virtuous Habits; and ſhould the Seeds of Paſſion be too deeply rooted in our Nature to be extirpated, Reaſon, we know, has Power to keep them in Subjection. This premiſed, I recommend to Parents the utmoſt Aſſiduity in ſhutting out the very Source of Injuſtice; that is, they muſt counteract thoſe Paſſions which tend to produce it; not only by inculcating the oppoſite Virtues, but by frequent Reflections on the Danger of cheriſhing irregular Deſires.

Juſtice is to be conſidered as general and particular; and tho' Mankind are apt to content themſelves with a general Juſtice, yet it can never claim the Merit of an exalted Virtue, unleſs we both know and practiſe it in particular. To attain this Knowledge and Love of Juſtice, Children are to be taught, even before they can ſpeak, to part with any thing they are in Poſſeſſion of, and this readily, and without Clamour: the Effect of which will be, that when a little more advanced, and they can diſtinguiſh their own things from others, they will not eagerly deſire the Property of a Brother, a Siſter, or Play-fellow. The next Step is, that Parents avoid with the utmoſt Caution every the leaſt Deceit,

Deceit, eſpecially about Money, and every thing which diſcovers to their Children a Fondneſs for it. There is nothing more ſurpriſing to me, than the univerſal Diſregard Parents have to the Preſence of their Children; a thouſand things in Life are neceſſary to be ſaid and done which they, particularly while young, ſhould not be Witneſſes to; and yet are Parents every Day and Hour ſo impolitic and ſo imprudent, as not only to diſcloſe their inmoſt Thoughts, but to tranſact the moſt improper, nay perhaps the moſt unjuſtifiable things before their Faces. As Children ſeldom have Judgment to diſtinguiſh, they can only catch Appearances. Now ſuppoſe a Man in a juſt Cauſe has play-ed the Politician, and by the Force of Stratagem recovered his Right; can it be a proper Subject for Children to be in the hearing of? But ſhould this Man have gone farther, and ſhould he boaſt a Conqueſt unjuſtly gain'd, perhaps to the Ruin of another; what Effect muſt this have on the tender Minds of Children? Children in general act by Imitation; therefore, as far as can be, they ſhould ſee nothing but what they may imitate. But farther, Children naturally think thoſe things right which they ſee done by their Parents; therefore they ſhould ſee no Action in them but what is really ſo. Farther ſtill, Children, even under a virtuous

Education, are ſurrounded with a thouſand Incitements to Ill; their Eyes and Ears are continually open, and continually receive corrupt Impreſſions, which dart to the Mind and Heart of the moſt innocent: where then can they fly for an Antidote to this Poiſon? To whom ſhall they have recourſe; or by whom ſhall they be furniſhed with Weapons for their Defence? By thoſe to whom they are bound by every Tye; Parents alone muſt ſtop the Torrent of every Evil to their Children, not only by virtuous Precepts, but by virtuous Example. For as it is a certain Truth, that the Influence of Parents is more than a Balance for a thouſand others, the Neceſſity of their oppoſing Vice with Virtue, is every way apparent: nor is it any where more ſo than in the noble Cauſe of Juſtice.

This Rule eſtabliſhed, I muſt again repeat to Parents the avoiding before their Children every Appearance of Deceit, and every Fondneſs for Money. If Children are taught to deceive, they will be induced to practiſe it for the Sake of Gain; and if a Love of Gain be cheriſhed in them, they will often uſe Deceit to acquire it. How apt are Parents to wiſh for Money in their Children's hearing; and this, not merely the Indigent, thoſe who want many of the Comforts,

Comforts, the Neceſſaries of Life, but thoſe who have already perhaps more than they make a good Uſe of. *Tom*, ſays a vain Father to his Son, had I ten thouſand Pound, you ſhould be the ſmarteſt Fellow in the Kingdom, ne'er a Lord in the Land ſhould out do you. Thus too, a doating Mother addreſſes her Daughter, What Pity it is my dear *Nancy* ſhould not keep her Coach; ſo ſweet a Girl! Oh! that I was but rich, you ſhould marry nothing leſs than a Lord. What muſt be the Effect of this Language? Muſt it not inflame the Heart, or fly to the Head and make it giddy? moſt certainly. Nor does it ſtop here; for when this irregular Love of Money is once deeply rooted, irregular Steps will often be taken to make it thrive.

But to purſue the Idea of Juſtice, let me not confine myſelf to the Paſſions, but ſpeak likewiſe to the Underſtanding. I will hope that Parents have ſhewn Children in Infancy the general Juſtice I have ſpoken of; the obvious Rules of Right and Wrong; and check'd in them every Shadow of Injuſtice: that is, that they have taught them never to meddle with Money, be it more or leſs, or with whatever elſe belongs to another; nor even to deſire it; nor to be fond of dwelling on it, counting it, or chinking it; (for Money has a ſtrange Effect on both

Eyes

Eyes and Ears:) never to put their Hands into another's Pockets; much leſs to unlock a Scrutore: never to evade the Payment or Acknowledgment of a ſingle Farthing; nor obtain unjuſtly even a Top, a Marble, or whatever can be called the Property of another. Farther, that as they advance, Parents inform them that there is a conſtant Intercourſe between Man and Man: that Providence has created ſome to labour one way, ſome another; that the various Wants of Life are to be ſupplied by the Care, the Induſtry, and the Sagacity of each in their ſeveral Stations; that the Poor are deſtined to labour for the Rich, and the Rich to employ and reward the Poor: that ſome in fine are born to govern, others to be governed. That this Intercourſe is called Society; and that Juſtice alone is the Band that connects and ties it; conſequently, that he is the moſt valuable Member of Society, who deſpiſing ſelfiſh or ſiniſter Views, who ſhunning the Tricks, the Frauds, the Villainies of others, reſolves to make Juſtice his Rule of Action. That to this End, beſides a general Knowledge of Property, and an Acquaintance with thoſe Laws which are made to defend it; beſides the adjuſting Profits in Trade, ſtating Accounts fairly, and paying Debts regularly; there are ſtill many things to be conſidered, ſome of which I will here endeavour

endeavour to reaſon upon, as they viſibly produce ſome certain kind of Injuſtice in their Effects, tho' their Cauſe is often hid from common Eyes, or they are diſguiſed by falſe or palliative Names.

The firſt Spring of Injuſtice is Pride: Children, as I have juſt obſerved, have their Minds impreſſed with a Love of Riches; whence naturally follows an undue Degree of Self-eſteem, accompany'd with a Love of Power, Show, and Dignity: now to effect theſe, a thouſand Stratagems are uſed; every Obſtacle which ſtands in the Way to Wealth or Preferment muſt be overturned; every Difficulty muſt be removed. Hence it is eaſy to ſee that unjuſt Means will often be uſed to gain the deſired End; and hence it is plain that thoſe who aſcend by indirect and violent Meaſures, cruſh down many others as they paſs. Parents therefore to obviate this, muſt teach their Children that nothing can be lawful which injures others; that they may indeed arrive at Honours and acquire Riches; but that unleſs they are obtained without Guilt, and poſſeſſed without Pride, they cannot be juſt: for even allowing that no undue Means are uſed to ſupport our Pride, there is Injuſtice riveted to the Vice itſelf; for the Proud, to raiſe themſelves,

themſelves, always attempt to depreſs or debaſe others.

Another Cauſe of Injuſtice is Sloth. Providence has created us to labour; the Head, the Hands, the Feet, all are given to anſwer in ſome Degree the ſame End; that is, the Preſervation of ourſelves, and the Benefit of others. None are born to be idle, none who are ſo can with any Truth be ſaid to fill up Life as they ought. Thoſe who have Talents are bound to cultivate them as far as they have Opportunity, that they may counſel, inſtruct, or aſſiſt others: thoſe who have Fortune cannot without Injuſtice neglect the Care, the Improvement, and the Diſtribution of it: thoſe who have no Fortune, but enjoy Health and Limbs, are Robbers of Society if they refuſe to work: and indeed among the various Objects of Sloth, thoſe who exerciſe neither Head, nor Hands, nor Feet, but lounge and fawn and beg for a Subſiſtence, no Matter whether in Rags or Finery, are of all others the moſt mean, at the ſame time that they are groſsly unjuſt The Virtues oppoſite to this are, Induſtry, Application, and Oeconomy; which Parents muſt raiſe in their Children betimes, and cheriſh with Zeal and Pains.

A third

A third Source of Injuftice is Luft. What I have before faid of an univerfal Regard to Decency both in Words and Actions muft not be confined to the State of Childhood, but be enforced by Parents on their Children as Rules that are never to be departed from; fince what is in it's Nature wrong, nothing can make right: for if Innocence be a Virtue, which even the abandoned will hardly difpute, every Deviation from it muft be more or lefs a Vice. As this then is a fetled Point, enlarging on it here is needlefs; my only Aim on this Head being to make fome Reflections on the Vice when manifeftly attended with Injuftice.

It has been the Cuftom of every wife Nation both in their Writings and Converfation, to inculcate and enforce the fineft Morals, the moft important Truths under an Allegory or Fable; and where the Simile is natural and the Expreffion emphatic, nothing is more powerful. Suppofe then a Father fhould lead his Son, as he approaches to Manhood, into a Garden, and thus addrefs him. "View here, my dear Child, "the Beauties of the Creation; fee how "abundantly the Earth is furnifhed with all "that can contribute both to our Ufe and "Delight. But befides the unmeafurable "Bounty of Providence, behold the Gar-

"dener's

" dener's inceſſant Toil; what pains he " takes to improve the Soil; with what " early Care does he water each tender " Plant; how watchful to ſecure them " againſt deſtroying Vermin, and how " anxious to defend his Flowers from Blaſts! " Now tho' Providence has given to MAN " a Power over all the Works of the Crea- " tion, 'twas never meant he ſhould abuſe " them. What then would you think of " him who ſhould pluck the choiceſt " Flowers here, purely for the ſake of de- " ſtroying them? But ſhould he go farther, " and exerciſe a wanton Pleaſure not only " in ſtripping them of their Beauty, but in " rendering them offenſive and odious to " all who ſee them? What, my Son, I ſay, " would you think of ſuch a Man? But " Oh! my dear Boy, ſhould this affect you, " ſhould this raiſe in you a Degree of Con- " tempt; with how much Indignation muſt " you behold the Wretch, who, with a " Complication of Crimes has deflowered " the faireſt Part of the whole Creation: " not an inanimate Roſe, or Pink, or Lilly; " but robb'd a ſpotleſs Virgin of her Inno- " cence! Tremble, my dear, dear Child, " tremble at the very Thought of ſo much " Baſeneſs! View with impartial Eyes the " guilty Deed! On one ſide the Deceit, the " Oaths, the Perjuries, and a thouſand cri-

" minal

" minal Inventions to gain the desired End; " on the other, the dreadful Change from " Innocence to Guilt; from Honour to In- " famy; from the Esteem of all, to the " Contempt of all; and what is stranger " still, forsaken and despised by the very " Seducer himself! Yet Oh! my Son, let " not these Reflections be made in vain; " but draw Profit from others Crimes: exa- " mine them in their true Light; be not " misled by those who palliate the blackest " Actions with the specious Names of Wit, " and Love, and Gallantry; but live in a " Resolution never to share in their Guilt; " never to injure another in the least Degree; " but above all resolve to suffer a thousand " Evils, to sacrifice every Passion, rather " than even stain, much less destroy, the " Flower of Innocence."

These are Sentiments our Sons must be warmed with; these are Ideas of Justice they must not be Strangers to, if we wish to make them good Men, or desire to fulfil our Obligations as Parents. Innocence, wherever it resides, is an inestimable Treasure; two things therefore Parents have to do herein, viz. to teach their Children neither to destroy another's Innocence; nor suffer others to sully theirs. The first has just been spoken of: I will only add, that

the

the ſame Regard muſt be paid to all Degrees, whether high or low: it is the Vice we are to keep in view, not the Quality of the Perſon. 'Tis no Extenuation of the Crime, that a Gentleman's Son ſeduced his Maſter's Cook; or that a young Nobleman has ruined only a Tenant's Daughter, or his Mother's Chamber-maid; no, no, there are no Diſtinctions in Virtue's Cauſe: that loſt, there are always ſome to weep; the pooreſt have their Parents, their Relations, or their Friends, to lament their ſad Miſhap; and thoſe who are robbed of what cannot be reſtored, have always their own Loſs to deplore.

The next Care of Parents on this Head is, that they labour to preſerve their Children's Innocence from being tainted by others. One would imagine when Parents had taught their Children every Virtue, and enforced them by their own Example, their Duty would be compleat; but far from it; they have ſtill the Obligation of repreſenting to them the Snares, the Artifices, the Villainies of deſigning People. In my laſt View I have ſhewn that our Sons, either hurried by Paſſion, led by falſe Notions of Gallantry, or Strangers to Right and Wrong, are often the Inſtruments, or liable at leaſt to be the Inſtruments, of others Deſtruction: in this

this I muſt touch on the Neceſſity Children are under of being defended from receiving Injuries. And here I muſt obſerve, that both Sexes are equally in Danger. The Girls indeed have by Nature and Education more Innocence, as well as more Tenderneſs; the Boys, tho' more robuſt, have more Temptations. Men are the Inſtruments, and dreadful ones too, which chiefly deſtroy our Daughters; but bad Women on one hand, and corrupt Men on the other, combine to deſtroy our Sons. Let Parents then point out to them the Dangers they are expoſed to, and furniſh them with every Means for their Defence; let them ſhew that the Colours Vice is painted in are falſe and deluſive; that however pleaſing the Appearances are, the Effects are bitter; that our corrupt Imagination is extremely apt to miſlead us, therefore they muſt not truſt to this Guide, but ſeek Security from Reaſon and Reflection; that they muſt not rely on their own Strength, by expoſing themſelves to thoſe who have the Subtlety and Cruelty to form Deſigns againſt their Virtue; and that, in theſe Caſes, the greateſt Proof they can give of their Courage is to run away, becauſe their Paſſions naturally incline them to ſtay; that thoſe, in a word, who wiſh to maintain their Virtue, muſt ſhun the Vici-

ous:

ous: and where the Affairs of Life unavoidably expoſe them to the Company of ſuch, let them by a conſtant diſcountenancing Deportment, ſhew their Diſapprobation of every unbecoming Word or Action; whereby they will check, and often prevent, any Attacks on their Innocence. But farther, to enforce the Virtue of Innocence, let Parents ſhew their Children the Obligations they are under of preſerving it; that beſides the Inſult offered to their Creator who made them rational Beings, and thereby diſtinguiſhed them from the Brutes, their departing from it is an Injuſtice to themſelves, an Injuſtice to their Parents, and to all thoſe who have laboured to correct the natural Corruption of their Hearts, by inſtilling into them every virtuous Principle.

A fourth Cauſe of Injuſtice is Avarice: which implies an inordinate Love of Gain. Avarice puts on a thouſand Shapes, and is to be found in Men of every Rank and every Age; but it is moſt apparent in the Rich and the Old: which is an Aggravation of the Vice; becauſe the one have more than enough already, and the other have not long to enjoy the Fruits of it, even ſhould they live to reap them. But what is moſt alarming in the Avaritious is, the extreme Danger

ger of going beyond the Bounds of Juſtice; and what *Dryden* * ſays of Wits and Madmen may, by the eaſieſt Change, † be apply'd without Impropriety to the Covetous and the Diſhoneſt. How many Schemes are formed, how many Devices uſed to raiſe a Fortune, or to add Hoard to Hoard? One circumvents another in Trade; and with more than ſavage Cruelty, abuſes the Power he has by keeping thoſe under that might otherwiſe flouriſh; and had rather ſee another ſtarve, than himſelf be deprived of what he does not want. A ſecond burns with a Thirſt of Gaming, and values himſelf for his ſuperior Parts, if he can trick another out of his Money at Play; regardleſs of the dreadful Conſequences attending the Loſs; and regardleſs of the Injuſtice of the Acquiſition. How do they poſſeſs their Minds who have raiſed their Fortune on another's Ruin? Do they ever reflect on the Miſery of their wretched Companion; or do they view the Diſtreſs of his Wife, his Children, and his ſuffering Creditors? Surely if the Gameſter did this, even he who wins, and wins by a fair Bet, and equal Lay, muſt tremble at Riches thus acquired: but

* Great Wits to Madneſs ſure are near ally'd:
And thin Partitions do their Bounds divide.

† Av'rice and Knav'ry ſure are near ally'd;
And thin Partitions do their Bounds divide.

if to this be added the Traps, the Snares, and other Artifices to draw in weak or unwary Men to their Ruin, what muſt we think of ſuch Wretches? We may both pity and condemn the Ruined, but we muſt abhor thoſe who cauſed it, however great their falſe Triumph may be. A third takes the Advantage of Diſtreſs or Weakneſs, and lends his Money, not with Kindneſs, but with a ſordid View: theſe are the Men who graſp at Mortgages for the ſake of foreclosing; and get Poſſeſſion of an Eſtate for half it's Value; who inveigle a Widow that they may ruin her Affairs, and enrich themſelves; or get a Guardianſhip that they may beggar the Children. A fourth, ſenſible what Power Riches give him, employs it to the harraſſing and depreſſing all beneath him; theſe are thoſe who to add to their ſuperfluous Wealth ſuck the Blood and Vitals of the Poor, by reducing their juſt Pay, and defrauding them of their Wages; or who with inhuman Scorn depreciate that Merit which others poſſeſs; or cruſh it in it's Appearance. But how ſhall Parents, who perhaps may not live to be Witneſſes to theſe Actions, prevent them in their Children? The Anſwer is eaſy. Imprint on them an early Love of Juſtice; and as they advance, ſhew them the various Ways of deviating from it; that by viewing theſe things in their

their true Light, they may conceive a juſt Horror of Crimes ſo deteſtable in themſelves, and ſo deſtructive to Society.

A fifth Source of Injuſtice is Slander. There are Men who would not game another out of his Money, nor forge a Deed, tho' they could obtain his Eſtate with Security, nor run him thro' the Body; yet ſhall, without Scruple, butcher his Reputation with Slander. An unbecoming Levity of Converſation and Behaviour is natural to many, who thereby do great Harm without once being aware of it; but this, tho' a great Evil in Society, is Innocence, if compared with the Malevolence of others. There are Men of ſuch rancorous Hearts, of ſuch malicious Natures, that they ſeem to have nothing human but the Form; Wretches, who, to gratify their Spleen, or to indulge a Pique, tear in Pieces the Good-name of thoſe whoſe Merit is perhaps ſuperior to their own. All the moral Writers condemn this cenſuring, cruel Humour; and a celebrated dramatic Poet † deſcribes

†——Who ſteals my Purſe, ſteals Traſh.
'Twas mine; 'tis his; and has been Slave to thouſands:
But he who filches from me my good Name,
Robs me of that which not enriches him,
But makes me poor indeed.——

SHAKESPEARE.

very

very beautifully the superior Loſs of Reputation to that of Riches. A Man that is robbed on the High-way ſees his Loſs, and knows the worſt of it; but he who is levelled at from afar, or receives a Stab in the dark, neither diſcovers his Enemy, nor knows where the Miſchief will end. In the great Family of the World, every one is furniſhed with Means for his Support, be it more or leſs; all are in ſome Degree poſſeſſed of Power, Genius, or Abilities to procure, if not a Fortune, at leaſt Subſiſtence; with what Face then does Mankind dare to fruſtrate the Intention of Providence, by robbing another of that Reputation which he is labouring to eſtabliſh, and by which alone he is enabled to ſupport his Wife, his Children, and himſelf. With what Pretenſions, or by what Authority do they preſume to ſtrip another of the Merit he is poſſeſſed of? If I have leſs Merit than another, let me labour to equal him; ſhould I perchance have more, let me not rob him of the little he is poſſeſſed of. But Men of this deteſtable Spirit imagine, that in making others little, they render themſelves great; and thus unjuſtly uſe the Power they are inveſted with, by abuſing their Hearers Ears; proſtituting their own Tongues to the Deſtruction of others; and, leſt Words ſhould ſometimes be ineffectual, they add Nods,

Nods, Winks, Shrugs, and whatever can exprefs Malice, Hatred, or Contempt. Pure Morality teaches us to throw a Veil over others Faults; but Juftice demands that we ftifle not their Virtues, much lefs pervert them: that is, we fhould be ready to acknowledge the Merit due to them, but cannot deny it without the bafeft Injury.

Behold then what Juftice requires of us! Parents who teach their Children a Knowledge of Property, who infpire them with a Refolution never to invade it in others, who teach them a Fairnefs in their Dealings, an Exactnefs in paying their Debts, and a juft Deteftation of the Tricks of fophifticating Goods, particularly Drugs, Wine, Food, and thofe things that often elude our Senfes, or affect our Health; who teach them to obey the Laws of their Country, in avoiding all clandeftine Trade, all Commerce in prohibited or contraband Goods, and make them afhamed of fuch Employments as require them to fteal their Way through the World, or fkulk about in the dark; thofe Parents, I fay, who do this, do well: but that is not enough; they muft check, nay conquer a babling cenforious Difpofition, and create in it's ftead that generous Tendernefs for others that they would wifh to meet with themſelves: but above all, they muſt inſpire their Hearts and Lips with Juſtice, and imprint on their Souls a Senſe of the Baſeneſs of Detraction, Calumny, and Slander.

Before I quit this Head, I muſt touch on a Species of Injuſtice diametrically oppoſite to that we have been cenſuring: my Readers will perhaps be ſurprized when I ſay it is Silence. So much is due to the Cauſe of Juſtice, that we cannot always be ſilent without a Breach of it. Men complain, and very juſtly, that true Honour is rare to be found; yet, while this is granted, we muſt obſerve, that falſe Honour reigns in it's ſtead; but my Purpoſe here is, to conſider how far it is an Act of Injuſtice.

When a Man ſets about a lawleſs Enterprize, his firſt Care is to engage what he calls a Friend to ſecond his Attempts, or at leaſt to promiſe him Secreſy; but, to make it ſucceed, the Party employed is to be a Friend on both Sides: here then is a manifeſt Injuſtice in the Silence of the third Perſon, however innocent he may be otherwiſe. But what is the Principle they act upon? Honour. What! ſhall I betray my Friend! has he not repoſed a Confidence in me? he has;

has; and I will be faithful to it. Who can reflect on the fatal Effects of this falſe Friendſhip, this miſtaken Honour, without trembling? Who is there, with any Knowledge of the World, that has not ſeen Sorrow, Guilt, Deſtruction brought on Families by the Connivance of a Servant, the Silence of a Brother, and the Weakneſs of a Siſter? What Barbarity in a favourite Maid to be the Inſtrument of a young Lady's Ruin, by conveying a Scrub into the very Family whoſe Bread ſhe eats; or at leaſt ſees her on the Brink of it, without ſpeaking a Word for her Preſervation? How dreadful are thoſe Friendſhips, how prepoſterous that Silence, where a young Gentleman ſees his Companion, his Fellow-Clerk, levelling at the Deſtruction of an innocent Girl, and not have the Soul to declare the guilty Deſign till too late? Or, finally, where is the Senſe, the Good-Nature, or the Juſtice of her who ſees a Brother taking fatal Steps, about to injure another's Virtue, or marry a Beggar, or ruin himſelf, and, as far as he has Power, his Parents too, without once ſtriking at the Root, by diſcovering his vicious Intentions and Practices? Who that can diſtinguiſh Right from Wrong, but muſt ſee the Injuſtice of this Silence? Parents therefore ſhould animate their Children with a Reſolution never to enter into these false Friendships, never to promise what is in it's Nature wrong, nor ever to promote or connive at another's Harm, if in their Power to redress or prevent it. But farther, Parents, in forming their Children's Minds, are in many Cases to adapt their Instructions to the Station of Life they are expected to act in. Those of Condition must not see their Parents injured, especially in a Matter of any Moment, and neglect to remove the Fault: those who are to serve, besides Duty and Respect, owe Justice; therefore must not only be faithful in their own Actions, but discover any real Injustice in those of others; and particularly they must detest with honest Scorn the being privy to an underhand Match. Laying Schemes, conveying Letters, Concealments from the Parents, or Denials where Danger is suspected, or otherwise contributing to the Ruin of a young Master or Lady, even tho' they could make their own Fortune by being in the Secret, are Actions ever to be shunned, as they are base in their Nature, and grossly unjust.

The last Source of Injustice is Revenge. I have said before, that pure Morality teaches us to throw a Veil over others Faults; I may with equal Truth say, it obliges us to forgive Injuries.

Injuries. For altho' it is a Juſtice due to ourſelves to maintain our Right, yet the ſame Self-Juſtice requires us to forgive thoſe by whom we have been wrong'd. If we can remove an Injury, we may, and ought; but Revenge is not the Weapon we are to uſe for that Purpoſe. Whatever fires our Revenge, is apt to cloud our Reaſon; Men therefore who meditate Revenge, ſeldom have Reaſon for their Guide; and he who forſakes Reaſon, is a bad Judge how far Revenge ſhould be carried. If we mentally ſurvey a revengeful Man, how melancholy is the View! What Agitations in his Mind! what Flutterings in his Heart! All Nature ſeems convulſed within him! and, in the Midſt of his Self-torture, his only Thoughts are, whether he ſhall ruin, or be ruined; murder, or be murdered! But if we go farther, and behold this Man in the Action he has ſo eagerly ſought for, or carry our Ideas to the Conſequences of it, we muſt tremble with Pity. His Countenance is an Index of his Mind: what Fury on his Brow; what Fire darts from his Eyes; what Malice, in confuſed, imperfect Accents, flows from his Lips; and what frantic Rage poſſeſſes his Soul! Sometimes a Duel is to repair the Injury; dreadful Situation! ſince whichſoever falls, the Calamity is inexpreſſible. Who can recall the Blood once ſpilt, the Life once loſt? who can conſole the wretched Survivor, when Revenge is glutted, and Reflection calls him back to himſelf? or can the Receiver of the Challenge draw Conſolation in his future Life, from a falſe Point of Honour? no, no; it is all Deluſion; and independent of the Crimes which gave riſe to it, the Deed itſelf is groſs Injuſtice. Revenge puts on many Shapes: ſome ſeek it not in Blood, yet, with equal Fury, hunt another to Ruin and Death by unjuſt Law-ſuits. What Havock does this make! How many fall from Affluence to Want, from Splendor to a Goal, thro' the Inveteracy of Revenge! Not all the Conceſſions of the oppoſite Party, not all the Tears of his Wife, nor the impending Ruin of his Children, can appeaſe the Revengeful: Savage-like, he quits not his Hold till his Fury is glutted, till his Adverſary is deſtroyed. Beſides theſe, there are many other Species of Revenge, leſs obvious indeed, but perhaps not leſs criminal: there are Men whoſe Fury is leſs, but whoſe Malice is equal: Men with cooler Heads, but with inveterate Hearts. Injuries, whether fancied or real, ſeize the Heart of the Revengeful, and having once taken place, a thouſand things are machinated for Retaliation of the Offence: every good Office ceaſes; ill Offices take

take place of them; cruel to their Character when abſent; arrogant and diſdainful to their Perſon when preſent; their Reputation torn to Pieces; falſe Conſtructions put on their moſt innocent Actions; and every ſiniſter Means uſed to ſtrip them of Fame, and Fortune; nay even of Bread. See here the dreadful Paſſion of Revenge; view the Cruelty on one Side, the ruinous Effects on the other. What Care then ſhould Parents take to baniſh it from their Children's Hearts, ſeeing it is the Source of Miſery to themſelves, and Deſtruction to others! Let them labour to ſtifle the firſt Reſentments; let them ſpeak to their Underſtandings as they advance. Youth is naturally full of Fire, and as now their Judgment is weak, they are eaſily miſled by falſe Notions of Honour; but where Malice is found to reſide in their Hearts, it will demand the utmoſt Pains to root it out: ſtill all ſhould aim at effecting it. To this End, beſides checking the earlieſt Reſentments, let Parents paint in the livelieſt Colours the Deformity of Revenge; let them ſhew how much it deſtroys their own inward Peace; let them counteract the Paſſion by encouraging in them Meekneſs, Clemency and Love; and above all, prove to them how much they ſink beneath the Dignity of Human Nature, how much they injure themſelves, and how unjuſt they are to Society in every Action that is accompanied with Revenge; but particularly where Life, Health, Fame, Peace, or Property are affected by it.

Thus much have I ſaid to ſhew the Neceſſity Parents are under of teaching their Children the Knowledge and Love of that great Bond of Society, Juſtice: it demands indeed much more Labour to diſcuſs every Point; but I perſuade myſelf, that if their Hearts are duly impreſſed with the Principles here laid down, they will be animated to know and practiſe every other Act of Juſtice which their various Stations in Life offer them the Occaſions of. Virtues beget Virtues; one Act of Equity will lead them to a ſecond; a ſecond will warm them to the Execution of a third; a Self-denial of little irregular things, will make way for the Entrance of Reaſon; and Reaſon exerciſed on the ſolid Principles of Juſtice, will enable them to conquer every lawleſs Deſire, every turbulent Paſſion.

Notwithſtanding what has been ſaid thro' the Courſe of this Attempt, of conquering our Paſſions, it is not to be underſtood that we are to be paſſive, ſpiritleſs, and inſipid; far from it; this would be fruſtrating the Deſign

Deſign of Providence. We are, under Reaſon's Guide, to enjoy our own Minds with honeſt Freedom; and he who has a warm Heart, a chearful Mind, and a frank Behaviour, bids faireſt for being a good Man. But what irreſiſtibly proves us deſign'd for an active State, is, the Virtue of Fortitude. Fortitude is Patience improv'd; it is Courage exalted; it is that Virtue which enables us not only to bear Sickneſs, Pain, Diſgrace, and Poverty, but arms us with Power either to conquer theſe Evils, or at leaſt ſo to weaken their Force that they may not bear too hard upon us. In viewing Mankind in general, or if each views himſelf in particular, it will be found that Life is imbitter'd a thouſand Ways; all have their own Troubles, all feel their different Sufferings; ſome indeed taſte ſo little of the Sweets of Life, or have them ſo ſtrongly impregnated with Sorrows, that they are ſcarce ſenſible of their Reliſh: Fortitude alone then is the Remedy for theſe Evils; and therefore ſhould be the Object of every one's Study. With this Weapon we are enabled to face every Danger, to encounter every Trouble, and to ſtruggle with every Difficulty: it is the Inſtrument Providence has kindly put into our Hands; and not to uſe it, is the higheſt Ingratitude, at the ſame time that it is being ignorant of our own Happineſs. Parents then cannot juſtify the Neglect of this Virtue to their Children: and it is from this Knowledge of Life, that I have already propoſed, in Compaſſion and Regard to their future Happineſs, that they familiarize them, with all the Tenderneſs of good Parents, to little Diſappointments while young; that they may be arm'd to bear greater as they ought. All irregular Deſires we ſhould diſclaim from our Hearts; but even with regard to thoſe which are in their Nature innocent, lawful, and reaſonable, how often are we diſappointed! How then will Children, as they advance, ſtruggle with Diſappointments, if Strangers to the proper Guide, if unacquainted with Fortitude?

But here I muſt obſerve, that many things are looked upon as grievous Evils, which, if conſidered in a proper Light, are no Evils at all: and to what is this owing? certainly to the erroneous Meaſures taken at ſetting out. The Eagerneſs of Children after every new Trifle, the Deſire of engaging in whatever is called Pleaſure, and the early Paſſion for Dreſs and Show, make them earneſt to have their Humour comply'd with. Now as many of theſe things are highly improper, gratifying their Demands muſt be an Error more

or

or leſs; but this is the leaſt Part of the Evil: the Habit of having all they deſire increaſes with their Years; and without conſidering whether the Things they ſeek are neceſſary or reaſonable, they purſue their Deſires, and are wretched when diſappointed. Hence ariſe many of the Paſſions which diſturb the Oeconomy of Families, and fill the World with Diſorder: Men diſappointed in their Buſineſs, and croſs'd in their Will, burſt into Rage, or contract a Fretfulneſs which makes them unhappy in themſelves, and painful to all who ſee or feel the Effects of it: and Women who have been uſed in Childhood to conquer their Parents, and in Youth all the World, who have been conſtantly addreſſed in the Language of Romances, and have been vainly taught to think the Men their Slaves; Women, I ſay, who are thus educated, are but very ill prepared to meet Diſappointments: the firſt Oppoſition throws them into Fits, whence follow Vapours, Melancholy and Indolence; the next kindles their Reſentment, which agitates the Mind, ſpoils the Features, by tearing off the natural Softneſs of the Countenance, and puts the ſweeteſt Temper into a Ferment; and, if a Huſband be the Object of it, 'tis great Odds but a ſhort Time creates either an unjuſt Coldneſs, or a fixed

Aversion. Mr. *Locke*, sensible of the Danger of irregular Indulgence, thus describes the Situation of a fondled Son. "He that "hath been used to have his Will in every "thing as long as he was in Coats, why "should we think it strange that he should "desire it, and contend for it still, when he "is in Breeches? Indeed, as he grows to-"wards a Man, Age shews his Faults the "more; so that there are few Parents then "so blind as not to see them, few so insen-"sible as not to feel the ill Effects of their "own Indulgence. He had the Will of "his Maid before he could speak or go; "he had the Mastery of his Parents ever "since he could prattle; and why, now he "is grown up, is stronger and wiser than he "was then, why now of a sudden should "he be restrained and curbed? Why must "he at seven, fourteen, or twenty Years "old, lose the Privilege, which his Parents "Indulgence till then so largely allowed "him?" From all this it is evident, that the early planting of regular Desires, checking the Growth of vicious ones, and subjecting Passion to Reason, are the great Means to lay the Foundation of Happiness in our Children, and the surest Fence against many Evils they would otherwise be exposed to: but if after all this, Sorrow, Pain, Dis-

appointment,

appointment, or Poverty be their Lot, let Parents teach them to meet it as they ought; teach them with the firmeſt Reſolution, with unſhaken Conſtancy, to bear up againſt the rude Attack; and teach them that the only way to leſſen the Evils they cannot avoid, is to adhere inſeparably to that heroic Virtue Fortitude.

I am now led to ſpeak of Temperance; the calmeſt Companion of the Heart of Man. Temperance is the Virtue that bridles our irregular Deſires; it is nearly ally'd to Prudence, and has a cloſe Connection with Juſtice; it calms Revenge, and quenches the Fire of unjuſt Reſentment; it checks the Epicure, and ſtops the riotous Hand of the Bacchanalian; it extinguiſhes or abates the Flames of Luſt, and baniſhes every lawleſs Action; it ſilences the flippant detracting Tongue, and gives in it's ſtead a pleaſing Moderation of Speech; it ſhuts the Door againſt Avarice, and proves experimentally, that Happineſs does not conſiſt in the eager Purſuit or Acquiſition of Riches, but in a contented Mind; it curbs that ſtrongeſt of all other Paſſions, Gaming, and diſtinguiſhes juſtly the Abſurdity and Folly of making that a dangerous Trade, which was only deſigned as a Relaxation and an Amuſe-

ment:

ment: Temperance, in a word, is the Parent of many Virtues; the Parent of Peace, Profperity, Health and Joy. But while thefe are Truths acknowledged and received, how comes it that we know fo little of the Practice of them? How comes it that in general thefe are mere Matters of Speculation? Alas! the Spring is tainted in the Source. We are intemperate in our very Cradles; no wonder therefore if we remain fo our whole Lives. We are born with irregular Appetites; and which, thro' Errors in Judgment, or miftaken Fondnefs, are daily rendered ftill more fo. But let us leave thefe melancholy Reflections, and confider the Advantages we enjoy, the Privileges we are invefted with. Providence, kind Providence, has given us Reafon for our Guide; and Reafon will conduct us to Temperance. —Nothing can be more ftrange to all Obfervation, than the Practice of forfaking Temperance; fince every Day's Experience proves to us, that Intemperance produces the very oppofite to what we feek. Suppofe when a Child is born, we afk the Parents what it is they wifh in that Child; they will anfwer, Life. But as Life alone, that is, mere Exiftence, may by Infirmity or other Accidents be very wretched, they will naturally wifh for Health and Happinefs. Well then, Life, Health,

Health, and Happineſs, are the general Wiſhes of Parents for their Children. Now let us ſee how their Wiſhes are likely to ſucceed. Their firſt Step is uſually a ſhameful Neglect of the Food of Nature, the Breaſt; the next, a blind Gratification of their Will; the third, an almoſt total Neglect of their Manners; and a fourth, the cheriſhing in them every irregular Affection. Where then is the Wonder that Parents are diſappointed? Life and Health depend on proper Food and other judicious Management on one part; and if ſick, an Obedience to Remedies on the other part; and Happineſs eſſentially depends in the firſt place on Health; in the next, on the due Government of our Senſes, Affections and Paſſions. See here how Mankind deviate from themſelves; how far they depart from their own Principles. But what then is the Remedy? nothing more obvious. Let Parents exerciſe their Reaſon in all the Steps they take for their Children's Welfare; let them examine Right and Wrong; let them not only avoid Paſſion, but labour to correct their own Errors of Judgment, that they may be the better enabled to prevent them in their Children; but particularly, let them fix in them the Knowledge, Love, and Habit of Temperance.

Theſe

These Rules will doubtless be an Infringement on those Liberties Parents usually take in indulging their Children's Stomachs; and it will be a greater in the Restraint it lays on their growing Passions: but they must convince them of the Purity of their Intentions by speaking to their Understandings; not all at once, but by Degrees, as they open and gain Strength; so that Step by Step they may point out to them the Loveliness, the Pleasure, and the Advantages of this uncommon Virtue. I say nothing here of the State of Childhood, because it is already understood that Parents have their Children's Health regulated by proper Management, and their Minds docile thro' the Force of Obedience; but when Dress, Pleasure, Company, Feasting, or whatever subjects us to be intemperate, come into Play, as they are Actions which always cause a Struggle, more or less, between Passion and Reason, it demands the greatest Care and Attention of Parents to win them to a Love of Temperance.

An easy Submission to our Lot in Life is one of the greatest Attainments towards Happiness. View a young Lady with a strong Passion for Dress; every new thing strikes her; one Companion has a richer Silk than herself; another has the sweetest Lace she

ever

ever ſaw; a third has Ear-rings ten times handſomer than her own; ſhe burns with Impatience to equal them, and that granted, new things ariſe, and the others are old tho' not worn out; that is, her Reliſh for them is loſt. Thus a continual round of Faſhions keep her inceſſantly anxious; and tho' perhaps ſhe poſſeſſes every thing, ſhe enjoys nothing. Not ſo the calmer well-inſtructed Fair; ſhe conſiders that Propriety of Dreſs is what ſuits her Station; and covets not another's Jewels: ſhe wears, without a Bluſh, a meaner Silk than her meaner Companion; and free from the Extremes of Negligence or Pride, ſhe is qualify'd for all the Dignity that Dreſs can give her; but is equally happy in an inferior Appearance. Thus too it happens with our Sons: One is in the continual Purſuit of Pleaſure, has a thouſand Contrivances to reach a Play, a Ball, or a Horſe-race; and is miſerable if theſe things are going on without him: while another, awaken'd by Reaſon, and check'd by Temperance, takes theſe things as they come; and neither inſipidly refuſes the Chearfulneſs of an Entertainment, nor is diſturb'd of his Reſt, or loſes either his Temper or his Appetite, if he is diſappointed. Such is the Difference between Paſſion and Reaſon, ſuch the genuine Effects of Temperance.

Temperance,

Temperance, as I obſerv'd before, is cloſely connected with Juſtice; that is, whatever thro' Intemperance affects our Health, or endangers our Lives, muſt be unjuſt. What can be more amazing than the falſe Judgment of Mankind even in the moſt obvious things! All allow that we have no Right voluntarily to throw away that Life which Providence has given us; on the contrary, we are bound to ſupport it, even under the Preſſure of Pain and Sorrow, to the laſt Moment. How comes it then that while this is acknowledged, while Men juſtly ſhrink with Horror at the very Thought of Self-murder, they have the Hardineſs to dally with ſome murderous Inſtrument? All the Arguments that are brought againſt Suicide, whether by Sword, Piſtol, Laudanum, or Arſenic, hold good, in ſome Degree, in the Point before us. The oftener a Building is ſhock'd, the ſooner will it decay; the more Violence is us'd to a delicate Machine, the ſooner will it be deſtroy'd; and no Machine is ſo exquiſitely delicate as Man. Now as every Species of Exceſs, Riot, and Debauchery, is a Shock given to our Frame, it muſt naturally impair our Health, and conſequently ſhorten our Lives. Many things tend to effect this, that Men in general are Strangers to; but

there

there are others they are too ſenſible of, yet attempt not to remove, nay plunge themſelves into. Here then appears the Neceſſity of Temperance; here we ſee the great Obligation of Parents to their Children in this Point: ſince they are not only accountable for their Happineſs, but even for their Health and Lives. To conclude, let Parents in inculcating this Virtue diſſuade their Children from every irregular Attachment, and convince them that no intemperate Affections are juſtifiable; that beſides avoiding thoſe irregular Paſſions which may be ſaid to reſide in the Soul, there are others that dwell on the Senſes, equally capable of deſtroying us; particularly an unhappy Attachment to ſleeping, eating, drinking, and many other things in their Nature not only innocent but indiſpenſably neceſſary; yet, by the frequent grievous Abuſe of them, made the Inſtruments of our Deſtruction.

Theſe are the things I had to offer on the Part of Manners; theſe are the Steps I have already in great meaſure taken with my own Children, and theſe the Sentiments I wiſh to inſpire them with. If therefore, as general Laws, they are equally applicable to others, my preſenting them in Print will, I hope, be conſider'd with the ſame Candour they

they are offered. But notwithſtanding what has already been ſaid, Parents have ſtill much to do. To keep up the Spirit of Government, they muſt conſtantly remember that Nature and Reaſon are to be their Guides: if we diſtort Nature, our Children will be prepoſterous Figures; and if we baniſh Reaſon, they will be Brutes or Monſters. Parents muſt remember too, that it is not for themſelves that they labour to train up their Children in Order, Obedience, and Knowledge; there muſt be no ſelf-pointed Views, no Pride, no Diſpoſitions to tyranniſe over their own Fleſh and Blood; theſe are Motives unworthy a Place in any Parent's Breaſt. Their principal Aim muſt be to make their Children happy, by making them wiſe and good; and if they ſucceed herein, ſo much Happineſs will be reflected back on themſelves as will amply reward all their Labours. But they muſt not ſtop even here; tho' this Deſign is noble, they ſhould have a nobler yet in view; that is, the univerſal Good of Mankind: 'tis too narrow a Good that ſeeks itſelf alone; Children muſt therefore be animated by their Parents with all thoſe Virtues that will make them dear and valuable to Society. Now what Chance is there that Children will come on the Stage of Life with the neceſſary Requiſites, unleſs

due

due Pains are taken to mould and temper their Hearts, to form their Minds, and cultivate their Underſtandings? Mr. *Pope*, after labouring to prove for what End we are in being, what Good we are to purſue, and what Evil avoid, concludes, "that all our "Knowledge is ourſelves to know." If then this Self-knowledge is of ſuch vaſt Importance for the ſecuring our Happineſs even in a moral Senſe, and is ſo very difficult to be attained; ſurely Parents are under the higheſt Obligation to their Children of improving every Means within their Reach, for the gaining this only true Philoſopher's Stone. The End, as Philoſophers agree, is the firſt thing in the Intention; but the Means to attain that End are ſurely, in the Caſe before us, either but little known, or little practiſed; elſe we ſhould not ſee ſuch daily and grievous Miſtakes committed in the training up our little Offspring; nor ſuch a continued Chain of Vice, Folly, and Ignorance, as is the general Reſult of this miſtaken Manners, this want of Self-knowledge.

But here I muſt caution my Readers not to bewilder themſelves in a Maze of fancied Difficulties; not to throw aſide theſe Inſtructions as uſeful or practicable to none but those of Genius, Learning, and great Abilities: the Light of Nature and Reason beams strongly on us all; and Parents, as I have before observed, have it greatly in their Power to regulate their Children's Conduct: for after all, it must be confessed, that it is not so much that Parents do not know, as that they want the Will, to act rightly. But I hope, that such as are really ignorant, will here, in some measure, be informed; such as already know, will here be induced to practise: since by avoiding the Errors too generally run into, so much solid Good will ensue. But, to return back again: where or how are we to begin? Why—(as has already been advanc'd) by Authority. Authority is undoubtedly the first Means towards attaining this great End; the other Means are, a steady Attention to the various Tempers of our Children; a strict Guard over our own Conduct; a watchful Eye on theirs; joined to a serious Practice of every Lesson for their Improvement: to which we are to add, such an Education as is suitable to our Sphere in Life.

EDUCATION.

EDUCATION is a very extenſive Subject; it is a vaſt Field to expatiate in; and has employed the Thoughts and Pens of many great Men, with whom I pretend not to vie: I confeſs myſelf far unequal to the Taſk; and perhaps the greateſt Service I can do my Readers, is to inform them, that, beſides the ancient Writers, the Archbiſhop of *Cambray*, *Tanaquil Faber*, Mr. *Locke*, Monſieur *Crouſaz*, and Monſieur *Rollin*, with ſome others ſtill later, have handled this important Subject. To theſe then I refer them, as great and uſeful Guides; but not to theſe alone; they muſt go farther; and apply to thoſe, whoſe Province it is to reduce the Theory of theſe to Practice: ſuch are many of our living Guides; who tho' they have not perhaps diſtinguiſhed themſelves by their Writings, are notwithſtanding deſervedly eminent for their Skill in teaching.

Nor is Education what I principally engaged

gaged in, in this Treatiſe; Manners alone, I have declared to be my Deſign; and if I can do the preſent or future Age any real Service by the Plan of puerile Government already laid down, I ſhall be happy in conſidering myſelf as a uſeful Member of Society. Still it will appear that Education and Manners have ſo great a Connection, that they are not always to be ſeparated: many of the Writers on theſe Subjects have conſidered them as one and the ſame thing; many juſt Sentiments are imbibed at the ſame time that we are acquiring Languages, and other Parts of Learning: and notwithſtanding a Truth which was advanced at our firſt ſetting out, that much Manners might be acquired without School-learning, yet it is not to be doubted that they ought to riſe in proportion to the Education beſtowed on us. Two things therefore I aim at in purſuing this Subject, without attempting to teach, or invading the Province of the Preceptor; the one, to point out what ſeems neceſſary for both Boys and Girls, in different Spheres of Life, to learn or avoid; the other, to ſhew how far the Education beſtowed on them is applicable to the Improvement of their Manners; or to their Engagement in any Art, Profeſſion, or Science.

As entering on the Subject of Education will naturally carry the Ideas of Parents back to the Childhood of their Offspring, I will, in Conformity with that, suppose, that the Rules already laid down chiefly regard the first Stage of Life; at most, that they are the Ground-work of a future Superstructure: this granted, I will suppose too, that Parents have employed these first seven Years in moulding their Children, and rendering them so far pliable, as readily to submit to whatever their Parents think proper for them to engage in. There is a strong Passion in many Parents to have their Children forward and early in their Learning; where there is really a Genius, a very great Propensity and Aptness to learn, this may certainly not only be allowed, but improved; yet in general I think very little Account is to be made of what they can learn before seven Years old: it is commonly Rote-work, and often forgot almost as soon as learned. However, let these things be taken as they are found: if a Child has a great Quickness and Facility in learning, let it by no Means be check'd; on the other hand, let not another be severely chastised, or it's Life rendered miserable, who has not the same early Aptness. Those who would avoid Error on this Point must consider, that a Child's Memory and Judgment are yet too weak to be much exercifed; that close Application and intenfe Labour are very unfit for this Infant Age; that it is putting their tender Minds too much upon the Stretch; and endangers either a fix'd Averfion to learn, or an incurable Dulnefs: let them farther confider, that fuch a quick Child as I have been fpeaking of, learns without the leaft Difficulty; and if they oblige one of another Caft to learn as much in the fame time, it is odds but they give him more Pain than his Frame can bear. Parents then muft be very careful to avoid thefe firft Miftakes in the educating their Children; fince from a natural Fondnefs to have them appear to Advantage, they often thruft them on things that are unfuitable to their Age, and fuch as they are by no Means qualified to undertake.

It muft not here be underftood, that nothing is to be attempted in the firft Stage of Life; that would be the oppofite Extreme of Error; and playful as Children ufually are at that Age, the leaving them wholly to themfelves for feven Years would be not only injuring their Capacities, but might endanger a Habit of Idlenefs: what I mean is, that all which relates to Education fhould

now

now be made as light, as eaſy, and as pleaſant as poſſible; that, as I have obſerved before, Parents ſhould take things as they are, and not be diſſatisfied or diſappointed, if they find no extraordinary Progreſs made.

But this firſt Stage being over, the Buſineſs becomes ſerious; they are now to enter the Schools. Parents of almoſt every Rank aim, or ſeem to aim, at giving their Children Learning; 'tis a natural Ambition, and, if rationally uſed, highly laudable. Thoſe of an inferior Claſs ſay, with a ſignificant Shake of the Head, 'Tis a fine thing to be a Scholar! True, it is ſo: but ſurely it is a ſad thing to be a learned Beggar; and worſe yet to be a learned Blockhead: an unlearned Cobler is a Prince to either of theſe. To judge of the Propriety of Education, we ſhould, I think, argue from a Knowledge of Life; for as no one ſurely will ſay that the ſame Degree of it is equally proper for all, it follows of courſe that it will be right or wrong, in proportion to our Knowledge or Ignorance of Mankind, and of thoſe Stations wherein it is ſo variouſly exerciſed. Now in viewing it in this judicious Light, it appears to me, that the Steps frequently taken by Parents in the educating their Children, are in many reſpects erroneous. Nor is this by any means to be aſcribed to the Teachers, but to the Parents; not to the Plan, but to the Execution: for as in the Order of Nature, every thing has it's own Sphere, it's Province aſſign'd it, which cannot be departed from without Error; ſo in the various Degrees of Mankind, if a proper Regard be not had to Situation and Abilities, the Miſtakes committed in educating our Children muſt be very many.

At the ſame time that I venture to think our Notions of Education ſometimes erroneous, I confeſs it is extremely difficult to fix preciſe Rules for a better; no wonder therefore if I err in the Attempt; and in that Caſe, I hope, the Goodneſs of my Intention will plead my Excuſe. But here let me aſk a natural Queſtion; What is it all Mankind aim at in the Education of their Children? certainly to give them ſuch a Degree of Knowledge as will qualify them to fill ſome certain Poſt, ſome certain Station in Life: in ſhort, to fit them for an Employment ſuited to their Condition, ſuch as will make them happy in themſelves, and uſeful to Society. This, I ſay, is, or ought to be our Aim: but how grievouſly do we pervert it? Parents often miſtakenly ſoar above their Reach; like Adventurers in a Lottery, all gape

gape for the higheſt Prizes; all ambitiouſly ſtrive to make their Children ſomething more than common, ſomething above themſelves; and by theſe Means often, very often, overturn and utterly ruin them.

The principal Aim of Parents ſhould be, to know what Sphere of Life their Children will act in; what Education is really ſuitable for them; what will be the Conſequence of neglecting that; and what Chance a ſuperior Education will give them for their Advancement to Poſts of Dignity. I grant, it is Pity that a fine Genius ſhould be uncultivated and buried in Oblivion; but ſurely it is greater Pity that Parents ſhould ſo generally miſtake their Children's Station, Genius, Capacity, and Inclinations, as they generally do; nay more, miſtake their own Capacity too; by engaging them in things above their Ability to conduct them through. The firſt thing many Parents do, is, blindly to magnify their Children's Parts; in conſequence whereof they engage them in ſuch Studies as ſquare with their Fancy; they then turn their Eyes on ſome few great Men, whoſe uncommon Merit, Genius, or Good-fortune, have rais'd them to conſpicuous Stations; and thus, in the Vanity of their Hearts, conclude their

Sons are to be Judges, Biſhops, Generals, and I know not what. But I would here earneſtly diſſuade Parents from this capital Miſtake; indeed it ſeems ſo glaringly abſurd, that I am ſurprized it ſhould be ſo common. But thoſe in inferior Stations will ſay, May we not then give our Children Education? yes certainly: but it ſhould be a ſuitable one. What then, may we not aſpire to raiſe our Children in the World? or muſt they, from Generation to Generation, remain Mechanics, Tradeſmen, or the like? Let me not be miſunderſtood. Every one ſhould look forward; there is a neceſſary Degree of Spirit becoming all Mankind; but then to be judicious, it muſt be rational: thus, at the ſame time that we avoid ſinking into Meanneſs, we muſt be very careful not to tower ſo high as to endanger our daſhing down into Error.

Education, tho' deſign'd to lead us to every Advantage, is often beſtowed to our Diſadvantage, by being the Cauſe of many Errors, we ſhould otherwiſe have eſcaped. Education is often waſted on us, either by being improper for our Station, or by engaging us in things we are unfit for. Education is a Term that often miſleads Parents themſelves; for many do not know either

either it's Extent or Ufe, nor know if their Children poffefs it or not. Thefe things confidered, it is eafy to conclude how common an erroneous Education muft be; and how much it behoves Parents to reflect on the neceffary Means to obviate the like Errors for the future.

I remember a Lady whofe Coachman was an Inftance of the Miftakes I have been fpeaking of. I am refolved, fays he to fome of his Acquaintance, to have one Gentleman in my Family at leaft. In order thereto, he gave his Son Education, and then put him to an Attorney: this entitled the young Fellow to drefs out, and keep, what he call'd, good Company; thefe led him to Pleafures, Gallantry, and many other Extravagancies; in fine, the old Man broke his Heart; and the young one in a fhort time was utterly ruined. But how much happier would he probably have been, had he kept to his proper Sphere, and been a Coachman too! It frequently happens, that honeft induftrious Men among the common Trades, as well as others, grow wealthy, and confequently are ambitious of giving their Children Learning; now as thefe People have ufually but a very fmall Share themfelves, they know little more of it than the Name: they ſend a Boy to School, and becauſe they hear him ſpeak hard Words, and ſee him hammering at a Latin Exerciſe, ſagely conclude that he has Learning; when it is fifty to one, that, comparatively ſpeaking, he knows nothing. It requires a great deal of Time, Diligence, and Application for a Boy to become a good Grammarian, tho' taught by the beſt Methods and the beſt Maſters; what then muſt be the Fate of thoſe who are under bad Teachers? and that there are ſome ſuch, I believe will not be diſputed. But ſuppoſing a Boy really acquires ſome Knowledge; let us ſee of what Uſe it will be to him: his Father is perhaps a Baker, and it is convenient to him to bring his Son up to his own Buſineſs; what does a Baker want with Latin? nothing. Beſides, continued Diſuſe will make him forget it; or, ſhould he retain it, of what Uſe could it be to him, but to make him pedantic and ſelf-conceited? But perhaps upon the Preſumption that this Boy is a Scholar, the honeſt Baker, deſirous that his Son ſhould cut a Figure, ſends him to the Univerſity, and he becomes a Divine: but what Pity is it that a good Baker ſhould be ſpoiled? The innocent young Man, tho' ſpirited up by his fond miſtaken Parents, has perhaps no Talents, no Genius,

nius, no Intereſt; what then muſt be his Fate? why—he muſt drudge, and court, and wait his whole Life, and at laſt gain nothing. What can be more miſtaken than this Conduct, and yet what more common? It may be urged, that theſe are Inſtances of illiterate Parents only, and that People in better Life know better things: now allowing that to be the Caſe, ſtill as Parents of this Kind are very numerous, they ſtand in great need of being ſet right, as the Errors they commit by this falſe Education are productive of many Evils.

Every Nation has it's Cuſtom of dividing the People into Claſſes. The *Police* of *France* divide them into Quality, Nobleſſe, Artificers, and Peaſantry. *England*, a mix'd Government, and a trading Nation, have the Nobility, Gentry, Mercantile or Commercial People, Mechanics, and Peaſantry. Were we to ſubdivide the People, we might run it to an Infinity: to avoid Confuſion therefore, I will ſelect five Claſſes; *viz.* the Nobility, the Gentry, the genteel Trades, all thoſe particularly which require large Capitals, the common Trades, and the Peaſantry. But tho' for the Sake of Perſpicuity and Brevity, I confine my Obſervations to theſe, yet they may occaſionally be applied to others; and tho' *London* may in genera be called the Scene of Action thro' my whole Design, yet is it equally applicable to, and intended for, the Benefit of the whole Kingdom.

Persons of Rank and Quality are, I doubt, placed in too high a Sphere for any Instructions of mine to reach them; or should this Attempt fall into their Hands, what Chance is there for it's being useful to them, since they seem to have every Advantage, every Help at command. Still as true Wisdom consists in seeking Instruction wherever it can be found, and as the lowest among Mankind may drop a Hint that may be useful to the highest, I will, with all due Deference and Respect, venture to speak my Thoughts; and if they reach the Ears of the Great, I dare hope, they will at least commend the Design, if they cannot applaud the Execution.

Human Nature (as daily Experience shews us) is, in the general, alike in all, from the Prince to the Peasant: the same Weaknesses attend us; the same Passions torment us; the same Diseases kill us: all are the Work of ONE GREAT ARTIST! all are born for the same great End! The Gifts of Fortune indeed are innumerably different;

rent; the Advantages of Education very many; and as a Train of Vices corrupts our Manners, ſo a Succeſſion of Virtues may be ſaid to enoble our Birth and purify our Blood. Hence it is we often ſee thoſe exalted Virtues in the Great and Noble inherited by their Poſterity; and hence too we often diſcover, even where Pains are taken to conceal it, an inbred Dignity, a Mein and Aſpect ſuperior to the Generality of Men. Still this Rule is by no Means univerſal; for the ſame Experience ſhews us, that great Men can do little things; even ſuch as the private and obſcure would be aſhamed of. And how ſo? becauſe Paſſion, not Reaſon, is their Guide. Parents then, we ſee, even of the higheſt Rank, are under an indiſpenſable Obligation of regulating the Manners of their Children. Philoſophers ſay, that all Paſſions are in all Men; but that their Predominance is unequal, and different in different Men: if ſo, the Great ſtand in moſt need of having them ſubdued, or at leaſt regulated, as the Power to indulge them is greater in them than in others. But granting that Parents of Quality are convinced of theſe Truths, and take all the Steps already recommended for train-up their Children in proper Decorum; granting too, that they deſign every thing

for

for their real Advantage; they have ſtill many things both to do and avoid which are not common to all.

Their firſt Care muſt be to avoid Sycophants, Flatterers, and Hypocrites; they are but too conſtant Attendants on the Great, and their Buſineſs is to diffuſe an imperceptible Poiſon (if I may be allowed the Metaphor) over both Parents and Children. Nothing is ſo amiable as Truth, nothing more deſirable, and yet nothing more difficult to reach the Great. If a Nobleman has a Child whoſe Parts are weak, whoſe Genius is ſlow and ſhallow, it is undoubtedly a Misfortune, but cannot be his Fault: the natural Blindneſs of Parents keeps them from ſeeing theſe Defects ſo clearly as another; but the unnatural, at leaſt unmanly Artifices of the Flatterer totally prevent their ſeeing them at all: and thus the noble Heir is miſtakenly taught to think himſelf what Nature has forbid he ſhall ever be.

Another Care is, that Youth of Quality, who have Parts and Quickneſs, be not ſuffered to waſte the firſt Flower of their Age in Idleneſs: it is a grievous Error, yet very common. I have already obſerved, that Parents who know nothing are injudiciouſly, and

and even anxiouſly ſolicitous to have their Children Scholars; and by a ſtrange reverſe Infatuation, Parents of Rank are often very indifferent about it. This Error is undoubtedly ſometimes owing to themſelves only by a ſupine Negligence in their own natural Temper; but it is much oftener owing to the falſe Praiſes given by thoſe that have both the Parents and the Child's Ear. A young Heir ſoon knows the Title, Dignity and Eſtate he is born to poſſeſs; too ſoon does he know his Independence, and too apt is he to grow careleſs about his Learning on this very Account; but if to theſe Impediments be added imaginary Excellence and Knowledge, thro' the daily Flattery of a Dependent, what is likely to be the Conſequence? why, that he will remain ignorant his whole Life. For who will take Pains to learn, that is firmly perſuaded he knows enough already? and that many of our young Noblemen are trained up in this Diſpoſition, nobody, I believe, will deny: it is true that Time may convince them of their Error; but it will then perhaps be too late to recover what they have loſt.

The Education of a Nobleman ſhould contain every thing that is both uſeful and ornamental. As he is more conſpicuous than others,

others, as he always ſtands on an Eminence, his Education ſhould be ſuch as may reflect a Luſtre on every one that beholds him. He is to be conſidered as a Pillar of the Laws, an Honour and an Ornament to the Age he lives in. To this End he is to ſtudy firſt, Languages; that is to ſay, two of the dead ones, *viz. Latin* and *Greek*; and of the living ones, beſides his Mother-tongue, *French* at leaſt. The Learned diſagree very much as to the Variety of Languages neceſſary to be acquired; ſome are of Opinion, that beſides theſe already named, *Italian*, *Spaniſh*, *Portugueſe*, and more yet, are becoming the Education of a great Man; and urge in their Favour, that the more Languages are gained, the more the Mind is enlarged: others diſſent from this, and maintain, that a great Variety rather confuſes the Mind than otherwiſe; that *Latin* and *Greek* are indiſputably the Languages of all learned Men; after thoſe, *French*, and at moſt *Italian*, are all that need be added, as every thing may be found in theſe, either originally or tranſlated into them: but they farther argue, that it is a great Waſte of Time, ſpent merely in the Acquiſition of Languages, when ſo many nobler Studies are to be purſued; Studies which at once ſtrike the Mind, and conſtitute true Science. This laſt Reaſon-

ing

ing has, I think, great Force; buthere for a Moment let me leave the Nobleman, to make an Obſervation on general Life. Languages, beſides being conſidered as general Parts of Education, are particularly neceſſary in certain Circumſtances of Life. If one, whether for Education or Buſineſs, goes to reſide in *Holland*, *France*, *Spain*, or *Italy*, it would be an Abſurdity not to attain the Language of the Country; ſo if another is to be a Merchant, ſurely he ſhould not be a Stranger to the Language of his Correſpondents; thus are theſe, and many other things more or leſs neceſſary, juſt as they are circumſtanced: and therefore ſhould Parents, beſides the Education they beſtow on their Children, as ſuited to their Station in general, join to it that which is neceſſary in particular. But, to return;

Beſides Languages, a Nobleman is to learn Philoſophy, both Moral and Natural; Mathematics; the ancient and modern Laws of our own Country; and the Cuſtoms, Laws and Manners of other Nations. He ſhould particularly be a Critic in our own Hiſtory, and our own Language; becauſe they are what in real Life he will have moſt occaſion to exerciſe. To this ſolid Learning ſhould be added the Embelliſh-

ments

ments of polite Literature, Poetry, Painting, and Music; and to compleat the Character, Dancing, Fencing, Riding and Architecture. Tho' this is going a considerable Way, it is much the least Part of what ought reasonably to be expected from him, considering the Light he stands in. It is of great Consequence that his Preceptor have a good Head; but it is of much more that he has an honest Heart. He is to humanize his Pupil's Soul, and form him for all those Actions that will give him a real, not a fancied Dignity. He should raise in him an ardent Love of his own Country; but, as every other Nation has it's Virtues as well as Vices, he should at the same time avoid the customary Prejudice of allowing them nothing. While he is taught to think and act nobly, he should be informed that the Knowledge, the Care and the Improvement of his Estate, are essential Obligations, and such as cannot be dispensed with. He must be easy of Access, without which Truth will seldom reach his Ear; nor will he be able to distinguish Merit from Demerit; or know how to right the Injured, or punish the Injurer. While he maintains his Dignity, he must be ready to condescend to Inferiors with an humble Deportment where necessary; and be taught to see and feel another's Woe: which

which nothing will more inforce, than convincing him of the Inſtability of all human Grandeur. His Dreſs and Behaviour ſhould be like his Quality, noble; yet perfectly free from Affectation, Vanity and Pride. He muſt be taught to know, that 'tis not for himſelf alone he is to live, but, from the politeſt Manners, a wiſe Conduct, and a benevolent Heart, to diffuſe Pleaſure and Joy to all that know him. Vice and Virtue are to be placed before him in their genuine Light; and the Beauty of the one made a Contraſt to the Deformity of the other. While he is taught to diſtinguiſh Honour from Infamy, Nobility from Meanneſs, the utmoſt Care ſhould be taken to ſhew him how much he would ſink beneath a Man, ſhould he become a Slave to any irrregular Paſſion. He ſhould, for Example ſake, as well as his own, be inſtructed to ſhun every thing that is mean, baſe or vicious; and, in a word, be endowed with all thoſe Virtues that will make him generous, noble, wiſe, and good. Much more might be ſaid on this Occaſion, much more might be added; but as the Great are ſupplied with far abler Helps from other Hands, I will only add on this Head, that if the Admonitions here offered be reduced to Practice, every other Virtue,

Virtue, even the moſt heroic, will become familiar and eaſy.

My next Topic is the Education of a young Lady of the firſt Quality; from which, if the Courſe of my Deſign did not make it neceſſary, I would gladly be excuſed: for as the moſt delicate Flowers require the tendereſt Treatment, ſo the conducting a Woman of Quality thro' the firſt Stages, and uſhering her into the World, is of all others the niceſt Part to act. Still, as Nature and Reaſon are my Guides; by them I hope to be enabled to offer ſome Aid, however ſmall, for the promoting this great End.

As all Parents have a Right to exerciſe a proper Authority, ſo all Children, however high their Rank, ſhould be taught to obey. Great Spirits may think Obedience mean; but Parents are to remember their Children's Happineſs is at ſtake: without Obedience they cannot regulate their Paſſions: and if not regulated, they have but little Chance for Happineſs. Misfortunes with a Coronet, Misfortunes with a Coach and Six, are ſtill Misfortunes; and it is the Buſineſs of every Parent ſo to conduct their Children, that they

they may on their part avoid them, or ſo to fortify them that they may bear them as they ought. But, as it is moſt agreeable to good Senſe, I will conclude that Parents of the higheſt Rank are convinced of this, and have employed the Infant Age of their Children accordingly. What next is to be done? What Education is moſt proper for a young Lady of the firſt Quality? Such ſurely as will diſtinguiſh her from the Crowd; ſuch as will more adorn her Mind, than the Jewels ſhe wears adorn her Perſon.

The Errors committed in the Education of the Children of private Perſons are many, from the Parents educating them above their Rank; ſtill there is one general Excuſe may be made for them, which is, that as the Turns of Fortune are ſometimes very great, they don't know what Occaſion they may have for it. But in Perſons of Quality the Caſe is different; they are already at the Summit, and their Education ſhould ſuit their Rank. As ſoon therefore as the firſt Stage is over, (not to mention what ſhe may have learnt during that Period) a young Lady's Time is to be eſteemed precious: Reading, Writing, Working, Dancing, *French*, *Italian* and Muſic are all to be taught her; and that not ſuperficially, as is too much

much the Cuſtom; not ſo as to puzzle and confound her Underſtanding, but to enlarge and improve it. A certain Author ſays, that there is not a Man in a thouſand who reads well; if ſo, and Men aſſert a Superiority of Knowledge, it will be no unfair Concluſion to ſay, there is not a Woman in two thouſand that does: but I hope this Gentleman's Aſſertion is not true, and then the Concluſion falls of courſe. Still it is very certain, that much more is required to read our Mother-Tongue well, than is commonly imagined; and as that is really graceful, a young Lady ſhould be taught to ſet a great Value on it. To know the Words and their Meaning is not ſufficient; ſhe muſt know the Pointing, the Emphaſis and the Cadence; and ſhe muſt know too, how, in different Parts, and on different Subjects, to modify her Voice, or ſhe will never read well. To read with Energy and Beauty, we ſhould know our Subject; and here the Underſtanding is concerned; this gain'd, we have nothing more to do but to keep cloſe to Nature; for the greateſt Fault committed in reading is, the throwing ourſelves out of Nature. As I have formerly attended the Lectures of ſeveral public Profeſſors, I remember one who committed this Fault of throwing himſelf out of Nature, as I have juſt obſerved;

obſerved; when he read, he put on a Tone of Voice not his own; when he laid down his Paper to explain what he had been reading, he was himſelf again; and thus was he in and out of himſelf, if I may be allowed the Expreſſion, ten times in an Hour. And yet this was a Man of Letters, a Man of Science, a Philoſopher!

The Hand-writing of a young Lady ſhould have an eaſy Elegance in it; a Medium between the *Italian*, which tho' beautiful to ſee is uſually wrote very ſlowly, and that Meanneſs of Hand too common in the Sex. Either of theſe Faults in a Lady's Hand-writing will appear in their true Light, if we conſider that the Cuſtom of writing familiar Epiſtles is one of the moſt important Steps in her Education. Nothing tends more to open the Mind, nothing bids fairer for gaining a Knowledge of the World, next to the ſeeing it, than the giving and receiving one another's Thoughts with Freedom, in a virtuous Intercourſe of friendly Epiſtles. Now an evident Obſtacle to this is the Manner of Writing; if a young Lady's Hand is a fine *Italian*, ſhe hates the Thoughts of writing a Letter, becauſe it will take up ſo much Time; and if it be a bad Hand, ſhe ſays her Scrawl is ſo frightful, ſhe is aſham'd that any body ſhould

ſhould ſee it. But there is another important Reaſon for familiarizing a young Lady to her Pen, which is that of writing correctly. For a fine Lady not to ſpell with exact Propriety, is frightful beyond Expreſſion; but when ſhe has gained that, ſhe poſſeſſes nothing till ſhe writes with Grammar, with Stile, and a ſuitable Turn of Expreſſion. Some, it is true, have by Nature a happier Turn this way than others, and may be ſaid to be born with a Talent for Writing; but tho' this be granted, yet certainly a great deal may be obtained by a due Care of their Education in this Point.

Needle-work is by no means below the Dignity of a Woman of Quality, therefore ſhe ſhould certainly be taught it; for tho' it may not be called a thing ſhe wants, yet the very Change of Employment is often a Pleaſure: beſides that the knowing it is really uſeful. I have ſeen a Woman of Quality at her ſick Lord's Bed-ſide, ſo far from being aſhamed to own ſhe could uſe a Needle, that what things of that kind were wanted during the Courſe of his Illneſs ſhe would let nobody do for him but herſelf; and thus at the ſame time that her Tenderneſs and Concern proved the Sincerity of her Affection, ſhe

ſhe proved that it was not below her Quality to be notable too.

Dancing I mention in courſe, tho' it is needleſs to recommend it here, not only becauſe I have elſewhere done juſtice to this Part of Education, but becauſe all are convinced of it's Importance, as an Accompliſhment which ſtrikes the Beholder's Eye, and gives more or leſs favourable Impreſſions in proportion as we excel in it. But here, to avoid Error, the End of Dancing ſhould be remembered; that it is not ſo much for the ſake of ſhining at a Ball (tho' that too may ſometimes be neceſſary) but to give an eaſy Air and Grace to all the Motions of the Body.

French, in it's Purity and Perfection, is a great Ornament to a Lady's Education; but that is not all: it is not only polite, but highly uſeful; both as ſhe may have frequent Occaſions to ſpeak it, and as there are many good Authors in that Language not yet tranſlated into ours.

Italian and Muſic for a fine Lady ſhould be inſeparable; for tho' it is allowed that our Muſic is vaſtly improved within half a Century paſt, yet the Critics in that way inſiſt,

inſiſt, that Muſic in our Language is incapable of equalling the *Italian*, from the great Number of Conſonants it abounds with.

When a young Lady is advanced thus far, ſhe has certainly done a great deal; but not enough. If ſhe is taught to think that the Great muſt be diſtinguiſhed by their ſuperior Knowledge, ſhe will be animated with a Deſire to acquire it; and not ſit down contented with an inferior Degree of it. Still, as deep Studies and very cloſe Application ſeem by Nature more the Province of Men than Women, ſo I have not urged the Study of the more learned Languages; and will leave this Point to be determined by the Parents and Preceptors. Hiſtory, 'tis true, gives us many Examples of Queens and Ladies of every Rank, who were diſtinguiſhed by their great Learning. Sir *Thomas More*, High Chancellor of *England*, in a Letter to his Daughter, commends her for the Purity and Elegance of her *Latin*; and Madam *Dacier*, Daughter of *Tanaquil Faber*, is well known (beſides her other learned Works) to have tranſlated *Homer* from the *Greek*: but theſe are rare Examples, and ſuch perhaps as ſhould rather be admired than imitated. Nature, I think, points

points out to us, that the Education of a Woman ſhould rather be ſprightly than grave; thus polite Literature ſeems a fitter Study for a Lady than Syllogiſms in Logic. However, that a Lady of Quality may by no means be deficient, ſhe ſhould have, beſides what is already recommended, a Knowledge of Arithmetic, Geography, and Drawing; to which may, with great Propriety, be added, at leaſt a general Acquaintance with Moral and Experimental Philoſophy.

The Sketch here given is not to be conſidered as the Edifice, but the Groundwork, the Foundation alone; the Superſtructure is ſtill to be raiſed. In order thereto a young Lady is to be nicely directed what Language ſhe ſhould ſpeak, and what ſhun: what ought to be her Sentiments, her Deportment, and her Actions. But firſt ſhe ſhould be taught to know that the World has it's Eyes upon her, and that in proportion as ſhe increaſes in Merit, ſo much nearer will ſhe approach to gaining univerſal Admiration and Eſteem. The Reaſonableneſs of this Admonition will appear, if it be conſidered how many Actions we do unworthy ourſelves, only becauſe we are unobſerved, or at leaſt think we are ſo; whereas by keeping our Attention awake,

 and

and conſidering ourſelves as always beheld, we ſhall often bluſh at the very Approach of Vice and Folly, and thus nobly fly from them. Yet this Conſideration of being beheld, tho' in itſelf a Virtue, muſt be carefully inculcated and nicely diſtinguiſhed, leſt it degenerate into a vain Deſire of Applauſe: her Buſineſs is to deſerve Eſteem, but not to look for it. We often ſee a half-bred Player ſtare about him when he has finiſhed his Speech, as if he would beg a Clap, a Smile, or a Nod of Approbation; but we never ſee this in a thorough bred one; he attends to his Part, to his Buſineſs, and nothing elſe; he knows that the beſt way to obtain and ſecure Applauſe, is to deſerve it.

I have ſaid a young Lady ſhould be nicely directed what Books ſhe is to read; indeed it is too nice a Matter for me to determine. Mr. *Addiſon*, in one of his *Spectators*, has, in a burleſque Way, given a Sort of Lady's Library; but I wiſh he had reverſed it, and told them ſeriouſly what Books would grace a Lady's Cloſet, and improve her Mind. For my own Part I think nothing is more difficult, even among Men, than a proper Choice of Books. Wiſdom and Virtue are the great Sciences we are born to learn; Books and Men are the Channels to convey the

the Knowledge of them to us. Now moſt Parents give their Children ſome general Cautions againſt bad Company, but Books are uſually thrown into one undiſtinguiſhed Heap: and tho' ſome perhaps are pointed out to us as good, we are not inſtructed to ſhun the bad; at leaſt they are ſtill open to our View. Witneſs the Swarms of lewd Plays, Poems and Romances, calculated to inflame the Minds, and corrupt the Hearts of the Readers: witneſs the Sophiſtry and falſe Reaſoning of many Writers, who take Pride in ſhewing how ingeniouſly they can deceive: witneſs the Loads of Lumber produced by thoſe, whoſe Talents have been miſtaken by making them Scholars without Genius: and witneſs too the Train of Trifles the preſent Age abounds with. From this clear and rational View of the State of Books, is it not apparent how liable we are to be miſled? True it is, that we may read our whole Lives and learn nothing, nay far worſe than nothing; learn Vice, Error, and Impiety. Since then this Point is of ſuch Conſequence to all, thoſe in exalted Stations of both Sexes ſhould have very able and faithful Guides herein; as from their Influence ſo much Good or Bad muſt flow. Still I muſt beg leave to caution Parents of the higheſt Quality, to imprint on their

Children's Minds and Hearts this Maxim, that all their Studies ſhould tend to make them wiſe and good. Convinced of this, as they advance in Years, their own Judgment and Goodneſs of Heart will, in great meaſure, inſtruct them what to read, and what to avoid.

A young Lady ſhould be taught to ſpeak her Mother-tongue with great Clearneſs, Purity, and Elegance; nothing coarſe, mean, or vulgar ſhould ever drop from her Lips; nothing uncouth, ſtrained, or affected; the one debaſes her Quality, and the other her Underſtanding. Great Ladies may perhaps think that their Greatneſs entitles them to ſay any thing; but where this happens, it is certainly an Error in their Education; or at leaſt it is one in their Practice. There is yet a third Error in Speech which Women of Rank ſhould carefully avoid; an Error conſiſtent with good Senſe, but good Senſe obſcured; that of catching every new-coin'd Word. The *Engliſh* being a living Language, is ſubject to great Variations and Changes; but is now deſervedly eſteemed in high Perfection, as it is certainly ſtronger, more expreſſive, and more copious than heretofore. Still there is Reaſon to fear, that every Change is not an an Amendment; and if it be, a Lady ſhould not be the firſt to adopt it: yet ſo it happens, that a Deſire to appear wiſe and learned ſometimes makes them over-ſhoot themſelves, and thus by aiming too high, they are liable to fall too low.

The Sentiments of a young Lady of Quality ſhould be noble, virtuous, and pure. While ſhe is ſurrounded with external Grandeur, ſhe muſt be taught to ſupport a Dignity of Mind, without which, all her Pomp will be mere Farce and Pageantry, and only tend to inflame her Vanity; ſhe muſt be taught to know, that the nobleſt Sentiments are thoſe which inſpire her with a Love of Virtue; and to be truly great, ſhe muſt condeſcend frequently to revolve in her Mind the Hardſhips, Sorrow, Pain, and Sufferings of the various States beneath her: above all, ſhe muſt be taught to maintain a ſpotleſs Innocence; and live in a conſtant Reſolution to ſuffer any thing, however great, rather than diſgrace her Birth and Quality by any Action unworthy of herſelf.

Her Deportment muſt anſwer her Quality, and be elevated, majeſtic, and noble; ſuch as will ſtrike us with Awe, at the ſame time that we ſee in it a Complacency and

Affability which charms us: ſuch as will not ſuffer even the moſt bold and abandoned to offer the leaſt Indecency or Rudeneſs, at the ſame time that it diſcovers a Heart ſuſceptible of the tendereſt Impreſſions. An eaſy Grace, a lively chearful Air ſhould accompany all ſhe ſays and does; but leſt this ſhould degenerate into Levity, ſhe muſt be inſtructed never to throw off, that great Ornament of the Sex, Modeſty.

Her Actions muſt be ſuch as will contribute to others Happineſs and her own; ſuch as will reflect a Luſtre on herſelf, and attract the Beholders of them to an unfeigned Eſteem for her: Generoſity, Benevolence, Charity, and Humility, accompanied with a Sweetneſs of Temper, ſhould alternately prevail: and if the Diſtreſſes of others ſometimes intrude too far upon her, (which from their great Severity they are apt to do) let her not add Miſery to Miſery, by dropping the Air of her Countenance, or uſe any Bitterneſs of Expreſſion, at the ſame time that ſhe refuſes to relieve.

I have here laboured to ſhew what Education is neceſſary to adorn a Woman of Quality; and will leave it to abler Pens to refine, to correct, and improve it. What I hope

hope and wiſh is, that the Plan here laid down may be deemed natural, practicable, and no way repugnant to good Senſe: nothing ſtoical, wild, or romantic; nothing, in ſhort, (allowing for the Difference of Genius, Health, and other Circumſtances) but what every Woman of Quality may and ought to be. But before I quit this Head, I cannot help remarking how injuriouſly Men often think and ſpeak of the Capacities of the other Sex. If all be true that they urge, (which with ſome is ſtill a Doubt) that the Underſtandings of Women are weaker than thoſe of Men, yet it by no means excuſes our excluding them from Education. Nature indeed ſeems to have formed the Men ſtrong in Mind and Body, that they may labour either with their Underſtandings or their Limbs as Occaſion requires; the Women more tender, for Employments of a gentler Kind: thus each have their ſeveral Provinces: allowing then the Woman to be the weaker Veſſel, that is, neither her Frame nor Faculties ſo ſtrong as the Man's, does it imply that ſhe has no Strength, no Faculties at all? by no Means. Experience ſhews us that the Sex have Wit, Judgment, and a Capacity to learn; how then can we juſtify our too general Neglect of them? But this Error is of great Conſequence even to ourſelves. If our Love for the Sex extends no farther than a groſs Senſe, we miſs our Aim if we expect to find Happineſs; or if we go ſo far as to conſider them uſeful in their domeſtic Capacity, that will not ſecure to us the agreeable: good Senſe, and good Temper, improved more or leſs by Education, ſhould be every Man's View in a Partner for Life; and where ſhall we find them, if their Education be univerſally neglected? A rational Man ſhould chooſe a rational Companion; but how will ſuch be found, if Pains are taken to keep them ignorant? Thus it is evident, that we are injuring ourſelves, and Poſterity too, by this unworthy Treatment of the Sex. Still it ſeems reaſonable, that as Men are to bear the Burden of Buſineſs, they ſhould have ſuperior Education, as well as ſuperior Strength; therefore the only thing here contended for, is, that every Woman ſhould have her Mind improved, her Underſtanding enlarged by ſuch an Education as is beſt ſuited to her Condition in Life: ſuch an one, in ſhort, as will make her laſtingly pleaſing by being both uſeful and agreeable.

The Tranſition from the Nobility to the Gentry is very eaſy; for whatever Difference there may be as to Rank and Title, it is certain

certain that many private Gentlemen have equal Ability to educate their Children as they pleaſe. The Plan then already laid down for the Education of a Nobleman, will in general hold good here. The eldeſt Son, to whom our Laws give the Eſtate, ſhould reſemble our young Nobleman as nearly as may be; not from a vain Deſire of being equal to him, (tho' it is the Way to make him ſo) but from a laudable Ambition of being excell'd by none in Learning and Virtue. Still there will ſometimes be great Difficulty to perſuade young Gentlemen who are thus ſituated to apply themſelves to Study: the early Knowledge they have of the Fortune they are to inherit makes them giddy; and they leave Study to their younger Brothers. What then is to be done? Parents muſt diſcard their outward Fondneſs for their Children, to prove their inward Affection; for how can they be ſaid to love them, while they ſuffer them to live in Ignorance? how can they be ſaid to love Virtue, yet lead their Children into Vice? Parents then muſt do violence to themſelves, they muſt be in earneſt, and conſider that the Education of their Children is an indiſpenſable Obligation. Parents, whatever be their Fortune, muſt exert a due Authority over their Children; muſt ſhew them they are ſerious, and convince them that they will not be trifled with. Dr. *Buſby*, the famous Maſter of *Weſtminſter* School, is ſaid to have made more eminent Scholars than any Man of his Time; the Reaſon is obvious, he was in earneſt; his Scholars durſt not trifle their Time away, or neglect their Studies: whether or no he carried it with ſo nice a Hand as never to err by his Rigour, I will not preſume to determine; but if he did, it is no Matter of Surpriſe, ſince every Man is liable to Error. Whoever conſiders the Depravity of our Nature, how propenſe we are to love Eaſe, and fly from Labour, will be convinced that Boys ſtand in need of every Help to make them diligent. The Authority of the Parents, the Authority of the Maſters, a Senſe of their Duty, and a pleaſing Proſpect of Reward, by the Acquiſition of Knowledge, muſt all combine to enforce their Compliance: and happy will it be for them if they can all produce the deſired Effect. But it will be happier ſtill, if the joint Endeavours of Parents and Teachers can create in Boys a Love for Study, and an ardent Deſire to gain Knowledge: then it is we ſee them go to their Book with as much Alacrity as they go to Dinner; then it is we ſee them ſtriving to excel; and the Knowledge they gain from

from a Love of Learning, makes them ſprightly and happy in themſelves and pleaſing to all that ſee them. Beſides, this Turn of Mind has ſomething in it ſo promiſing, that it is what every thinking Parent would wiſh for, and ſhould earneſtly ſtrive to inculcate; yet he muſt not be ſurpriſed if he does not always find it; and indeed Experience ſhews us, that it is generally neceſſary to govern Children with a tight Rein: for early Indulgence does them incredible Miſchief; in particular, it gives them a Reluctance for Study very hard to be conquered.

When theſe firſt Difficulties are got over, Parents ſhould then apply themſelves to their Children's Underſtanding: the joining Reaſon and Authority together will give double Weight to their Injunctions. Suppoſe then a Father addreſſing his Son, let us ſee what Reaſon will dictate. "Do you "know, my Dear, why you go to School? "why I engage you in Study, and "threaten you ſo ſeverely if you neglect "it? is it for my Sake, think you? or "is it becauſe I take Pleaſure in giving "you Pain? no; it is for your Sake alone "that I thus urge your Obedience. Pro-"vidence has made me the Inſtrument of "your Being; therefore, as your natural

"Guardian,

" Guardian, I am accountable for your
" Education: Learning is the Road to
" Knowledge; Knowledge will lead you
" to Virtue; and Virtue to Happineſs.
" Need you then any other Inducements to
" learn than the Duty you owe to me, and the
" Advantages that will accrue to yourſelf?
" no ſurely; I truſt you will want no other
" Motive." Is not this Method both rational and natural? I think it is undeniably ſo; and that, by theſe eaſy Means, Parents may, in general, promiſe themſelves great Comfort in their Children by guiding them as they ſee proper. Children, if moulded while young, readily yield, like Wax, to the Impreſſion; yet now they are merely paſſive: but when Reaſon gains Strength, when they ſee their Parents acting with a generous Affection for their Good alone, then it is that they are animated with a Love of Duty, and with a Deſire to become every thing that they would have them be.

Every Gentleman of Fortune ſhould certainly give all his Sons the Education of Gentlemen; and therefore the younger Brothers are, in the fundamental Points of Education, to accompany the eldeſt: but tho' this be granted in general, yet there are certain particular Rules to be obſerved; ſome

ſome one Point to be excepted againſt, another to be purſued, with many other things, according as Circumſtances vary, all which require the Parents Attention. I have juſt obſerved, that the Foundation of their Learning ſhould in all the Sons be becoming the Stock they ſpring from: but the eldeſt muſt be graced with every Ornament. He muſt be taught to know, that poſſeſſing a Fortune ſuperior to his Brothers, obliges him to acquire ſuperior Qualifications. He is to conſider himſelf as one deſigned to do Honour to his Family, and to his Country; and be convinced, that if he neglects to cultivate his Mind, he will be a Diſgrace to both.

Parents of this Claſs have, with regard to their younger Sons, two principal things to do: firſt, they are carefully to attend to their Genius, Temper, and Inclinations; and next they are to reſolve on an Employment ſuited to them: this ſettled, they are to purſue their Education accordingly. The three learned Profeſſions, Divinity, Law, and Phyſic, require not only deep Erudition, but require too a Species of Learning proper to each; beſides, as theſe are Employments of the moſt ſerious Nature, and of the moſt weighty Conſequence, not to give them all the Qualifications that human

Wit

Wit is capable of attaining, is surely a grievous Error. Yet are there sometimes other Errors too material to pass unobserved: not those of the Head, but of the Heart. It is in general hoped, that were due Care is taken in forming the Manners, the natural Corruption of the Heart may be corrected; but where that is neglected, or our Endeavours to effect it prove fruitless, which, it is to be feared, they sometimes will, the utmost Care should be taken in the Choice of an Employment for Life. It is a Rule in Life, that where we cannot do any great Good, we should do no Harm; and therefore it should be a Rule with Parents to place their bad Children, if they are so unhappy as to have any, as remote from Mischief as possible. Now to apply this to the Matter in hand, we must observe, that to fill up these important Stations with all their just Requisites, we must not only have a found Education, and a clear Head; but we must also have an upright Heart: that is, we must resolve to banish every finister Aim, and have no Views but those of Justice, Probity, and Honour. To what must we ascribe the general Reproaches thrown with so much Freedom on Professions which have in their Nature the strongest Claim to Respect, as their Foundation is Virtue,

Truth,

Truth, and Juſtice; but to the corrupted Channels the Stream paſſes through? For tho' Men's Judgments frequently err, and falſe Conſtructions are often put on the beſt Actions; yet it is to be feared the Complaints are ſometimes but too juſt. Men ſtrongly tempted by irregular Paſſions, whether Pride, Avarice, Revenge, or others, will naturally incline to gratify them: hence then appears the Neceſſity, in theſe Profeſſions particularly, of well-regulated Hearts: that on one ſide no Injury may be done, and on the other, that no Cenſure may be juſtly incurred.

It is to be preſumed that the younger Sons of every Gentleman's Family (unleſs by any lateral Means they have an independent Fortune) are to engage in ſome Profeſſion or Employment, in order to their Advancement in the World; and it is perfectly right that they ſhould: for by this means they may not only fill up their Time like reaſonable Creatures, but become capable of doing Honour to ſome Profeſſion, be uſeful to Mankind in general, and often raiſe a Fortune equal to their elder Brother. Now beſides the learned Profeſſions; the Sea, the Army, and the Exchange, with many others, needleſs to enumerate, are open for them to engage

engage in; and hence farther appears not only the Neceſſity of conſidering their Fortune, but of attending to their Genius, Temper, and Inclinations.

Nothing is more talked of than the Neceſſity of conſulting our Children's Genius; and I think verily there is nothing ſo little underſtood, or ſo little attended to. I know that many People ſay, there is nothing more eaſy to diſcover than the Genius of Children; but if we view the continual Errors committed in this Point, we ſhall have reaſon to think otherwiſe. What is more evident than a general Partiality of Parents to their Children? and what will naturally be the Conſequence of it? certainly a falſe Eſtimation of their Capacity. However, difficult as I think this Knowledge is to be obtained, either from general Partiality, Want of Penetration, or the natural Inconſtancy of Youth; yet let us not throw aſide our Attention, nor wildly give up our Children to Chance; but rather let us improve the Reaſon Providence has endowed us with, and labour to draw ſuch Concluſions as will moſt conduce to their real Happineſs. To act therefore with Judgment in this weighty Matter, Parents muſt not, becauſe a Boy ſays he will go to Sea, immediately ſend him;

him; nor becauſe another ſays he will be a Soldier, directly buy him a Commiſſion. One perhaps only wants to get away from his Studies, and the other thinks it a fine thing to wear a laced Coat. Youth is naturally giddy, and what they like to-day, they will often diſlike to-morrow; Parents therefore would be grievouſly miſtaken, were they to take every Start of Fancy, every premature Requeſt of their Children for Genius. Still it is certain that they have many Ways of diſcovering what they are capable of, and what they are inclined to; therefore our Prudence and Judgment are to go hand in hand with theſe Diſcoveries. For Inſtance: if we ſee a Boy of intrepid Courage, loving, ſeeking, and enduring Hardſhips, and dwelling with Delight on maritime Affairs, at the ſame time that he has virtuous Diſpoſitions, and both loves and applies to his Books; we need not heſitate to breed him to the Sea. So if we are convinced, that another ſeeks a Commiſſion from true Honour and Courage, and from an ardent Deſire to ſerve his King and Country, we may encourage his laudable Ambition; but if we diſcover that his Motives are thoſe of being conſpicuouſly dreſs'd, of ſauntering and dangling one part of his Time away, and raking and gaming another part; if we ſee too, that his only Fear, is the Fear of having occasion to fight; we should certainly reject his Request, and oblige him to apply another way: nay more, we should convince him how mean a Soul he must have, to seek so inglorious a Life. In like manner, if we see a Boy whose Head is manifestly turned for Business, whose Cast of Temper argues Method in every Action, we may pretty safely conclude we hit his Genius, by making him a Merchant. But there is a capital Mistake Parents frequently commit, that is, their being influenced by some oblique Interest; which often tends to ruin their Children. For Example: the Family has a Living in their Gift, and a Boy must be bred a Clergyman on purpose to fill it: or there is an Uncle a Bishop, therefore the Nephew must be a Bishop too; tho' perhaps he has no more Genius nor Chance for it, than he has of being Emperor of *Morocco*. Thus another, who would have been an Adept in the Mathematics, and have done Honour to the Science, or whose Sprightliness would have made a Figure in polite Literature, is cramp'd with the Study of the Law; not because he likes it, but because it is a Profession that may raise him to be a Judge; perhaps Lord Chancellor: tho' he has as little Chance for either as the

Clerk

Clerk to a Juſtice of Peace. A third, in Nature's ſpite, is made a Phyſician, only becauſe his Parents have ſeen a *Mead*, a *Hulſe*, or a *Wilmot* ſtanding at the Top of the Profeſſion; and therefore conclude their Son will have equal Genius and equal Merit.

Here then it is evident, that Parents are often miſtaken, not only by Inattention to the Genius of their Children, but by over-rating their Parts; by fixing a Profeſſion for them, perhaps as ſoon as they are born, or by blundering them into an Employment which their Education is not equal to. On this laſt Point let me explain myſelf. Suppoſe I have not over-rated a Boy's natural Parts; ſuppoſe too that I have at great Expence kept him at School for ten Years; it does not from hence follow that he is learned: I muſt know if he has applied and improved theſe Years to his real Advantage; that is, whether his Learning is deep or ſuperficial; I muſt know too the Tenor of his Studies, for even of thoſe who are very diligent, all Parts of Learning are not equal Favourites; ſome are ſprightly, ſome grave, ſome in ſhort more ſtriking to them than others: laſtly, I muſt know if the Nature of his Education be adapted to the Employment I am about to engage him in. Without

out Attention and Regard to theſe Circumſtances, it will be impoſſible to keep clear of Error in the Diſpoſal of our Children for Life: and as not only themſelves, but Society too, muſt feel the good or bad Effects of our Choice, it is of the higheſt Conſequence that it be judicious.

But Genius is not the only thing to be conſidered in the fixing our Sons for Life. Mr. *Pope* has a Poſition, * which does not tally with general Obſervation; for according to him there will hardly be a Man in ten thouſand qualify'd for the Station he is in. True Genius is, I think, but rarely to be met with; plain natural good Senſe, carefully improved by Education, will certainly enable the Generality of Men to become Proficients in any ſingle Art or Science: that is, as by well directed Steps they are capable of acquiring great Perfection in one Way, ſo would they have been equally perfect had their Steps been directed another Way. Our Defects in general are not ſo much owing to the Want of Parts, as to the Want of cultivating them; hence appears that amazing Weakneſs in ſome Parents, in ſhewing a Boy as a Prodigy, when

* One Science only will one Genius fit;
So vaſt is Art, ſo narrow human Wit.

every

every other Eye can ſee there is nothing uncommon in him; and hence too appears the Folly of others in neglecting thoſe Improvements ſo eſſentially neceſſary for him.

From what has been here advanced it is pretty evident, that a young Gentleman of moderate Parts well improved, is capable of becoming whatever is pointed out for him, provided he is diligent. But here it is my earneſt Requeſt, that Parents reſolve to make their Children happy; and this they cannot do but by complying in ſome meaſure with their Temper and Inclinations; for it is on this chiefly their Felicity depends. The ſame Boy (as I obſerved before) would become an Adept either in This or That Employment, but it is perhaps one only that will make him happy: therefore it is not always Genius, but Inclination, that requires our Regard.

The ſeeming Reſemblance of Genius and Inclination may make ſome People take them for the ſame thing. Genius is a natural Gift, a Power in the Soul to do what another, without that Genius, cannot do: Inclination is a natural Propenſity to purſue ſome certain Employment, whether we have Genius to execute it or not. We are told of of *Cicero*, that no Man had a ſtronger Inclination to be a Poet than himſelf; yet with all his great Abilities he had not a Genius for it. So in our own Times, we have ſeen Men with the greateſt Itch of Writing produce nothing that argued Genius: ſome fond of Muſic almoſt to Diſtraction, without a Power of acquiring it: and others with a Paſſion for Painting, whoſe Genius amounted to nothing more than to dawb. On the other hand, there are Men poſſeſſed of Genius, but devoid of Inclination; ſo true is it, that however ſimilar they appear, they are really diſtinct in themſelves, ſometimes very near to, at other times very diſtant from, one another. But to return to our Subject. As we have obſerved, that uncommon Genius is not to be always expected, and as we have ſhewn, that general good Capacity ſeldom is wanting; nothing more remains but to learn what Employment will ſuit our Sons Temper and Inclinations, and then compleat their Education accordingly. For ſurely it is wrong to inſiſt on a Boy's applying to the Law, when the Delight of his Soul is the Study of Phyſic and the Knowledge of Nature. Or is it not wrong to pin another down to the Study of Divinity, when Commerce engroſſes his whole Attention; or his dauntleſs Heart burns

burns to traverſe the Ocean? and is it not equally wrong to make a Boy a Merchant, who delights in the Study of the Law? moſt certainly. Theſe therefore are the things we muſt attend to, theſe the general Steps to be taken or avoided; and as none but general Rules can be laid down, the particular Exceptions every Parent's Judgment muſt ſupply.

A young Lady of the ſecond Rank comes next under my Conſideration: but as I have dwelt pretty largely on the Woman of Quality, I have not occaſion to ſay much here. One material Diſtinction to be made in a Lady of this Claſs is, whether ſhe is an only Child, an Heireſs, no Brother in the way to enjoy the Eſtate; or whether ſhe is only a younger Child, and is to ſhare the Fate of her younger Brothers or Siſters. In the firſt Caſe, I would recommend that her Education approach to that of a Woman of Quality, ſince it is highly probable ſhe will become one; at leaſt if her Education, Conduct, and Deportment correſpond with thoſe of ſuperior Rank, ſhe will always be Company for them: but, in the other Caſe, that is, where a Brother ſweeps away the Eſtate, it is certain that her Edncation

need

need not be ſo brilliant, nor ought to be ſo expenſive as in the firſt. Yet let not this damp a young Lady's Spirits; I do not mean to make her leſs happy, nor recommend the leaſt Neglect of her; far from it. A State Coach with three Footmen anſwers no better than a plain Coach with one, for all the Purpoſes of a Coach: and a Diamond Necklace keeps a Lady no warmer than a Necklace of inferior Value. Thus it is with the Education of a Woman of Quality; it is in ſome meaſure merely ornamental, without being eſſential to her Happineſs. Still it is fit it ſhould be ſo. When the Superſcription of a Letter begins with Her Grace, or Right Honourable, when a Coach or Chair appears with a Coronet, 'tis fit that due Deference and due Diſtance be obſerved; and to ſecure this, 'tis fit that her Education have a ſuitable Dignity. But, as I have juſt obſerved, this is not eſſential to her Happineſs: and if thoſe in private Life, and of moderate Fortunes, aim at equalling theſe either in external Appearances, or in too exalted an Education, they are pretty ſure of running into Error; for Happineſs much depends on an Education ſuited to our Condition in Life. Thus while I eſteem it a Misfortune for a Woman of Rank not to appear

appear to the utmoſt Advantage, it ſeems no leſs a Misfortune for a young Lady in private Life vainly to aſpire at equalling her.

Still I warmly urge, that no contemptuous Neglect be ſhewn her; let her be taught as thorough a Knowledge of her Mother-tongue as if ſhe were a Princeſs; let her too write, and dance, and ſpeak *French* to Perfection: Muſic too I recommend, but not to Perfection. Here, I am afraid, my Readers will ſtart, and think that either the Author or the Printer has committed an Error; but a little Patience, and we ſhall, I hope, underſtand one another. When we conſult a Phyſician, or a Council, they take the Fee, and give us their Opinion; which Opinion we may either reject or follow as we pleaſe. When I ſat out in this Undertaking, I declared myſelf not a Lawgiver, but an Adviſer; as ſuch then let me be conſidered. I ſpeak my Mind freely, and like an honeſt Lawyer give my Opinion honeſtly; where the Advice is good, follow it; where erroneous, reject it: thus ſhould all reaſonable People do, taking along with them this Caution, not to condemn raſhly and precipitately, but weigh the Matter well; and neither laviſhly beſtow unjuſt Praiſes, nor unfairly rob Merit of it's Due. This premiſed, I return to my Subject. It is very certain, that a young Lady of this Clafs fhould learn Mufic; it gives her a fprightly pleafing Air; it is a fine Relaxation from more ferious Employments; and it greatly contributes to keep up a Chearfulnefs thro' the whole Family: but I would not have her ambitious to excel; and I think Parents ought not to covet it. To attain Mufic to great Perfection, and to ftudy the *Italian* for that Purpofe, is a Work of great Labour, Time, and Expence; too much by far to gain what at laft amounts to no more than an Amufement. Ladies of great Rank and Fortune have every thing at their Command, therefore fhould aim at Perfection in all they undertake; but thofe in more private Life, have certainly other things to do. They are, by all the Rules of Prudence, to be taught to work: they fhould be taught to know too, that they muft reduce their Theory to Practice. They are to ftoop likewife to domeftic Cares; whereby they will often be enabled to boaft a Happinefs which greater Ladies are Strangers to. But fuppofing that either to gratify herfelf or her Friends fhe engages deeply in the Study of Mufic; Parents are here often cajoled out of their Money, and their Senfes too, by their Daughter's fancied Excellence: and the fame Man that is lavifh in his Praifes to the fond Father's Face, will perhaps in the

very

very next Company ſwear the Girl ſqueaks like a Pig. There is a great deal of Inſincerity, nay the groſſeſt Flattery, attends this kind of Study; and Parents in general have need of better Eyes than common to ſee thro' it. However, not to injure the young Lady's Capacity, I will grant that ſhe really does excel: ſtill I ſay, her Time might have been much better employed in acquiring more uſeful Knowledge: ſuch as is properly ſuited to her Station. There are yet other Inconveniencies attending this Study when a Lady excels, or has the Reputation of it; that of expoſing both her and the Parents to a great deal of gay Company at leaſt, if no worſe; ſuch as tends to diſſipate the Mind, to ſhut out Reflection, and thereby check or prevent the Knowledge of more weighty Obligations: and it often likewiſe expoſes them to a great deal of ill-timed Expence: which, as every Day's Experience ſhews us, frequently does great Harm, but ſeldom any Good.

It is certain that every populous Place, eſpecially a polite City like *London*, ought to have ſome Entertainments of this Kind; and Perſons of Quality and Fortune ſhould give due Encouragement to them, as the Performers make it their Bread, and labour their whole Lives to excel, that they may give them the utmoſt Entertainment in their Power: all this, I ſay, is highly reaſonable, if reaſonably uſed. But will not a Concert, an Opera, or an Oratorio always furniſh this? moſt certainly. Is it worth a young Lady's while, whoſe Fortune perhaps will be but ſcanty, to conſume a great deal of Time and Money, and at laſt fall ſhort of a Stage-performer? by no Means: any more than it is an Honour to a Man of Quality to be called the firſt Fiddle in the Kingdom; or for a Gentleman to boaſt that he can beat his Coachman at driving.

If to the Steps already laid down of a young Lady's Education of this Rank be added Arithmetic, Drawing, and Geography, I think every thing will be done that her Parents need wiſh; and enough, if well improved, to enable her to make a very advantageous Figure. Still ſhe ſhould be taught to know that this is only learning the Road; and ſhe herſelf, with theſe Guides, is to take care not to go wrong: good Company, good Books, and an Attention to her own Actions, are to compleat her. She ſhould not aim at more deep or learned Studies, which probably would only make her affected or pedantic; make her a Pain to herſelf, and diſguſtful to all who converſe with her, particularly her own Sex. Knowledge

ledge does not confift in Words, but in Things; and a Language, merely as a Language, conveys only the Knowledge of Words. If on this Foundation, and with thefe Materials, fhe builds with Care, with Diligence and Judgment, I dare affirm, that thefe alone will furnifh her with every Means of being wife and happy.

I am now to treat of the third Clafs of People, the Men of Trade and Commerce, in which I comprize the Merchants, and all thofe that are ufually diftinguifhed by the Epithets of genteel Trades and good Bufineffes: fuch as require Figure, Credit, Capital, and many other Circumftances to conduct and fupport them: But I confefs there is no fmall Difficulty herein. In fome Countries the Gentry and the Men of Trade are as diftinct People as if each were a Kingdom by itfelf: *England*, a trading Nation, connects more clofely the whole Body of the People; links them, as it were, in one continued Chain, and brings them nearer to a Level. The Man of Trade marries the Daughter of the Gentleman; the Gentleman the Tradefman's Daughter: and again, the Gentleman makes his Son (the younger at leaft) a Man of Trade. Hence arifes the Difficulty of feparating them; nor can it indeed be altogether done. The Reputation and Value of Trade has convinced Gentlemen of the Uſefulneſs and Neceſſity of an Alliance with it; and Trade is greatly indebted to the many and great Fortunes thrown into it from the Produce of Eſtates: thus are they blended and interwoven; and thus are they become reciprocally beneficial. Still, according to the general State of things, regarding the various Ranks in Life, I think we may make one ſenſible Diſtinction without Offence; that is, Gentlemen may be ſaid to ſtoop or condeſcend to Trade, and Trade may be ſaid to aſpire not only to an Alliance with Gentry, but to become Gentry too. Thus while I honour Trade, I would by no means fail to pay a due Reſpect to Gentry; and therefore give them that Preference they are intitled to.

Birth, Education, and Manners, may be ſaid to conſtitute the Gentleman. Birth alone, tho' a Claim, is too poor a one to deſerve that Title; Education adds indeed a Luſtre to Birth; but both together are not ſufficient without Manners: that is, to complete the Gentleman, they ſhould all unite. To adjuſt this Matter fairly, we may without Impropriety urge, that Manners alone will give us a better Claim than Birth and Education together; and why? becauſe theſe are not in our Power to chooſe. For Example:

Example: It is not my Fault that I was not born a Nobleman, nor did I choose my own Education, but my Parents for me; yet when once I have learnt to know Right from Wrong, if I chuse the Right, and labour to maintain it for Virtue's Sake; surely some Degree of Merit is mine: therefore, to use again the good old Bishop of *Winchester's* Motto, MANNERS MAKETH MAN. Still, as I observed before, to perfect the Character, all should combine: and thus if the Man of Trade depends on his Acquisitions only, he will find himsely greatly mistaken. There is a pleasant Story told of King *Charles* II. I think not unapplicable here. An unbred Citizen becoming very rich, made a Friend at Court, who informed the King he desired much to be made a Gentleman; That, says the King, with a Smile, is not perhaps in my Power; but tell him, I'll do better, I'll make him a Knight. Thus at the same time that he conferred an Honour, he ingeniously reproached him, by shewing, that, to make a Gentleman, required something more than even Money or Title. The principal thing then that Men of Trade have to do is, to keep clear of Self-sufficiency; and avoid that Arrogance and Conceit which Money is apt to create. Their frequent Marriages and Intermarriages with well-bred People, are ſome Means to effect this; and educating their Children ſuitably is another. Thus the riſing Generation at leaſt will be improved; and hence appears the Neceſſity of good Education and well-regulated Manners for this Claſs of People: that as they inſenſibly, as it were, become allied to their Betters, they may be taught properly to coincide with them.

Many Reaſons prove the Neceſſity of good Education for People of this Claſs. In a Society of Men, ſuppoſe a Coffee-houſe, we ſee a promiſcuous Croud of Gentlemen and Men of Trade; in an Aſſembly of Women, we ſee mixed with the Gentry, not only the Wife of the Merchant, but that of the Brewer, the Diſtiller, the Druggiſt, and the Draper; and it is highly neceſſary that theſe ſhould have ſuch Education, and their Manners ſo regulated, as will make them fit Company for thoſe. But there are more weighty Reaſons yet. Every Man converſant in Life, muſt have obſerved, not only the many calamitous Falls from high to low; but alſo the frequent Progreſſions from low to high; and where theſe Advancements are the Fruits of honeſt Induſtry, I rejoice with them in their Succeſs. A Citizen grown rich by Trade, reſolves to approach to the Gentry; and his firſt Advance

is

is uſually to the Center of the Town. Here for a while he ſits down, and with ſweet Content enjoys the Fruit of his paſt Labours; but perhaps it is not only for a while; the Heart of Man is reſtleſs, and he burns to taſte the Manners of the Court: thus he flies to St. *James's Square*, *Groſvenor Square*, *Berkley Square*, or one of the ſurrounding Streets; thus the Son gets a Poſt, and the Daughter marries a Lord; and thus the next Generation or two reaches the Summit of Grandeur and Honour. If things are ſo, and daily Experience proves they are, is it not highly neceſſary to ſet out with a good Education? moſt certainly. Still it ſhould be a ſuitable one. A Man of Trade may be qualified to keep his Betters Company, without vainly aſpiring to be like them; for that would be rendering him unfit for the very Trade he is engaged in. Every Man may and ought to look forward; but if every Man anxiouſly dwells on future Greatneſs, and continually dreams of Poſts, Titles, and Palaces, it is the certain Way never to reach them: for tho' the Advancements juſt pointed out are, I think, literally true, yet are the Inſtances but few in compariſon with the whole. Therefore the Buſineſs of Parents is, to give their Children firſt a juſt Senſe of their preſent Station; then to guide their Education, and regulate their Manners accordingly; that done, leave the rest to Providence.

I hope this Reasoning upon the close Connection of Gentry and Trade is clear and express; and proves what I advanced, that they are not to be wholly separated. Whence it appears, that the Education both of Boys and Girls of this Class must in general be like that of the preceding. Still some Judgment, Prudence, and Self-knowledge are necessary to guide Parents herein.

The first wise Caution is, that Parents consider their own Fortune, and the real Prospects before them: it is not enough that a Man be of such or such a Trade, to entitle him to train his Child equal to another of the same Trade; for if this be taken as a Guide, many grievous Errors will be committed. What can be a greater Misfortune than to educate a Boy like a fine Gentleman, and not be able to support it? or to train a Girl with the Expectation of keeping her Coach, and have little or nothing to give her? yet is this often the Case. Another Caution is, not to neglect such an Education as may be at least solidly useful, if they cannot reach the ornamental Part; for as Carving, Gilding, and Painting may at any time be added to adorn a well-

well-proportioned Room, ſo a ſound Education is every Day capable of Improvement: and as the Viciſſitudes of Life are many, it is right that Children ſhould on every proper Occaſion be able to prove the Goodneſs of the Stock they ſpring from. To ſet this Matter in the cleareſt Light, let us ſuppoſe any two of the ſame Buſineſs, no matter what; one has a large Trade and ſmall Family, the other a ſmall Trade and large Family; the Trade being the ſame, our Idea of both the Men will at firſt Sight be alike; but if we come to a nearer View, and thence draw a Compariſon, we ſhall find it very unequal: for tho' a Merchant is ſtill a Merchant, yet while one has great Difficulty to give his Daughter a ſingle thouſand Pound, the other can with Eaſe give his twenty thouſand. Thus, tho' each ſhould educate his Children ſuitable to his Character, yet each ſhould at the ſame conſider his Abilities.

Many other Rules laid down in the preceding Claſs hold equally good in this. The Genius and Frame of Mind are to be attended to; particular Studies are to be appropriated to particular Employments; the Diſpoſition of Soul ſhould be nicely ſearched into, that every thing mean, narrow, or baſe, may be ſubdued by the Principles of a

generous

genererous Education. Moſt young People, even of both Sexes, place their Happineſs in external Appearance, but Girls have naturally the ſtrongeſt Paſſion for Dreſs and Show; now Parents can never make the Education of their Children ſolid, unleſs they reverſe this Diſpoſition, not only by teaching them the Emptineſs of this falſe Happineſs, but by teaching them where to find the true. There is indeed an Appearance ſuitable to every Station, which to neglect, would be ſinking into Meanneſs, and be a Diſreſpect to thoſe we live among; that then ſhould be regarded, but that alone; for all above ſhould be made indifferent to us: Happineſs is in the Mind, and to improve the Mind is the Way to reach it. Nor is Happineſs more among the Great, with all their Grandeur, than among the Little; and if it be, the Fault is in ourſelves; ſince nothing is truer than the Maxim, which ſays, that Happineſs does not conſiſt in enlarging our Poſſeſſions, but in contracting our Deſires. Nothing therefore can be more dangerous in the educating our Children, than cheriſhing in them a Paſſion for Dreſs, eſpecially the raiſing them above their Abilities. Children ſhould be taught to know, that it is not how they look, but what they feel, that deſerves Solicitude: thus too in eſtimating Riches; it is not what we loſe,

but

but what we ſuffer, that merits our Regard; ſince we may ſometimes loſe a great deal, and ſuffer nothing.

Parents, in educating their Children, are to make them pleaſing and uſeful. It is the Opinion of ſeveral ingenious Writers, that the firſt Appearance of a Stranger makes the ſtrongeſt and moſt laſting Impreſſion on us; that as they ſhew to more or leſs Advantage at firſt Sight, ſo do we think more or leſs favourably of them ever after. Now, tho' I do not think this is univerſally true, ſince Experience ſhews us that ſome who ſtrike us at firſt never give us any Pleaſure in their Company afterwards, and others who have nothing very pleaſing in the Beginning of our Acquaintance, improve upon us at every Viſit, and inſenſibly gain our Eſteem; yet it is certain, that our Deportment ſhould always be ſuch as may diſpoſe People to think favourably of us, and never ſuch as can juſtly offend. But here I muſt obſerve, that young People are very apt to proſtitute this Diſpoſition, by uſing it only occaſionally; whereas, to make it a Virtue, it muſt be exerciſed univerſally, and become a ſettled Habit; in ſhort, it muſt flow from the Heart. A young Gentleman is to pay a Viſit to a great Man, to a rich Aunt, or to ſome Perſon of Diſtinction, of whom perhaps

perhaps he has Views or Expectations; what Pains are taken to make a graceful Appearance, how exact is his Deportment, how nice is his Behaviour, and how pleasing his Conversation! The Visit paid, the Mask is thrown off, and he is a very Bear to every one else; nay perhaps even to his Parents, to whom he owes all that he enjoys. So too a young Lady who is to make her Appearance at an Assembly; no Player studies more to get their Part before they come on the Stage, than she to attract her Beholders; but then, like them too, when her Part is over, she often falls below herself. But have Actions like these any Merit in them? can it be a Virtue never to be civil but where we expect to gain by it? ought we not to give every thing it's proper Name, and call such Behaviour Dissimulation and Hypocrisy? most certainly. To obviate then this Error in our Children, and prove the real Use of Education, let Parents be very careful to teach them an universal good Behaviour; not partial, narrow, or confined, but such as will shew itself at all Times, on all Occasions, and to all Degrees of People: and if, as has been observed, the first Impressions generally make for or against us according as we behave, Youth must be taught to consider themselves as continually seen by somebody or other for the

the firft time; and therefore they muft always demean themfelves in fuch manner as to deferve Efteem, if they ever hope to gain it.

The other Point of Education is to make our Children ufeful: therefore nothing that can contribute to it fhould be omitted. A young Man, befides the firft Education beftowed on him, befides the Pains taken by his Parents to engage him in fuch a Station as gives him the faireft Profpect of Happinefs to himfelf, muft be inftructed to employ his Talents to the Benefit of others; and in all things, as far as is confiftent with Prudence, Juftice, and Self-prefervation, promote the Happinefs and Advantage of every one within his Reach. Here let me add, that while our Laws give the Men fuperior Power, a Father fhould be very careful to fix in his Son a tender Regard to the oppofite Sex; not indeed to become their Slaves, or degenerate into Effeminacy; not to be the Dupe of thofe who ftudy to allure; but to have a juft Senfe of their Merit, their Innocence, and their Virtue: and thence refolve never to defpife, infult, or opprefs them, nor ever to impofe a Hardfhip on them too great to bear. A Girl, on the other hand, is to be taught, that a Degree of Subjection is allotted her; but that it

muft

muſt never be baſe, nor ever need be mean. She muſt know too, that the Fruits of her Education are to appear in her Actions; to this End, beſides her Knowledge of Books, the Exerciſe of her Needle, her Pen, and her Figures, ſhe is to underſtand the Management of a Houſe, be acquainted with the various Seaſons of Proviſions, the Price of Markets, Skill in Carving, Demeanour at Table, and, in a Word, the whole Oeconomy of a Family. Laſtly, ſhe muſt know that her Province is to pleaſe, and that every Deviation from it, is thwarting Nature; but that the chearful Exerciſe of thoſe Obligations her Station requires, will beſt ſecure Happineſs to herſelf, and the Eſteem of all who behold her.

I flatter myſelf that what I have here ſaid, will furniſh my Readers of this Claſs with ſome Help to guide them thro' the Difficulties that naturally attend their Duty as Parents. And if to this they add the Exerciſe of their own Judgment, by varying the Rules as they ſee neceſſary, their Children will undoubtedly receive much Improvement; and reflect great Honour on themſelves, who thus aim at the general Good, not only of their own Offspring, but of all Poſterity.

I have

I have here enlarged on the Steps neceſſary to be taken for educating three Claſſes of People, and now proceed to treat of the fourth; which comprehends a very large Part of the Kingdom, but *London* particularly; *viz.* all the inferior Trades, and many others, that, according to the Cuſtom of aſſociating together, we may conſider as forming one Diviſion: Men, very valuable in their Way, and of boundleſs Uſe to Society: tho' by the Wiſdom of Providence born rather to Labour than to Idleneſs; to be obedient to the Laws, than to be the Diſpenſers of them.

I am well aware that Difficulties will occur to me on this Head, and thereby ſometimes break the Order of my Deſign; but, as I have elſewhere obſerved, when Exceptions from general Rules are reaſonable, it is perfectly right to adhere to them. It would be Affectation in me to call myſelf ſuch a Stranger to the World, as not to know the Influence of Money: Mankind is apt to contract a Degree of Eſteem for all who poſſeſs it; and the Poſſeſſor ſeldom fails to ſet a ſufficient Value on himſelf for it. Thus it often happens that Men, whoſe Buſineſs is but mean, grow wealthy, have perhaps an only Child, and think they have a Right to educate it as they pleaſe; for my own

own Part I do not mean expreſsly to oppoſe it, becauſe it may be nipping a promiſing Fruit in the Bud; but Parents of this Claſs ſtand in need of more Knowledge to conduct themſelves herein than commonly ſpeaking they are poſſeſs'd of.

Nothing is more frequent than for Men in different Stations to ruin themſelves by raſhly aſpiring; and he who has Reputation and Credit in one Sphere, is perhaps undone if he moves beyond it. But while we ſee that Money is apt to make Men even of good Underſtanding and good Education giddy, no wonder that thoſe of obſcure Birth, no Education, and a Life of ordinary Employment, ſpent moſtly in ordinary Company, value themſelves for their Poſſeſſions far beyond Deſert. To this is owing that vain Strut, that ſupercilious Air, and Contempt of others, ſo frequent in People of this Claſs; and hence too ariſe thoſe Errors they daily commit, by an oſtentatious Education of their Children; by vainly aſpiring to equal their Betters, and often to ſurpaſs them, at leaſt in Appearance. I had occaſion, ſome Years ago, to make a Viſit to a young Lady of Faſhion and Fortune at one of our Boarding-Schools near Town, where the beſt dreſs'd Girl in the whole Houſe was a Poulterer's Daughter.

Can

Can there be any thing more abſurd than this? yet is there any thing more common? It is a general Obſervation, that ordinary People dreſs their Children finer than People of Faſhion; and why? only becauſe they will ſhew the World they are able to do it, and therefore will not be outdone. Parents are not aware how deſtructive this falſe Pride, this vain miſtaken Fondneſs is to their Children: and the firſt Effect it has on them is, to make them aſhamed of their Parents, thoſe very People who thus miſlead them. Can any thing be more prepoſterous and unnatural? yet is it undeniably true.

There is an unhappy Propenſity among Mankind in general of being aſhamed of their poor and mean Relations, even among the Good; it is a Spark of Pride very hard to be extinguiſhed, yet it may and ought to be done. And conſidering that ſcarcely a Family in the Kingdom is without them, more or leſs, it is Matter of Surpriſe that ſuch Pains ſhould be taken to ſtifle and conceal them: eſpecially too if we reflect how much real Honour it does ourſelves to cheriſh, to countenance, and to eſpouſe them. Still it is true, that there is this Propenſity, this Weakneſs in Men, either from their Nature, or their Education. Shall we then, inſtead

inſtead of keeping under this Pride in ourſelves, lead our Children into it too? ſhall we deck them out ſo far above themſelves only to deſpiſe us? and to make them falſely happy, make ourſelves truly wretched? nothing can be a greater Folly, and nothing requires more the Parents Care to avoid. I remember I once called to ſee a Friend who was an Apothecary; a young Fellow, my Friend's Apprentice, was at Work behind the Counter, and out peep'd a laced Waiſtcoat. (I muſt obſerve it was in thoſe Days when a laced Waiſtcoat ſtood for ſomething, for it has now, I think, loſt all it's Significance.) As the Appearance was unuſual, I enquired who that young Gentleman was; and, to my great Surpriſe, was informed he was the Son of a Coachman; and the Lace he wore was taken off his Father's Livery. Thus what was before no better than the Badge of Dependence, is now turned into an Inſtrument of Contempt and Ridicule. In how many of theſe things do the Weakneſs and Folly of Parents appear? would ſuch a Boy own his Father on the Coach-box? or would he not rather, with an audacious Cock of his Hat, paſs contemptuouſly by him? nothing better could be expected. And yet People who take theſe Steps wonder their Children are

not

not good; wonder they are proud, vain, and untoward, when they themſelves have made them ſo.

Another Effect attending this miſplaced Indulgence, this falſe Education, beſides the making them aſhamed of their Parents and Relations, is, the Influence it has on the Children's future Lives: the Parents, it is true, are often made wretched, but the Children are not happy. Every thing raiſed above itſelf is in a precarious tottering State; the Building, whoſe Foundation is weak, is every Day liable to fall; and the Man who pretends to what he cannot maintain or ſupport, is in perpetual Danger of Ruin. Self-ſufficiency and Money may make his Outſide paſſable; but if he is all Meanneſs, all Ignorance within, he can never procure a Grain of Eſteem, nor ever be ſolidly happy. Children may in time diſcover their Parents Miſtakes and their own Misfortune, but will then perhaps have no Remedy to apply. Happy had it been for them had their Education ſuited their Condition in Life; they would then have laboured with honeſt Chearfulneſs; and by keeping within their proper Sphere, have had their Labours crown'd with Succeſs.

My Readers of this Claſs will, I am afraid,

afraid, be apt to miſtake me, and think I deſign to keep them in a low dependent State; ſuch an one as they call being unhappy; far from it: I would not have undertaken this Treatiſe at all, had I not deſigned the real, the univerſal Good of Mankind. Without Vanity I can ſay it, no one has a more diſintereſted, a more general Love of human Nature than myſelf; thouſands have ſuperior Abilities, but few, perhaps none, have ſuperior good Wiſhes for the Happineſs of Society; and ſhould this very Performance prove a Trifle, the Fault may be in my Head, but it is not in my Heart: my Intention is good, if my Power is weak. Let this then ſerve as an Apology to all my Readers, but let thoſe of this Claſs in particular be perſuaded, that my Deſign is to augment the Happineſs of their Children, not to leſſen it. But then, they muſt reſolve to ſeek Happineſs where it can be found; if they wander into a Maze of Difficulties, and get into a Sphere they are utter Strangers to, they will moſt probably miſs of it; but if they confine themſelves within their own proper Orb, they need not fear to find it. Still there is Reaſon to apprehend, that Men of every Rank, and even among the loweſt, will value themſelves not for what they are, but for what they have; and while People miſtake

miſtake Head for Brains, and Money for Merit, the beſt Advice will often be uſeleſs.

But great as this Folly is, there is a much greater reigning. Money, as I have already obſerved, is extremely apt to intoxicate Mankind; and it's Influence is but too viſible both in high and low Life: but there are thouſands of this Claſs of People who pride themſelves in educating their Children learnedly and expenſively, without the leaſt Pretenſions upon Earth. If a Gentleman upon the Decay can get his Son educated ſuitable to his Birth, Regard to his Family, and Regard to his Education, may obtain him a genteel and profitable Employment: ſo too, if a Man in an inferior Station is convinced he can purchaſe his Son a Place or a Commiſſion ſuitable to his ſuperior Education, there is certainly room to juſtify him, tho' we blame his Vanity; but that People without the leaſt Expectations, that are conſcious they cannot give their Children a Shilling, who have not the Honour of a Family to ſupport, nor a Reputation to maintain, ſhould run theſe ſtrange Lengths, is amazing! The Truth is, Pride and Ignorance are their Guides; they ſcorn to be outdone by their Neighbours, tho' all the while they really don't know what it is they are doing.

It

It is to be presumed that Children while Children, and while educating, are in general Strangers to what may be their future Fortune on the part of their Parents: now if they are taught to think themſelves equal to their Betters, taught to expect mighty things, and at length find nothing, it is, I think, a grievous Calamity on one ſide, and groſs Injuſtice on the other: and yet is this evidently a daily Error.

The ſame things that yield us great Good, are often productice of great Evil. Food, deſigned by the Laws of Nature to preſerve Life and Health, is often made the Inſtrument to deſtroy it. Education, deſigned to lead us to Happineſs, by enlarging and improving our Underſtandings in ſome certain Way, is often made the Inſtrument of our Deſtruction. Hence appears the Neceſſity of a temperate and a judicious Uſe of both; and hence too we ſee, that the Education ſuitable for one, is very unfit for another. But I will now point out what Education appears to me to be generally proper for People of this Claſs; and where ſolid Reaſons make particular Exceptions neceſſary, it is my Advice that Reaſon take place of general Rules.

I will ſuppoſe then that my Readers deſign

ſign with me the real Good of their Children; and neither mean to neglect them, nor to hazard their Ruin by overdoing things. To this End Boys are to be taught Reading, Writing, Arithmetic, and Drawing; to which may be added, a Knowledge of Maps. This Plan, tho' comprized in a few Words, contains all they need, nay all they out to learn. It is uſual in the common Buſineſſes to put Boys Apprentice at about fourteen Years old; now ſuppoſing they begin to learn at ſeven, they have Work enough cut ought for ſeven Years at leaſt; which if well attended to, and their Time be well employed, is capable of turning to great account. I mean not to give offence to any one, but as the Province I am engaged in obliges me to ſpeak my Thoughts, I may offend without Intention: and honeſt Truth, in a Matter of this Importance, is not to be diſguiſed. My Advice then is, that Boys of this Claſs never once attempt to learn *Latin*. What do they want with it? or what uſe can they make of it? will it enable a Man to make better Shoes? will it aſſiſt a Taylor in cutting out a Coat? or will it give a Barber a keener Edge to his Razor? Parents, when they ſend a Boy to School, are often guided by the Maſter what he ſhall learn; he, naturally fond of advancing his Scholar, puts him into *Latin*; and

P thinks

thinks him ſhabby without it. But is it not poſſible that this Gentleman may be a Man of real Merit, a good Grammarian, nay a compleat claſſic Scholar, yet a very bad Judge of Life? moſt certainly. The Boy is thruſt headlong into things he does not want, and neither Parents nor Maſter conſider the End: for tho' it is certain that Parents cannot always tell what their Children will be, yet thoſe of this Claſs are pretty ſure they want not deep Learning.

Of all the Miſtakes committed in Education, none is equal to that of our being thruſt into an Employment for which we are unqualified; eſpecially too if it be one of a ſerious important Nature; now no People on Earth are ſo liable to this as the Claſs we are treating of; for as they are apt to take a Remove beyond themſelves for profound Knowledge, they plunge their Children into a Labyrinth of Difficulties, by engaging them in a Profeſſion or Science far beyond their Power to reach.

I have already urged, that, in the Caſe before us, a learned Education is needleſs and improper; but this is ſaying too little of it, and treating it too mildly: we may go farther, and ſhew that it is even hurtful, by being an Impediment to more uſeful

Know-

Knowledge: and farther ſtill, that it is not always what it is taken for. A Boy in common Life has perhaps about ſeven Years Schooling; the greateſt Part whereof is employed in learning *Latin:* his *Engliſh* is notoriouſly neglected; and Writing and Arithmetic he gains but imperfectly. Now I beg leave to aſk, whether theſe three laſt are not more uſeful to a Boy of this Stamp than *Latin?* and whether it is not a Misfortune to ſpend his Time in gaining what he has no uſe for, and omitting what he wants? But it is an Error in me to call it gaining, when in Reality it is loſing: for after a Boy has been puzling his poor Brains, and been tortured with *Latin* for ſeveral Years, it is ten to one that, comparatively ſpeaking, he knows nothing: that is, nothing radical, and to the Bottom; nothing, in ſhort, but what one Year's Apprenticeſhip will entirely efface. As a Proof that this is no Exaggeration, loſing Learning is not only the Fate of Boys in common Life, who ſeldom get more than a Smattering, but it is confeſſed by every Gentleman, by the deepeſt Scholars, that a long Diſuſe of a Language, or almoſt any Branch of Learning, will in great meaſure wear it out of our Memories: or at leaſt take off that Facility which conſtitutes Perfection. A Relation of mine was ſent to *London* ſome Years ago to be educated fit for Busineſs; a Friend had the Care of him; who, after ſending him to learn Reading, Writing, and Accompts for ſome Time, reſolved to compleat him by putting him for a Year to *Merchant-Taylors* School to learn *Latin.* He did ſo; and that finiſhed, he was put Apprentice to a Cabinet-maker. But what availed his *Latin?* juſt nothing. In three Months time he ſaw'd and planed it all away; he was not a Pin the better for it; but he loſt a Year of precious Time, that might have been very uſefully employed in improving what he had before learn'd, and in applying himſelf to Drawing: a thing abſolutely neceſſary for the very Buſineſs he was put to, and which, to my own Knowledge, he has often lamented the Want of. Now this is not a ſingle Inſtance, an accidental Miſtake, but a general Error; hundreds and thouſands of which might be every day produced: the Conſequences whereof are always more or leſs wrong, and ſometimes very fatal.

I have obſerved that uſeful things are neglected, to run in purſuit of what to them is uſeleſs; that is, they leave a certain Good for a precarious one. But we may reaſon ſtill farther on this Head with great Utility. Mankind is by Nature aſpiring and ambitious; and where Wiſdom and Prudence accompany our Steps herein, they are highly laudable.

laudable. But if, inſtead of theſe, Ignorance and Vanity are our Guides, we are pretty ſure of going wrong. A Man of mean Extraction, and illiterate, takes theſe miſtaken Steps already pointed out, in bringing up his Son; whence a falſe Pride is ſtamped on both, and is ſure to increaſe with the Boy's Learning. The Father's Care is to keep his Boy from diſgracing his Education. "*Jack*, (ſays he) I have be-"ſtowed Learning on you, to make you a "Man; look forward, and I don't fear but "you will make your Fortune." And the Son at the ſame time takes care to think himſelf a better Man than his Father. But let us conduct him on; he is now a Gentleman; becauſe he has, or fancies he has, Learning. He muſt dreſs fine, and keep Company with his Betters; this leads him to Expences he cannot afford; no matter, he is a Gentleman, and muſt appear like one. His Father, after rumaging his Brains for a genteel Employment, at length puts his Son to an Attorney. But that's a dull Life, he likes the Stage better; and after having ſeen Plays by the hundred, he concludes himſelf equal to any thing, and turns Player: where perhaps his higheſt Character is to ſpeak the Prologue in *Hamlet*'s mock Play, or to be the rueful Apothecary in *Romeo and Juliet*. It is too well known what kind of Lives theſe Gentlemen lead; they are moſtly riotous, extravagant, miſerable, and ſhort. Now can it be denied that theſe, and ſuch as theſe, are the fatal Conſequences of this falſe Education? ſurely daily Experience convinces us it cannot. But as I labour for the public Good, ſo I deſire to do the ſtricteſt Juſtice. I will grant then that a Boy of this Stamp, and thus trained, does all on his Part to advance himſelf; that he is prudent, temperate, and virtuous; ſtill he has neither Bottom, Intereſt, nor Friends; it is an hundred, perhaps a thouſand to one, if he arrives at any thing higher than being a Hackney-Writer, an Uſher to a School, or at moſt the ſlaviſh Maſter of an inſignificant one.

Permit me here a ſhort Digreſſion. There are no People in the World, whom I at the ſame time both honour and pity, ſo much as Schoolmaſters and Preceptors; thoſe particularly to whom we owe the moſt eſſential, the moſt ſolid Part of our Education. There is ſomething ſtrangely inconſiſtent in Mankind, or they could not ſee a Maſter inceſſantly ſlave, and toil, and ſweat to inſtruct others, and leave him at laſt without Reward. The Man who is qualified for a Teacher, muſt have laboured many Years in the Purſuit of Knowledge. If we would

wiſh

wish this Man to do Justice to our Sons, we certainly should do Justice to him; that is, we should prove, at the same time that we desire our Children to be made wise, that we have so much Gratitude as to make him happy, by rewarding him as he deserves. From this ungrateful Disposition, or, from a very misplaced Frugality, it often happens that Parents do not seek the best Teachers, but the cheapest; whence not only follow the fatal Consequences attending a bad Education, by a seeming one passing for real, but also that many, who are by no means qualified, undertake the important Task. To return then to my Subject, we cannot doubt but that some of these unqualified Teachers are the Fruits of this false Education we have been speaking of; Men, who tho' unequal to the Task they are engaged in, would have been distinguished as eminent Proficients in another Way, and been very valuable to Society; while in this, the highest Honour they arrive at, is perhaps the holding forth with a dictatorial Air in an Ale-house.

Many are the evil Effects this false Education produces; for thro' the Mistakes of Parents, the Pride of Children shews itself very early, and daily gathers Strength: they soon look down with Scorn and Contempt on the mean Bufinefs of their Father; and foon afpire to what they have not the leaft Chance to reach. But as they have been injudicioufly taught to afpire, we cannot greatly wonder at their miftaken Conduct: hence we fee them fpending their Lives not merely in Trifles, but in Riot, Extravagancies, and Debauchery: averfe to Employment, averfe to Labour; too learned to be induftrious, too ignorant to be wife. But how much happier would they be to know themfelves, and keep within that Self-knowledge! How fweet is that Bread which is earn'd with honeft Induftry! How much happier is the Man that labours at his Loom, than he who with miftaken Pride, defpifing it, is perhaps reduced to be dependent on others! Could then Parents in general of this Rank, but learn Content in their Stations, and keep their Children from foaring beyond their Reach, they would fecure much Comfort to both, befides contributing to the Happinefs of Pofterity.

My Readers will remember that the Scheme of Education for Boys of this Clafs, is Reading, Writing, Arithmetic, Drawing, and a Knowledge of Maps. I will now fhew what Advantage may be made of thefe, and endeavour to prove, that this is fo far rom being a contemptible Education, that when

when attained to Perfection, it is not only uſeful, but very extenſively ſo.

Mr. *Addiſon* ſays, that every Man who reaſons is a Logician, tho' he has never ſtudied the Rules of Logic: ſo too we may ſay, that every Man who ſpeaks grammatically is a Grammarian, tho' he has not been taught Grammar. What I here mean is, that a due Attention to Children, and proper Inſtructions with regard to *Engliſh* only, will enable them to make a very conſiderable Figure both in Reading and Speaking. Nature furniſhes us with the Faculty of Speech, but the Mode of it in great meaſure depends on the Place we are born in, and the Language we are accuſtomed to hear. The Court, and the learned Part of a Nation, certainly ſpeak the pureſt Language; the Vulgar and the Illiterate ſpeak the coarſeſt, and the moſt corrupt: but there are many Degrees between, who may be ſaid to have the Power of chooſing, as they frequently hear both. It is then the Parents Buſineſs to be greatly attentive in this important Point; eſpecially as Experience ſhews us that a great Man can be vulgar, and a little one polite, and the Medium can neglect the Advantages in his Power by adhering to the wrong Side, when with equal Eaſe he may attain the right. I have already cautioned the Great never to fink beneath their Quality; and while they learn to be humble, they muſt carefully avoid being mean. I have alſo recommended to the Gentry to approach as near to the Quality in good Behaviour and polite Language as poſſible: and to thoſe of this Claſs, I ſtrongly urge, that every thing coarſe, vulgar, and incorrect, is not only improper, but highly unbecoming; is not only abuſing the Faculties Providence has furniſhed them with, but is debaſing their Nature. If then the Parents of this Claſs enter upon the Education of their Children with juſt Reflections (which all, more or leſs, are capable of making) the natural Conſequence will be, that they will ſeek ſuch Methods as are moſt conducive to their acquiring a thorough Knowledge of their Mother-tongue.

It may be urged that a compleat Knowledge of the *Engliſh* cannot be acquired without *Latin*; but, with all due Reſpect, I beg leave to diſſent from this: I have ſeen a good *Latin* Scholar greatly deficient in the Knowledge of *Engliſh*, and a very correct *Engliſhman* who did not know a Word of *Latin*. But nice grammatical Rules are not ſtrictly the Province of Boys in common Life, and much may be done without them. A good Maſter will enable them to read in a very expreſſive and ſignificant Manner, at the

the ſame time that he makes them acquainted with his Subject. He will teach them the different Types, why a *Roman*, why an *Italic* Letter is uſed; where the Accent is to laid on different Words, and on the ſame Word in different Senſes; where capital Letters are to be uſed, and why; the different Stops, which we call Pointing, and their Force; the Cadence, or Falling of the Voice, in ending a Sentence, or a Paragraph; and, what is the greateſt Beauty of all, where to lay the Emphaſis or Streſs on every Expreſſion, ſo as to give it it's utmoſt Energy. Farther, he will teach his Scholars to keep cloſe to Nature; and not ſuffer them to borrow a Whine, a Tone of Voice from that almoſt univerſal Deſtroyer of Nature, Affectation. He will ſhew them that the only thing which can be granted in this Caſe, is a certain adjuſting, or rather a little Elevation of the Voice in Reading, above Speaking; and that they come neareſt to true Reading, who would be ſuppoſed to be Speaking, were a blind Man the Hearer. He will ſhew too, that, according to Nature, all Subjects do not require equal Energy in Reading; and conſequently the Voice muſt be modify'd and varied, on ſuitable Occaſions: for as we are ſuſceptible of various Impreſſions; and as Joy, Grief, Anger, and other Paſſions, are differently expreſſed

by

by us without any previous Study, purely from the Force of Nature, ſo a good Maſter will ſhew, that a Prayer, a Hiſtory, and a Poem, have each ſomething different in their Nature; and that to give them their due Propriety, Force, and Beauty, each muſt be read in a different way. Beſides theſe, the Maſter will ſhew his Scholars, that in order to ſpeak to Perfection they muſt obſerve firſt, what Language their Betters ſpeak, and by comparing it with that of the Vulgar, they will be enabled to diſtinguiſh, not only good from bad, but Propriety from Impropriety; whence they will inſenſibly learn, Gender, Number, and Caſe; Perſon, Mood, and Tenſe, with many other things relating to Grammar, without once ſuppoſing that they are acquiring them. Secondly, he will direct them in the Choice of ſuch Books as will give a double Reliſh to Reading, by the Goodneſs of the Language they are wrote in. And laſtly, he will recommend their ſeeking Opportunities of hearing their Betters read, that they may compleat by Imitation, what Inſtruction has laid the Foundation of.

But to give all the Satisfaction in my Power, I beg leave to obſerve, that as Grammar (if I may be allow'd the Expreſſion) is the Soul of every Language, it may, in in essential Matters, be taught in *English* as well as in *Latin:* it is true, that, in compound Words, and some of the Derivations, both *Latin* and *Greek* are necessary, and indeed many other Languages; but they are only so for Gentlemen and professed Scholars; and tho' a mere *English* Scholar cannot give all the Derivations of Words, yet he can give all the Meanings, and all, or most of their Rules; and thereby be enabled to acquire a considerable Degree of Perfection, a pretty thorough Knowledge of his own Language; and sometimes a Knowledge superior to those who in other respects are superior Scholars. Should it still be urged, that if Boys learn *Latin*, a Knowledge of *English* will be a necessary Consequence, and that Grammar in *Latin* is Grammar in *English*; I am ready to grant it: but the Point here maintained is, that what is called a learned Education is unnecessary and often hurtful to Boys of this Class, nor have they Time to acquire it. Besides, there are always Difficulties in referring or applying grammatical Niceties from one Language to another; Difficulties which are not within the Province of every one to get over. If therefore Boys of this Class, instead of engaging in *Latin*, which, as has been shewn, they have not Time to acquire, nor in general have any use for it

if

if they did, would apply to the Study of *English* only, and make the moſt of that, they may improve to a great Degree; vaſtly more than is uſually done, becauſe prevented by an injudicious Application to the *Latin*.

Thus much have I ſaid, in ſome meaſure to do Honour to the Language of my own Country; but chiefly with a View to remove the Errors too generally run into by inferior People, partly from their Vanity, and partly from their being Strangers to the many and great Advantages which this Branch of Education only is capable of affording. I know that innocent well-meaning People are often miſled in educating their Children; and have heard many ſay, that a Boy muſt learn *Latin* to enable him to ſpell *Engliſh*; but this is a vulgar Error, and henceforward, I hope, will be removed. But yet farther to prove the Uſefulneſs of our Language in the real Concerns of Life, we may add, that by this alone may be learnt, from thoſe whoſe Province it is to teach, every Duty, every Obligation we owe to God and Man; by this we are enabled to read the ſacred Writings; by this we can become acquainted not only with the Hiſtory of all *Europe*, both ancient and modern, but of the whole World; and particularly

ticularly with the Hiſtory of our own Country: by this we are furniſhed with Books containing Helps in Building, Planting, Gardening, and many other things of great Uſe to Mankind; and by this, in a word, we are furniſhed with vaſt Abundance of both Inſtruction and Delight; not only from the excellent Tranſlations from *Latin*, *Greek*, *Spaniſh*, *Italian*, *French*, &c. but from the original Writings of many of our own Countrymen: Men, whoſe Genuiſes were perhaps inferior to none. Here, without Flouriſh, Parade, or Exaggeration, my Readers will ſee how noble an Uſe may be made of our Mother-tongue; how much Pleaſure it will yield us, how much Knowledge it will convey to us; and hence, I hope, Parents will be induced to conſider it in the Light it deſerves.

Boys are next to engage in Writing; and I earneſtly recommend that it be cloſely attended to, and conſidered as a Matter of great Importance. The preſent Method of teaching, and the Kind of Hand now uſually wrote in Buſineſs is, I think, admirable; the Merchants of *London*, and ſome of our public Offices, ſhew great Perfection in this Way; and I would recommend that every Boy both learn and practiſe a mercantile Hand, as it is at the ſame time uſeful and beautiful.

beautiful. Every Man who is acquainted with Life must daily see the too general Defects of Hand-writing. If a Bricklayer, or any other Workman, brings in a Bill, what a pitiful Figure it makes; nay, it is sometimes so very bad, that none but the Writer himself can read it; and where we see one wrote out in a masterly Way, it is ten to one but he has, at considerable Expence, employed somebody to do it for him. Now this must surely be considered as a grievous Misfortune, both as it is an Inconvenience, and a Loss; and which ought carefully to be prevented in the rising Generation. Besides, if we reflect on the unforeseen Advantages which many meet with who are fine Penmen, we shall be convinced how necessary it is to excel in this Art.

We come now to Arithmetic, which includes a large Field of Knowledge. The Use of Figures is so universally known and allowed, that it seems needless to urge any thing in their Favour. Men of all Degrees want their Aid; they are the first Introduction to the Mathematics; and the Knowledge of them is more or less necessary from the Prince to the Peasant. If a Man fails in *Holland*, they immediately say, he has not kept good Accounts; in Truth People of almost every Rank stand in need of their

Help;

Help; and their Ufe and Power thoroughly known and attended to, would preferve thoufands from Ruin. Parents then cannot do too much to inftruct their Children in this important Branch of Knowledge; efpecially if they confider on one hand the Confufion and Perplexity which attends the Ignorance of it, and on the other hand the many furprifing Turns for the Advancement of their Fortune, when poffeffed of the Knowledge of it. All young People, as I have before recommended, fhould be taught Method, and nothing more likely to initiate them in it than a mafterly Knowledge of Figures. Befides, Debtor and Creditor, Lofs and Gain, are by no means confined to the Merchant; every Man, however low his Trade, or however narrow his Dealings, while he does trade or deal, fhould underftand what he is about: and he has no other Way than this of attaining that neceffary Knowledge. I am very fenfible, that fome Men, even in Trade, have got thro' the World, and made good Acquifitions, without any confiderable Degree of this Kind of Knowledge; but we may truly fay of fuch, that Fortune ftood fo very near them, that they ftumbled upon her: tho', for one who has thus fucceeded, a thoufand have mifcarried. But my Aim is, to have the rifing Generation fo educated, that either

Misfortune

Misfortunes may be prevented, or, if they do come, that their own Conduct may be irreproachable: and, I say again, no way more likely to effect this, than knowing thoroughly and attending closely to Figures. But farther, this and the foregoing Branch of Knowledge are strong Recommendations in various Stations of Life: many, even from nothing, have by these Qualifications become great Merchants; our *East-India* and other Companies frequently want Boys who write and account in a masterly Way; and when young People set out in the World and act for themselves, the Knowledge of their Affairs, from their Skill in Figures, is often a Restraint upon them, and a Curb to their Passions; by keeping them from what they see they cannot afford.

I shall now speak of that important, tho' much neglected Branch of Knowledge, Drawing. It is matter of Surprise to me that a thing so obviously useful, and in many Respects so indispensably necessary, should be so generally disregarded. Young Gentlemen at an Academy indeed sometimes learn a little Drawing; but neither so often, nor so compleatly as they ought: but it is not of those I now mean to speak, but of that large Body of Youth comprehended in the fourth Class of People. As Parents cannot know certainly

tainly what their Children will be, it is fit that, according to their Station, they ſhould be ſo educated, as to be prepared for whatever may ſuit their Circumſtances, their Capacity, and their Inclinations: to this End, beſides Reading, Writing, and Arithmetic, I earneſtly recommend Drawing. To prove it's Uſe, let us firſt view the various Branches of Building; where we ſhall immediately ſee the Neceſſity of underſtanding it. It is my Advice to all Parents, without Exception, that they implant in their Children an ardent Deſire to excel; not to engage them in things they are unequal to, not to fill their Heads with Chimeras of fancied Power and Abilities, but that they labour with unwearied Induſtry to become perfect in their Way, be their Profeſſion, Trade, or Buſineſs what it will. Thus, if a Boy is to be a Bricklayer, a Carpenter, a Smith, or any other Trade relating to Building, it is right that he ſhould be animated with a Deſire to become perfect, and not ſit down contented with a ſcanty, ſuperficial Knowledge of his Buſineſs: and, to attain this, Drawing ſhould be made as familiar to him as Writing; which would greatly tend to his Advancement in the World: for how often does it happen that a Gentleman wants his own Conceptions and Deſigns explained and improved; which are eaſily

done

done by a mafterly Workman, but are entangled and made worfe by a Blunderer. Drawing fhews us the Difference between Beauty and Deformity; as Features, Mein, Afpect, Stature, and the Power of Light and Shade. It teaches us the Ufe of Lines, Angles, Squares, and Circles; it teaches us the Rules of Proportion, what Bafe is proper for an Edifice of different Dimenfions; what conftitues a regular, what an irregular Building; it diftinguifhes true Tafte from falfe; it affifts our Fancy, and enlivens our Imagination; it is the Foundation of Architecture, and therefore neceffary for every Branch of Building: for tho' there are general Rules and Principles in each Order of Building, yet is there great Latitude for what we call Fancy, Tafte, and Judgment: and thus the whole Beauty and Propriety of an Edifice may be faid to depend on the artful blending of the feveral Orders into one perfect Superftructure.

Thus much for the Ufefulnefs of Drawing in Building; but I fhould injure this Art if I ftop'd here, for it is ftill far more extenfive. It is not enough that a Gentleman builds himfelf a Houfe, it muft be furnifh'd too; and if he be a Man of Fortune and Tafte, he will not be contented with what is merely ufeful, but will add the ornamental

mental likewiſe: hence appears the Neceſſity of the Artificers in this Way learning to draw in order to excel. If an Upholſterer be ſent for, it is an Advantage to him not only to give the proper Dimenſions of Furniture, but to diſplay the ſeveral Ornaments and Fancies in uſe, and even ſtrike out new Deſigns of his own; that he may convince People he is a Maſter in his Way: he cannot ſhew a Piece of Damaſk or printed Linen, but the Draughtſman appears in it; and it is right that he ſhould be equally knowing in his own Buſineſs.

But if we take a more general Survey of things, in order to give us a true and ſolid Eſtimation of real Life, we ſhall find this Art of ſurpriſing Uſe. How many Trades are there ſubſervient to the Arts and Sciences? all thoſe who make Maps, Charts, and Globes; all thoſe who make mathematical Inſtruments, and the vaſt Apparatus for the different Parts of Experimental Philoſophy; ſo too Engravers, Sculptors, Painters, and Anatomiſts; all theſe, with many others, needleſs to enumerate, ſtand in need of Drawing: So vaſt is it's Uſe, and ſo neceſſary is the Knowledge of it!

The laſt Step of Education for Boys of this Claſs is Geography, or the Knowledge

of

of Maps. Geography makes us acquainted with the whole Surface of the Earth; the whole terraqueous Globe: it is first divided into Quarters, viz. *Europe*, *Asia*, *Africa*, and *America*; again, these Quarters are subdivided, so as to make us acquainted with particular Provinces, Kingdoms, States, and Empires: hence it is easy to see the Pleasure and Use that arises from this Knowledge. Men of every Rank are liable to leave their native Country; and indeed it is often the only Way to their Advancement. What a Pleasure then must it be to be acquainted with a Road we never saw? to travel in a Country without Pain from our Fore-knowledge of it? which is really the Case with an Adept in Geography. But supposing our Travels exceed not the Bounds of our own Country; it is a Subject of great Delight to be thoroughly acquainted with that. Or farther yet: supposing we do not travel at all; Geography has still it's Use: it assists us in the Knowledge of History, and thereby adds Instruction and Pleasure to our Reading: in fine, it makes us acquainted with the whole World, without going out of our Closets.

My Readers are, I hope, by this time convinced, how advantageous these Steps of Education are for many of the Purposes of Life;

Life; nay they are ſuch as ſome in better Stations are in great meaſure Strangers to, tho' they may be poſſeſſed of Qualifications otherwiſe uſeful. If then to this be added virtuous Diſpoſitions, a docile Mind, a becoming Behaviour, and, in a word, that genuine Manners recommended to all, I think Parents in general of this Claſs may promiſe themſelves much more Comfort in their Children than they uſually find.

Girls too of this Claſs are capable of being very valuable; but again I muſt caution Parents to be aware of thoſe Banes of Happineſs, Idleneſs, Pride, and Vanity. Idleneſs is juſtly called the Root of all Evil; and Pride and Vanity are empty nothings: or if they can be ſaid to produce any thing, it is Evil. Girls of this Claſs have many things within their Reach, and if well attended to, may attain them. They may read and write to great Advantage; and learn ſo much of Accompts as will be neceſſary for conducting their Concerns, and underſtanding thoſe Affairs they may in future Life be engaged in. They may and ought to work to Perfection, but principally the uſeful Parts: and tho' the ornamental is highly commendable, yet it muſt not here be encouraged to the Prejudice or Neglect of the uſeful. When this Foundation is ſolidly laid, let them be carefully inſtructed in the Management of a Houſe, according to what has already been obſerved in the foregoing Claſs; from whence they will receive ſuch a Fund of uſeful Knowledge, as when joined with good Demeanour, will procure them not only the Eſteem of their Equals, but that of their Superiors. Let Parents farther inſpire them with Diſpoſitions daily to improve their Minds; to maintain with firmeſt Reſolution the niceſt Innocence, even amidſt the rudeſt Attacks, ſhould they occur to them; and laſtly, to ſupport themſelves with a chearful Mind in that State which is allotted them. In fact, Happineſs is much more within their Reach than they commonly imagine; but if they neglect to conſider the Advantages they enjoy beyond thouſands who are beneath them, and anxiouſly dwell on the Splendor of thoſe above them, it is the certain way never to find it.

Notwithſtanding what has been ſaid on this Claſs, Allowances are ſtill to be made as Circumſtances vary; and if the Plan be in general practicable, it is all that can be expected. Education is in ſome meaſure accidental; and it is right to embrace thoſe Advantages which Accident offers, provided they do not interfere with more uſeful Knowledge, for then they are no Advantages.

For

For Example: nobody ſhould neglect their Mother-tongue; yet if they are ſo ſituated that they can add *French* to it, they ought by all means to do ſo. In the preceding Claſſes *French* is conſidered as a neceſſary Part of Education chiefly from it's Politeneſs, and the Advantage of reading *French* Authors; but according to the preſent Age it is far more uſeful. *French* is now ſo univerſal, that a Man who ſpeaks it can do Buſineſs with whatever Foreigner comes in his Way; or ſhould he go abroad, he can tranſact his Affairs in any Country, or on any Exchange in *Europe*. But it is ſtill farther neceſſary. *Moliere*, in one of his Comedies, introduces a Converſation, where a Servant is accuſed of flattering his Maſter: "What can I do? "replies he: I am to pleaſe, I am to ſecure "my Service by keeping in his good "Graces, and I have no other way of do-"ing it: therefore, continues he, it is not "the Fault of me who flatter, but of him "who will be flattered." So in taking a View of Life we may ſometimes obſerve, that to ſecure the Intereſt and Favour of the Great, the Taylor, the Milliner, the Shoemaker, and many others, are expected to introduce their Modes under a *French* Tongue. But to do juſtice to the Wiſdom of our Nation, this is far from being general; therefore a general and close Application to the *French* for the fourth Class does not seem either necessary or practicable; because to some it would be useless, in others it would be forgot again, and by many it would never be attained.

Another Part of Education which is oftentimes merely accidental, is Music. If a Man plays on any Instrument, it will be delightful to him to employ his Son's leisure Time in giving him something of so agreeable an Accomplishment; or if he can improve his Daughter's Ear or Voice, by giving her a pleasing Manner in Singing, she should not be deprived of it; for these things make young People sprightly in themselves, and pleasing to others. But then Care must be taken that they stop here: they must not engage in an expensive and laborious Study of Music, unless it is to be their Trade; nor must they be attached to it so as to neglect other Obligations, or so as to engage them in irregular Company: and above all, great Care must be taken that they be not tainted by that Torrent of Corruption, bad Songs.

There is indeed a Step of Education for this Class, as well as all the preceding, which

which I think of Importance, could it be obtained without the uſual Inconveniencies attending it; that is, Dancing. I conſider Dancing as conducive to Health; I conſider it as ſometimes a Means of preventing Deformity; and where there is no danger of that, all muſt ſee that it is the great Means of making young People of both Sexes ſtand, and walk, and ſit, and even look and ſpeak to advantage. Mr. *Locke*, ſpeaking of a docile Mind, and good Diſpoſitions, as ſuperior to every other Conſideration, ſays, "Parents ſurely muſt "have a ſtrange Affection for *Latin* and "*Greek*, who will prefer them to their Sons "Virtue." So too I may ſay of Dancing; if we cannot get the Good without the Bad, it is better to let it alone. Firſt, it is, for a great many People, too expenſive; nothing indeed to thoſe of Fortune, and in great Buſineſs; but to others, more ſo than is convenient. Next, it is apt to inflame young People's Vanity, as well as increaſe the Expence of their Apparel. A Boy who learns to Dance is diſſatisfied unleſs he has Pumps, white Stockings, laced Hat, and many other things not neceſſary to his Station; and a Girl rejoices when the dancing Days come, only becauſe ſhe is to have her Silk Coat on. A third Objection is, the Danger of their contracting a Passion for Dancing; for tho' young People may sometimes very innocently divert themselves with an Evening Ball or a Country Dance, yet an eager Desire for these Engagements, especially to those of lower Rank, and to those who live in *London*, are extremely dangerous. Still, as this Qualification seems really necessary, if the Expence of the Master can be submitted to, the other Difficulties may, I think, be got over. But here the Manners are concerned: Children must obey, and wear without a Struggle, and without a Blush, such Apparel as their Parents judge fit for them. If besides this, they are made sensible that every Step in their Education is taken purely for their Good, and are carefully instructed never to abuse by an inordinate Attachment what is bestowed on them only for Use; if Parents I say do this, they may in general hope that all their Children learn will turn to good account.

The Province I am engaged in, and the tender Regard I pay to all human Nature, demands that I speak of a fifth Class of People, usually term'd the Peasantry: tho' I think the principal thing to be done here, is to admonish those in higher Spheres to behave

have with Juſtice and Humanity to them, rather than to addreſs themſelves. If we ſpeak of Education, here it will naturally carry our Ideas to the Spade, the Plough, or the Team; and which may without Impropriety be called Education to them. It is a true Saying, that there is a right way and a wrong in doing every thing; if ſo, it is an uſeful Part of Education to inſtruct them how to till the Earth with greateſt Eaſe to themſelves, and with greateſt Profit to thoſe who employ them. As early and conſtant Labour is the Province of this Claſs, there is but a ſmall Share either of Time or Abilities for Inſtruction; ſtill as they are by Nature ſuſceptible of it, thoſe who have Power cannot employ it better than by beſtowing it; ſo far at leaſt as may open their Minds to diſtinguiſh Truth from Falſhood, Right from Wrong, Innocence from Guilt. If to this were added, at leaſt the Power of reading their Mother-tongue, it would at times be an Entertainment and a Conſolation to them; and it would remove, in ſome Degree, that total Darkneſs and Ignorance they muſt otherwiſe remain in.

But here, for the Sake of Inſtruction, I muſt depart from the ſtrict Propriety of the Word *Peaſant*, to touch on another Species of Rustics; that is, those of the lowest Class of People, in *London* particularly. These People possess indeed the Ignorance of the Peasants, but they seldom equal them in Innocence. Many are abandoned to every Vice; many indeed are honest and industrious; but even among those who are themselves good, their Children, thro' an early false Fondness, or the Corruption of others, are usually ignorant, untoward, and vicious. Whence we daily see and hear in the open Streets such things as are Insults on Mankind; such as must shock the Ears, and make the Heart tremble; and such as cannot but be a Reflection on any civilized Nation. We say, it is easier to obey than govern; and, in this Case, it is perhaps easier to propose a Remedy, than to put it in Execution. But to cure an Evil among the Little, we must address ourselves to the Great; for if they have either their Example or Countenance, all Attempts to remedy it are fruitless. Next we must turn our Eyes on those in Power, as Magistrates, and Men in Office; if these exercise their Authority with Justice and Fidelity, much may be done: but if they not only neglect this, but give ill Example too, little is to be expected. Thirdly, the Children of these People are to have some Degree of Education;

tion; the Boys, Reading, Writing, and the first Rules in Arithmetic at least; which, if carefully taught them, will qualify them for many useful Employments. The Girls should at least read and work at their Needle. But all this, tho' indispensably necessary, is too weak to effect the Purpose designed. The Perverseness of the Will, the Unruliness of the Head, and the Corruption of the Heart, are still to be conquered. Manners alone then is the effectual Remedy: and as, to cure a Disease, we must strike at the Root of it; so, to rectify the Morals and Misbehaviour of the Corrupt, we must, on solid Principles of Reason and Reflection, awaken the Mind, and regulate the Heart.

CONCLUSION.

A Citizen of *Athens* advifing with *Xenophon* about whither he fhould fend his Son for Education, It is my Counfel, anfwered *Xenophon*, that you fend him to *Sparta*. To *Sparta!* fays the *Athenian*; is rude and uncultivated *Sparta* then preferable to *Athens*, the Seat of Arts and Sciences? Yes, replies the Sage: at *Sparta* he will learn a Science worth all the reft, he will learn to obey. According to this Philofopher then, Obedience alone is a Science productive of every ufeful Knowledge; whereas, without it, all other human Knowledges are often ufelefs, if not, in general, dangerous Acquifitions.

Certain it is, that much may be hoped from fetting out right, and every thing is to be feared from a wrong Beginning. Parents therefore who aim at making their Children wife, fhould aim at previoufly making them good. That is, (to recapitulate the chief of what has been faid) they muft make their Wills

Wills pliant and tractable, by teaching them an early, very early Obedience: next, they should mould their Hearts, imprint on them a Love of Truth, Honour, Justice, and every other Virtue: lastly, they should form their Minds and Manners, by shewing them the several Duties of their Station, and how to fulfil them.

The first Duties of Children are in great measure mechanical: an obedient Child makes a Bow, comes and goes, speaks, or is silent, just as he is bid, before he knows any other Reason for so doing than that he is bid: the Dawn of Reason shews him general Duties; that is, that he owes to his Parents and Guides Obedience, Respect, and Love: when his Mind is farther opened, and his Judgment has gained Strength, he sees (if led by faithful Teachers) that he is born for an important, nobly important Purpose; and tho' many particular Obligations, which he was before a Stranger to, present themselves to his View, yet is he convinced that they are nothing but what, under Reason's Sway, he is capable of answering. Farther, he sees that the Exercise of all moral Obligations are rendered light by being reciprocal; and from a Sense that his own Support, Comfort, and Happiness requires

requires the Aid of others, he chearfully and willingly labours for others. Laſtly, he ſees, that tho' irregular Paſſions ſometimes raiſe Tumults in the Soul, and ſtruggle for the Maſtery, yet from the Happineſs of a well-tempered Heart, the conſtant Exerciſe of Reaſon, and the Reflection he muſt needs make on the daily Inſtances before him of Vice puniſhed and of Virtue rewarded, he may not only be enabled to give Virtue the Aſcendant, but to give it on the pureſt Motive; that is, for the Love of Virtue. All this, I ſay, unleſs Children are by Nature untractable, or are overpowered by the Torrent of corrupt Example, will generally be the Effect of well-regulated Manners: and, poſſeſſed of all this, who can doubt but that they will then be wiſe? or who can think that while thus much is wanting they ever can be wiſe?

Mankind, as has been obſerved before, naturally deſire their Children's Proſperity and Happineſs; but if they ſeek it in any other Road than this, they muſt not wonder if they miſs of it: rather may they wonder in good earneſt, if they ever find it. Still is the ultimate Point untouched: for, beſides that our Paſſions are to be regulated, and our Actions to be innocent in themſelves,

ſelves, and valuable to others; to make them perfect, they are farther to be animated by a right Intention: for, ſays a learned and ingenious Author, "the Intention is "the Pulſe of the Soul." Many Actions, in themſelves indifferent, are rendered hurtful by an Error in the Intention; and even thoſe which ſeem calculated by Nature to produce the moſt ſignal Advantages to others, as well as to us, are often, for want of being properly directed to their right End, both fruitleſs to thoſe they were deſigned to benefit, and even detrimental to ourſelves. Here then we are to know, that moral Duties are of divine Origin; and if Nature ſhews us the firſt Laws of Right and Wrong, the Author of Nature implanted them in us. But our Obligations to the GREAT CREATOR of us all will irreſiſtably appear, if we duly ſurvey ourſelves and every thing around us; for as thence we ſhall ſee that from Him alone we receive all things, ſo thence ſhall we be convinced that to Him alone all ſhould be referred. Thus it is evident, that to fill up the Meaſure of our Duty, three things are neceſſary: firſt, we are to be carefully informed what is Right, and what is Wrong; ſecondly, we are inviolably to adhere to the one, and avoid the other; and, thirdly, the Right we

do

do muſt be done from Principle; which can no otherwiſe appear in us than by honouring and ſerving the Author of our Being, and of all the Bleſſings we enjoy: theſe naturally lead us to believe in him, to hope in him, and to love him; and theſe are Acts which conſtitute Religion. But here, with all due Reverence, I drop my Pen; leaving the Conſideration of our Duties in a religious Light to thoſe whoſe Province it is to point out, explain and enforce them: to thoſe, in a word, to whom the Office is given from above.

FINIS.

Titles in This Series

MARRIAGE

The General Nature of Marriage

1. Thomas Salmon. A Critical Essay Concerning Marriage. London, 1724.
2. Letters on Love, Marriage, and Adultery; Addressed to the Right Honorable the Earl of Exeter. London, 1789.

The Forms of Marriage, Legal and Illegal

3. Henry Swinburne. A Treatise of Spousals, or Matrimonial Contracts. London, 1686.
4. Simon Dugard. The Marriages of Cousin Germans, Vindicated from the Censures of Unlawfullnesse, and Inexpediency. Oxford, 1673.
   with
   John Quick. A Serious Inquiry into that Weighty Case of Conscience, Whether a Man may Lawfully Marry his Deceased Wife's Sister. London, 1703.
   with
   James Johnstoun. A Juridical Dissertation Concerning the Scripture Doctrine of Marriage Contracts, and the Marriages of Cousin-Germans. London, 1734.
   with
   John Fry. The Case of Marriages between Near Kindred. London, 1756.
   with
   John Alleyne. The Legal Degrees of Marriage Stated and Considered, in a Series of Letters to a Friend. London, 1775.
5. Henry Gally. Some Considerations upon Clandestine Marriages. London, 1750.

with
A Letter to the Public: Containing the Substance of What hath been Offered in the Late Debates upon the Subject of the Act of Parliament, for the better Preventing of Clandestine Marriages. London, 1753.
with
Henry Stebbing. An Enquiry into the Force and Operation of the Annulling Clauses in a Late Act for the better Preventing of Clandestine Marriages, with Respect to Conscience. London, 1754.
with
Henry Stebbing. A Dissertation on the Power of the States to Deny Civil Protection to the Marriages of Minors Made without the Consent of their Parents or Guardians. London, 1755.

Divorce and Adultery

6. Marriage Promoted. In a Discourse of its Ancient and Modern Practice, Both under Heathen and Christian Common-Wealths. London, 1690.
with
A Treatise Concerning Adultery and Divorce. London, 1700.
with
Conjugium Languens: or, The Natural, Civil, and Religious Mischiefs Arising from Conjugal Infidelity and Impunity. London, 1700.
7. George Booth, Earl of Warrington. Considerations Upon the Institution of Marriage. London, 1737.
with
The Present State of Matrimony: or, the Real Causes of Conjugal Infidelity and Unhappy Marriages. London, 1739.
8. F. Douglas. Reflections on Celibacy and Marriage; in Four Letters to a Friend. London, 1771.
with
Considerations on the Causes of the Present Stagnation of Matrimony. London, 1772.
9. Trials for Adultery: or, the History of Divorces. (In seven volumes). London, 1779.

SEX

General Sexual Knowledge

10. Nicholas Venette. Conjugal Love; or, the Pleasures of the Marriage Bed. London, 1750.

11. Aristotle's Masterpiece or the Secrets of Generation. London, 1700.
with
Aristotle's Masterpiece in Three Parts. London, 1725.
with
Aristotle's Problems. London, 1710.
with
Aristotle's Last Legacy or His Golden Cabinet of Secrets Opened for Youth's Delightful Pastime. London, 1720.

The Dangers of Masturbation

12. Onania, or the Heinous Sin of Self-Pollution and All Its Frightful Consequences in Both Sexes Considered. London, 1710.
with
Onania . . . London, 1723.
with
A Supplement to the Onania. London, n. d.

13. S. A. Tissot. Onanism. London, 1766.
with
M.D.T. Bienville. Nymphomania, or, a Dissertation Concerning the Furor Uterinus. London, 1775.

Venereal Disease: Causes and Treatment

14. A Treatise of All the Degrees and Symptoms of the Venereal Disease in Both Sexes. London, 1708–09.

15. Jean Astruc. A Treatise of the Venereal Disease. London, 1737.

16. William Buchan. Observations Concerning the Prevention and Cure of the Venereal Disease. London, 1796.

Prostitution and the Sexual Life of the Town

17. The Wandring whore. Parts I–VI. London, 1660–61.
18. The London-Bawd, with her Character and Life. London, 1711.
19. John Dunton. The Night-Walker: or, Evening Rambles in Search of Lewd Women. London, 1696.
    with
    Edward Ward. The London Spy. London, 1709.
    with
    Edward Ward. The Amorous Bugbears: Or, The Humours of a Masquerade. London, 1725.
20. Hell upon Earth: or the Town in an Uproar. London, 1729.
    with
    Satan's Harvest Home, or the Present State of Whorecraft. London, 1749.
21. Select Trials at the Session House in the Old Bailey. London, 1742.
22. Robert Dingley. Proposals for Establishing a Public Place of Reception for Penitent Prostitutes. London, 1758.
    with
    Saunders Welch. A Proposal to Render Effectual a Plan to Remove the Nuisance of Common Prostitutes from the Streets of the Metropolis. London, 1758.
    with
    John Fielding. An Account of the Origin and Effects of a Police Set on Foot by His Grace the Duke of Newcastle in the Year 1753. London, 1758.
    with
    An Account of the Rise, Progress, and Present State of the Magdalen Hospital. London, 1776.
23. The Covent Garden Jester, or the Rambler's Companion. London, 1775.
    with
    Harris's List of Covent-Garden Ladies: or, Man of Pleasure's Kalender, For the Year, 1788. London, 1788.

Sodomy (Homosexual Behavior)

24. The Tryal and Condemnation of Mervin, Lord Audley Earl of Castle-Haven. At Westminster, April the 5th 1631. For Abetting a Rape upon his Countess, Committing Sodomy with his Servants, and Commanding and Countenancing the Debauching his Daughter. London, 1699.
 with
 The Women-Haters' Lamentation. London, 1739.
 with
 A Faithful Narrative of the Proceedings in a Late Affair between the Rev. Mr. John Swinton and George Baker. London, 1739.
 with
 John Kather. Genuine Narrative of the Conspiracy, Kather, Kane, Alexander, Nickson, etc. Against the Hon. Edward Walpole, Esq. London, 1751.
 with
 The Trial of Samuel Scrimshaw and John Ross, for a Conspiracy in Sending Threatning Letters to Humphry Morice, Esq; of Dover-Street: With an Intent to extort Money from him. London, 1759.
 with
 The Trial of Richard Branson, for an Attempt to commit Sodomy, On the Body of James Fassett. London, 1760.
 with
 Robert Holloway. The Phoenix of Sodom. London, 1813.

THE FAMILY, CHILDREN, AND SERVANTS

Childbearing and Childrearing: The Role of the Physician

25. Jane Sharp. The Midwives Book. London, 1671.
26. Francis Mauriceau. The Diseases of Women with Child and

in Childbed. London, 1710.

27. Guillaume de la Motte. A General Treatise of Midwifery. London, 1746.

28. Jean Astruc. A Treatise on All the Diseases Incident to Women. London, 1743.

29. Walter Harris. A Treatise on the Acute Diseases of Infants. London, 1742.
with
The Nurse's Guide: Or, the Right Method of bringing up Young Children. London, 1729.
with
William Cadogan. An Essay upon Nursing, and the Management of Children, From their Birth to Three Years of Age. London, 1750.

30. James Nelson. An Essay on the Government of Children. London, 1756.

31. John Hill. On the Management and Education of Children. London, 1754.

32. William Buchan. Domestic Medicine. London, 1772.

33. Lady Sarah Pennington. An Unfortunate Mother's Advice. London, 1817.

Children and Servants: The Advice of the Clergyman

34. William Fleetwood. The Relative Duties of Parents and Children, Husbands and Wives, Masters and Servants. London, 1705.

35. A Present for Servants from their Ministers, Masters, and Other Friends. London, 1787.
with
Eliza Haywood. A Present for a Servant Maid. London, 1743.

36. Thomas Seaton. The Conduct of Servants in Great Families. London, 1720.